The Woman beneath the Skin

The Woman beneath the Skin

A Doctor's Patients in Eighteenth-Century Germany

Barbara Duden

Translated by Thomas Dunlap

Harvard University Press
Cambridge, Massachusetts
London, England
1991

Originally published in 1987 by Klett-Cotta as *Geschichte unter der Haut:
Ein Eisenacher Arzt und seine Patientinnen um 1730.*

This book is printed on acid-free paper, and its binding materials
have been chosen for strength and durability.

Library of Congress Cataloging-in-Publication Data
Duden, Barbara.
[Geschichte unter der Haut. English]
The woman beneath the skin : a doctor's patients in eighteenth-
century Germany / Barbara Duden ; translated by Thomas Dunlap.
p. cm.
Translation of: Geschichte unter der Haut.
Includes bibliographical references and index.
ISBN 0-674-95403-3
1. Women—Medical care—Germany—Eisenach—History—18th century—
Case studies. 2. Storch, Johannes Pelargius, b. 1681—Diaries.
I. Title.
RA564.85.D8413 1991
618'.0943'09033—dc20
91-4673
CIP

Preface

This is a study of how people of another time experienced the body. As a historian I describe how a doctor and his women patients in the German town of Eisenach around 1730 envisioned the inside of the female body, and how these ideas shaped their actions and gave meaning to their experiences.

For more than a decade my work has dealt with the female body in history. From the supervision of prostitutes in Berlin and the reform of midwifery in Prussia, my research led me to the problem of gender- and class-specific ideas about childbirth, and eventually into the still largely unexplored eighteenth century. In the summer of 1982 I happened upon eight large volumes entitled *Weiberkrankheiten* (Diseases of Women). They are the work of Dr. Johannes Pelargius Storch, who in his old age excerpted case histories from a twenty-year span of his diary and compiled them into a handbook of instruction for younger colleagues. In each of the more than 1800 cases Storch recorded, in a few brief lines or over many pages, the ailments of a woman and his own thoughts about her condition. Since he diligently padded his case studies with learned references and comparisons, the women's complaints are buried among quite fantastic details. Bits and pieces of medical theories that would have been circulating at the University of Halle are combined with elements from popular culture; self-evident bodily perceptions appear alongside things that struck me as utterly improbable. Until now historians of medicine have been at a loss what to make of this strange hodgepodge. In their view this work contributes nothing to the history of gynecology, since Storch did not physically examine his female patients, rarely performed autopsies, and therefore had nothing to add to the knowledge of his profession.

I perused the volumes with a sense of bewilderment. In each "case" the small-town doctor reported in High German what a patient had just revealed to him—presumably in the local Eisenach dialect—about her blood, labor pains, heart constriction, or head cold. Even through the eyes of a man and the doctor's German I began to hear the personal stories of hundreds of different women, and I realized that I had before me an exceptionally rich source for the history of the female body. These records of authentic women's complaints, though undoubtedly distorted and condensed by the doctor, soon began to undermine my own certainties about the permanence of the female body and how it is experienced by a woman. And so I immersed myself in this source with the hope of giving a history to the female body.

To gain access to the inner, invisible bodily existence of these ailing women, I had to venture across the boundary that separates the body, and especially the inner body beneath the skin, from the world around it. From every intellectual perspective the body and its environment have been consigned to opposing realms: on one side are the body, nature, and biology, stable and unchanging phenomena; on the other side are the social environment and history, realms of life subject to constant change. With the drawing of this boundary the body was expelled from history, and the problem of how it has been perceived fell outside the sphere of social history.

How the life inside the body has been experienced across time is not a subject normally included in the domain of historical studies. Today bodily processes are studied and explained by doctors, physiologists, neurologists, and other scientists. Since they present their findings as normative descriptions, older descriptive and explanatory models, considered obsolete by scientific standards, cease to be the concern of scientists and are left to historians of science. Today the world of the past is divided up by exclusive disciplines, which determine the nature of historical phenomena. Deeply embedded biases have supported this fragmentation of the past, preventing a redrawing of intellectual boundaries, and the strict intellectual and institutional separation of the "social sciences" from the "natural sciences" has established this dividing line as a permanent feature of the scholarly landscape.

As a historian I am therefore faced with a paradox. Scholars study the physical conditions of people in the past and examine patterns of fertility, birth practices, nursing habits, and the frequency of intercourse in different historical cultures. But what people in a different age and culture thought about the inside of the body, about the hidden sphere under the skin, about stomach, breast, blood, and excrement, about the "life inside the body," is virtually unknown and rarely looked at.

Not long ago Georges Duby called upon historians to redefine the domain of history, to open up the "boundless sphere of total history" and include, for example, the history of honor, bread, suicide, and birth. To take up Duby's bold challenge demands first of all that we examine the assumptions and prejudices that have created the narrow boundaries of historical inquiry and have excluded sensory perceptions, hunger, pleasure, and pain from historical life. Such a critique of the intellectual traditions in which a nonhistorical body has been opposed to the historical world is just as important as a critical examination of the concepts and analytic methods that may enable us to create a radically new historical dimension for the body and its cultural representations and images. The first step toward understanding the complaints of the women of Eisenach was therefore to realize that my own certainties about the body are a cultural bias, one which perhaps I could even learn to transcend. I had to create some distance to my own body, for it was clear that it cannot serve as a bridge to the past.

One of the historian's most tenacious mental habits is the strict separation of biology as an immutable sphere of life from society and culture as spheres that are variable and changeable over time. In this dichotomy between nature and history, the body is assigned to the category of nature and biology. As a result, histories of the human body examine cultural variations of the body's manifestations and attributes: the history of sleep and food, of sexuality and disease, of age and death. But the vehicle of all this activity, the body itself, is always thought of as a physiologically stable entity. To us the body is essentially an anatomico-physiological collection of organs. Its inner processes, its secretions, fluids, and excretions, its sexual patterning and "vital events"—birth and death, menstruation and menopause, nursing and ejaculation, procreation and pregnancy—are always thought of as physiological processes. This mental demarcation of a socially "raw" corporeality has created barriers between historians and the body.

I hope to break down these barriers in my commentary on the diaries of Johann Storch. Chapter 1 examines the scholarly literature. Its focus is on body perception and its epistemology, not on eighteenth-century social history or the history of medicine. My aim was to get a sense of the methodological approaches that the contemporary social sciences use in dealing with the problem of body perception. This chapter is intended as a conceptual framework for the remaining chapters: the commentary on the women's complaints. Only by examining the varied and often circuitous approaches through which scholars have tried to grasp the history of the inner body could I gain a certain distance from the work of Storch, which allowed me to observe my source without imposing my preconceptions on it. Chapter 2 describes Johann Storch and his style of writing. Chapter 3 discusses his small-town practice and examines the conversations between the doctor and the women. Chapter 4 invites the reader to experience what was once a very real perception of the inner body, one so strange that it was some time before I could accept that it had ever existed.

This work was begun at the Institute of Modern History at the Technische Universität Berlin. I am deeply indebted to Professors Reinhard Rürup and Karin Hausen for their patient support. Many thanks too, especially to Professor Hausen, for the many insights we were able to gain in our close collaboration. Finally, I am grateful for their courage in accepting my work as a contribution to the historical sciences.

I owe a great deal to conversations with Jane Marquis, Regina Schulte, Heide Wunder, and Susanne v. Paczensky. I also must single out four colleagues, because many of their ideas became my own, and without their encouragement this work would not have been finished: Ruth Kriss-Rettenbeck, David Sabean, Ludolf Kuchenbuch, and Ivan Illich.

B.D.

Contents

The Woman beneath the Skin

ONE

Toward a History of the Body

Two Methods—Two Bodies

The study of how the modern body emerged and the study of how people of a vanished world perceived their bodies can be seen as two separate tasks. Even though these two aspects of body history are inextricably intertwined, it is methodologically useful to separate them. The historical conditions that shaped our modern body perception did not emerge until the second half of the eighteenth century, and it was some time before they became part of a common framework of perception. It is true that the first steps toward describing the human body as the kind of object that would become so self-evident to the nineteenth century already had been taken in France during the time of Descartes and in England during Harvey's later years. But even with so innovative a scientist as Harvey this did not go beyond theoretical treatises. In Germany as well the new epistemological forces began to have a broader impact only in the first half of the nineteenth century. Until the late eighteenth century medicine was characterized by profound discontinuities that separated experimentally derived insights, theoretical understanding, and the practical application of new knowledge.

As I surveyed the literature on body perception, I became convinced that it was essential to separate these two aspects of body history. To study the making of the modern body is to study the gradual unfolding of something that is now self-evident. But the historian who seeks the body of past ages is confronted with a tenacious stream of images and motifs that have persisted over millennia. At times they seem to blend and merge, but occasionally, remarkably, they reemerge in their original form. It is quite difficult for a historian to apply analytic tools to an object that seems beyond time and history.[1]

And yet the quest for a vanished body perception cannot be separated from the sociogenesis of our own body. To understand how the modern body came into being is an essential first step toward the very different task of reconstructing an extinct body perception. After all, my body determines my perceptions; above all, it shapes my notions and images of corporeality: of pain and pleasure, taste and lust, aging and disease, pregnancy, birth, and death. Unless I become aware of the historical origins of my own perceptions, I am *a priori* cut off from approaching the vanished reality of the "corporeal self." I cannot be too careful *not* to use my own body as a bridge to the past. I "have" a body. None of Storch's female patients "had" a body in the same sense. Down to my very language and physical form I am a possessive individual.[2] The fundamental obviousness of my body has become second nature to me, more so perhaps than any other part of my thinking. To approach the women's complaints recorded by the doctor in Eisenach, Germany, from my own body consciousness would profoundly prejudice my understanding of what these women were saying. With a growing amazement at the strange body perception in Eisenach came the realization of how difficult it would be to construct a satisfactory interpretation of this source. That prompted me to explore the field in which other scholars have tried to tackle similar problems.

The work of scholars from very diverse disciplines proved unexpectedly relevant and important. At the same time, it was a surprise to see what a gap opened up between my endeavor and those historians who have made the "body" the specific object of their study—for example, historical demographers.[3] Without classifying the literature that influenced my own approaches in studying the genesis of the modern body and Storch's work, I will first indicate the difficulties that confront the effort to historicize the body. Next I will outline the paradigm of the modern body and follow this with a brief overview of the literature dealing with this paradigm in general, and by a more detailed discussion of the scholarship from my own perspective. Only then will I list some of the approaches that scholars have used, primarily in the last thirty years, in an attempt to reconstruct how the body was experienced, what it meant, and the attitudes that people had about it.

THE CONSTRUCTION OF THE MODERN BODY

When I speak of the sociogenesis of the modern body, I am referring to the past two hundred years, when people began to describe, treat, become aware of, and satisfy an entity very much like the body I "have," this body with which I identify as a woman. Before I could listen to the women of Eisenach, I had to understand that my body—through which I am rooted in a nonhistorical nature—is a unique historical creation that I must set aside. In a work inspired by the ideas of Michel Foucault, David Armstrong examined the transformation of medical knowledge in Great Britain after World War II. Reflecting on his days as a medical student, he begins with a central insight: "I doubt if it ever occurred to me or my fellow medical students that the human body which we dissected and examined was other than a stable experience." He goes on to recall how amazed he was that past ages had been so ignorant of things that today are so obvious. How was it possible that earlier generations "had failed to see the clearly differentiated organs and tissues of the body?" How was it possible that they had "failed to apply the most rudimentary diagnostic techniques of physical examination?" Slowly it dawned on him that he was asking the wrong questions: "The problem was not how something which is so obvious today had remained hidden for so long, but how the body had become so evident in the first place."[4] Armstrong has echoed my own experience in reading Storch's work: a continuous astonishment at the self-evident manner in which we take the body for granted as an unchanging biological reality.

Foucault described the discovery of this biological reality as a unique creation arising from the interplay between the "medical gaze" and the material it both examined and fabricated. It was only toward the end of the eighteenth century that the modern body was created as the effect and object of medical examination. It was newly created as an object that could be abused, transformed, and subjugated. According to Foucault, this passivity of the object was the result of the ritual of clinical examination. The clinical, investigative gaze fixed and crystallized as "the body" that which it perceived. The gaze of the doctor was like a dissection; the sick patient was now treated in a way that once had been conceivable only with dead bodies. Foucault repeatedly pointed out that the impact of this new clinical discourse about the body can be seen in two ways by the historian: it repressed, censored, masked, abstracted, and alienated modes of perception; at the same time it had the power to create new realities, to constitute new objects, to introduce new, inescapable rituals into daily life, rituals whose participants became epistemologically dependent on the newly created objects.[5]

As a result, a new body perception became commonplace, which Figlio has described for the late eighteenth century as follows: "it involved a degradation of the notion of a self extended into a unique and inviolable corporeal volume, to one in which the self only loosely possessed a body."[6] This isolated, objectified, material body was seized by a dissecting gaze that embraced not only the entire body, not only its surfaces, but also its recesses and orifices. It penetrated inquisitively into the inside, evaluating the palpated organs and relating them to a visual image of the organs of cadavers. This gaze turned the body, and with it the patient who possessed it, into a new kind of discrete object. The clinical examination fabricated the body and made possible the creation of the private body, but this body could still be read only through the grid of the "anatomical atlas." The reality of this "body" was the product of these descriptions, and not vice versa, for what took hold was the belief that these clinical descriptions truly grasped and reproduced "reality."

Thus in the course of the nineteenth century the body gradually emerged as a multilayered description, with each layer made up by the text of a different science. But this modern body was not the result of developments in medicine. Nor was it the product of what Foucault has described as the *grand renfermement,* the process of "the great confinement," which, in the wake of an increased social stratification in all spheres of life, affected not only the body, but also the insane, delinquents, and homosexuals. Instead, the genesis of the modern body can be seen as the quietly ignored and overlooked flip side of the entire history of the last century. The modern body is consistent with other aspects of the modern image of man, the *homo oeconomicus.*[7] Looked at from a distance, the thematic principles from which the social, physical, and biological worlds have been woven turn out to be the same "fabric"; they are spun from the same historical material.

REFLECTIONS ON THE HISTORY OF MATTER AND FORM

At present there is no accepted way of classifying scholarly contributions to the history of corporeality, nor is there a clear definition of the object it is investigating. This object, the body, is constituted only at the point where different fields of scholarship converge. My first step therefore was to start compiling an analytic bibliography of the auxiliary resources for a history of the body. In the process I became convinced that it would be necessary to immerse myself in studies that might seem quite unrelated at first glance: Steinberg's studies on the depiction of Christ's genitalia; seventeenth-century devotion to the Sacred Heart; Zur Lippe's essay on perspective and the art of fencing. At the same time it became increasingly difficult to avoid seeing history only through the mirror of the body. What follows is not a summary of the literature I have surveyed. Instead, my aim is to use selective examples to point out the main perspectives within the existing scholarship that contributed directly to my interpretation of the work of Johann Storch. In most instances the contributions to the history of the modern body that were of use to me were buried in the historical scholarship that deals with how the "natural body" was described, disciplined, manipulated, or given more efficient medical treatment. Because the body is usually considered a natural given, this kind of history is very often a legitimation of the history of medicine. It tends to make the healer into a timeless figure, to naturalize the "doctor" along with the body. As a history of ideas it often attributes prophetic powers to the gaze of the scientist by linking together the succession of scientific concepts into a progressive discovery of "facts." In presenting history as a progressive enlightenment, it often cannot but let the body emerge from a story of gradual discoveries. One of its axioms is the assumption that there are so-called "natural facts" which can be isolated and discovered and whose continuous discovery and accumulation has gradually created the state of knowledge we have today.[8] In this way medical and scientific history becomes the story of how the "real" body is "discovered." Cultural and social history examine how the body is culturally shaped, and how a wide range of environmental factors influence it. The history of *mentaliteés* and psychohistory in turn place the emphasis on the internalization of these influences. A part of women's history, along with some work from a patient-oriented history of medicine, can be read as the history of resistance to the well-intentioned, professional distortion of the body.[9]

In all these approaches Bachelard's distinction between the historicity of matter—the body experience itself—and its form is rarely, if ever, made explicit.[10] I too fell short of doing it justice, since it demanded time and again that I turn my thinking upside down. But this distinction was helpful for my understanding of corporeality in Eisenach, and it is no doubt fundamental for a history of corporeality in past times and for a critique of the modern body. All the studies I have mentioned implicitly presuppose something like a nonhistorical (biological) matter of the body, which is then molded by time and class, on which "culture is imprinted" or which is "culturally shaped."[11] The matter itself always remains a given. But if we start from the assumption that the imagination and perceptions of a given period have the power to generate reality, we can approach phenomena that are usually rendered invisible because of some a priori axiom of what is natural. After all, Storch reports bodily manifestations that are anatomically improbable, and he corroborates them with socially respectable, nonsuperstitious sensory testimony. I cannot and do not wish to clarify whether the *chirurgus* who recorded a periodic menstrual flow from a wound and the *physicus* who on several occasions saw a nun from Eichsfeld urinating through her mouth were describing something real. But if Bachelard teaches me to take the imagination seriously as a source of material reality, I do not deny the possibility that the thinkable actually becomes reality. In his early writings Bachelard repeatedly returned to this fundamental distinction between two complementary aspects of the imagination: a formal and a material one. The form and the matter of our imagination cannot be separated, for one cannot exist without the other. In a series of essays Bachelard investigated this material, matter-generating power of the imagination, and he very deliberately took as his theme the four basic material elements of the universe—earth, water, fire, space. The blood that flowed from the wound of a girl in Eisenach in March 1725 and signified her menstrual blood, is "real" to the extent that in Eisenach a variety of materials "bled." In this sense the material that bleeds, no less than its form, is created only by the observer's gaze. Hence matter itself is historical. [12] In criticizing the historians' shallow concept of reality, poets and philosophers have for years made demands on historians which the latter have not yet answered. In 1926 Malraux formulated this demand in *La tentation de l'Occident:* "You believe that there is something permanent in what you call man, but that is not so. You are like serious scientists who carefully note every movement of fish, but who have not yet discovered that fish live in water." [13]

This fundamental challenge to the "reality of the historians" is not meant to detract from the importance of their work. I have learned even from works of historians who write about bodily phenomena, but always with a preconceived notion of their unchanging naturalness. Even when the preconception of a natural corporeality made the historical images that were examined seem "erroneous," a "false doctrine," [14] I have found things to help in my own approach.

Before I describe, later in this chapter, the resources and tools for my history of body percepts, I will discuss selectively the contributions to the making of "my" modern body. My discussion is not intended as a historical outline. Instead, it is structured around points of reference that I derived from the scholarly literature. [15] I will touch on three aspects: the history of the new society's disempowering grasp of the body; the defining and recasting of the body through the medical gaze and the grounding of a single, orthodox concept of the body in a monopolistic medicine; and the connection between the development of broader social themes and the new image of the body.

The Genesis of the Modern Body

THE DISEMPOWERMENT OF THE BODY

The industrial body stands in the focal point of a powerful and diverse service organization. The body of the north Italian women described by Accati was itself a source of power, for "she who can give life, can also give death." In mid-seventeenth-century Friaul this wisdom was a social truism.[16] But in the wake of the Counter-Reformation the priest of the village of Polidoro demanded for "mother church" the power to bestow the life that really mattered to ensure salvation from eternal death. Accati describes the outbreak of a power struggle, in particular the shift of the source of power from the body and the utterances of women to the institution of the Church and its written word. The power over thunderstorms, which old women had long been able to command (undoubtedly with the toleration of the Church) by baring their buttocks, and the power of a virgin to influence weather by opening her bleeding vulva toward heaven were no longer simply accepted as strange and mysterious powers. Instead, they were now regarded as threats to the institutional power of definition and were demonized. What took place was a "persistent devaluation of the magic of the body, which was a part of popular culture."[17]

The power of life and death was embodied above all by women in their capacity as "vessels of life and death,"[18] for this power was grounded in the ambiguity of their womb.[19] Owing to their own periodicity and fertility, women represented powers whose help the village looked for and feared. Women accompanied the passages of life, the entrance and the exit (birth and death); they washed the newborn and the dead; they nursed the children and the sick. Women were "the wellspring of popular culture," and this was inherent in their flesh and confirmed daily by a thousand gestures.[20] After all, their bodies housed the forces and substances that could produce good as well as evil: blood, the periodic flow, the afterbirth, the amniotic fluid, and finally the "mother" (womb), which, like an oven, could bring forth and take life.[21] This power and task of infusing life and destroying it was embodied in woman; through her every gesture and many of her words the village community was anchored to an unwritten, invisible order. From the seventeenth century on, a new, bureaucratic power was employed to destroy this cosmic anchoring of popular culture, to describe the female body, to interpret its ambiguous power as a demonic threat, and to explain its very nature as "natural" weakness.

Muchembled describes the war of destruction that was waged during this same period against the body-based power of the self-sufficient peasant society in Flanders, and he examines the rituals of a new justice which imprinted its gaze upon the bodies of its subjects. The "body," he writes, "becomes more and more a stake of power. It is no longer sufficient that the body is productive. Beyond that, it must be minutely subjected, controlled, and dominated. Between the sixteenth and the eighteenth century the culture of the elites invents and applies a 'political technology of the body.'"[22]

In a stimulating essay on blood and how it was envisioned in Italy during this same period, the historian Camporesi quotes from the execution ritual of one Baldassare, the man who had murdered the Prince of Orange (1584). The execution was stretched out over four days: a few hours each day on a stage in full view of the public. According to Camporesi, what took place was the dissection of a living body, in which the act of justice was "celebrated" first by dislocating the body on the scaffold, then by burning its skin, and finally by penetrating inside the body and drawing out the intestines. It would seem, at least from the perspective of the state, that the infliction of torture as such was secondary to the solemn act of taking control by means of the anatomy of the condemned. The symbolism of the punishment was conveyed by opening and exposing the innermost flesh. Indeed, anatomy was at this time still a public ritual that linked the punishment of an executed or condemned person to the demonstration of the structure of the human body.[23] Only gradually, over the course of the eighteenth century, was anatomy transformed from a public exposing of the inside of a human being "as such," to a procedure in which doctors acquired professional knowledge in a closed dissection chamber.[24] An expression from the Thuringian dialect reveals that our interpretation of the political meaning behind the anatomizing, the "dissecting" inflicted on Baldassare corresponds very closely to a deep-rooted and tenacious aversion felt by those people and subsequent generations: peasants near Jena ordered that their corpses be guarded in the villages to keep them from being "rolfinked."[25] Rolfink was one of the first German anatomists, a professor at Jena and court anatomist in Weimar. Linebaugh has described how the horror which late-eighteenth-century Englishmen felt at losing their bodies to the London anatomists was a compound of various motives: religious ideas about resurrection; fear that an improperly executed hanging might leave the condemned in a state of apparent death; hope of escaping the gallows through a cleverly knotted noose; and the desperate wish to escape the further intrusion of the state's power even after one had been hanged.[26]

I have strung together these acts of undisguised violence—witch persecution, the scaffold, and anatomy—to indicate the strategic importance of the body and the symbolic value of its integrity. During those two centuries when the power of the state was being established, a time which also saw a new and unparalleled regulating and ceremonial demarcating of the corporeality of the European upper class, great importance attaches in my view to an interconnected, twofold development: in scientific work and corporal punishment the inside beneath the skin was exposed. In this way the connections, deeply rooted in popular culture, between this (invisible) interior and the macrocosm were eradicated. The act of dissection, which exposed things, and the reduction of the body merged into one process. The "state" was able to gain power from this opening and isolating of the body because the "biological" body and the "social" body were connected, had a correlation in the culture's consciousness; whatever was done to the former was never done only to a "private body," like that of Baldassare. "The surgeon . . . who undertakes the dangerous task of making visible the hidden depths of the body, who lays hands on the order which God has established in the bosom of his creature, is in a way a Luciferian person," writes Marie Christine Pouchelle to express how unthinkable anatomy was in the Middle Ages.[27]

A violent process began in the seventeenth century, one in which the body as the embodiment of localized social vitality was symbolically broken: in the witch trials the body of woman was demonized, deatomized on the scaffold; by being displayed as an anatomical patchwork, it was deprived of its meanful opacity. Before the body could be constituted as the object of descriptive observation, it first had to be devalued as a vehicle of symbolic meaning.

Foucault has described a series of revolts to free the condemned "patient"—as he was called—from the hands of the executioner.[28] But the resistance to the demonstrative individuation, the *de - finition* of corporeality and its display, had not only psychic but also social reasons.

The society of the seventeenth century did not yet have room for a corporeality that was isolated, "disembedded" from the total network of social relations. This becomes evident in reading Calvi. Calvi describes how the city of Florence prepared itself against the approaching plague in 1630 and subsequently survived the epidemic.[29] Under the pressure of this threat, the existing networks of otherwise separate healers became intermeshed; frictions increased between the "zolfatori, beccamorti, biri, specifici, cerusini," who sprang up everywhere; the offices responsible for settling conflicts were overtaxed. Calvi reveals the varied activities that unfolded during the plague, the "scourge of God," and in which the candlemakers, the amuletmakers, and the intercessors were no less important than the apothecaries, the *medici,* and the gravediggers. Relations which we today, with our medicalized gaze, would all see as "body-related," were so polymorphous and polycentric to the citizen of Florence, as well as to the city administration, that he does not even seem to have a "body" at all.

The transitions from daily afflictions—evil and corrupting fevers, suppurating boils, watery stool—to the plague were as unspecific and vague as the boundaries between the corruption within the body and the decay of the entire cosmos (pp. 71 ff.). The plague was perceived as a disease not only of the biological body, but also of nature and the social body. In a concentric approach through these bodies, on which the signs of the poisoning were observed, Calvi describes how the physical body, an "open organism," was also exposed to the same evil influences. The putrid vapors penetrated through the openings to the inside: through the pores—the pores of a hot-blooded person being more open than those of a melancholy person—through the mouth and the nose, and then pushed on to the center, the heart. A constant exchange took place between the inside and the outside, "a relation of osmotic exchanges with the elements." Efforts to cure the disease concentrated on calming the disturbed exchange between inside and outside with unguents, fumigations, massages, herb pouches, and precious stones placed near the heart, while making sure not to clog the sensitive mechanisms of "reciprocal exchange and filtration between the inside and outside" (p. 77). In this cosmos the skin does not close off the body, the inside, against the outside world. In like manner the body itself is also never closed off; it is composed of material that is no different from the world surrounding it.[30]

MacDonald has found similar correspondences between inside and outside and a complete blurring of the boundaries between "mental" and "physical" afflictions in England in the second half of the seventeenth century.[31] In analyzing what villagers reported to their astrological physician, he carefully refrains from using modern psychiatric concepts. The villagers complained that the evil corrupted their humors and took possession of them, made them deranged. Or they spoke less dramatically of extraordinary sadness, apathy, frenzy, which stood under an unfavorable influence of the stars. The notes show clearly that "madness" was only a heightened form of conditions that lurked inside every person as passions, fears, sadness, and gloominess. This world knew no "insanity," even less one that would have been clearly "mental" or clearly "physical." "Physical" or "mental" norms did not exist; consequently there was no distinct pathology. The sufferings that were laid out before Dr. Napier were part of the day-to-day village experiences. Moreover, in the first half of the seventeenth century this perception was not yet class-specific. Robert Burton observed that, "There is in all melancholy *similitudo dissimilis,* like men's faces, a disagreeing likeness still; and as in a river we swim in the same place."[32] MacDonald examines, on a local level, the disintegration of this common perception. Toward the end of the period he finds among the elites a clearly defined notion of "insanity." The demons, heavenly inspirations, evil insinuations, and supernatural influences of old had become "saecularized" and, as medically defined phenomena, enclosed in the body of the insane person, the only place they could now be found.[33] The first public hospitals, to which the sick were sent in a departure from the previous practices in the region, treated insanity according to medical theories. MacDonald analyzed the papers of Dr. Napier exclusively from the viewpoint of "mental disorder." But his study of the people in Great Linford (Buckinghamshire) who were "troubled in the mind," also shows the presence of a body internally undivided and externally unbounded. The "body" as a discrete óbject of social control during times of plague or in daily personal hygiene had not yet taken shape.

DISCIPLINING THE BODY

This body, the vague corporeality of popular culture, became offensive in the course of the eighteenth century—increasingly so as the new creation of a "bourgeois body" progressed, and as a growing number of enlightened writings probed the relation between body and environment. The factors that contributed to the new creation of the body were extraordinarily complex. How they emerged and established themselves and what kind of social relations they embodied have not been adequately studied. Nevertheless, I shall at least outline some of these factors.

Labor was only very gradually discovered as an economic value, not merely as a precondition for the processing of goods, but as a scarce production resource, a factor in the competition among nations. The subject body thus acquired economic value. The human being became an economic factor also as a physical entity; his life span and his physical ability to work became statistically measurable quantities of the national economy.

Around 1770 the study and cultivation of the body politic became, at least in the intention of administrators, the task of "policy." In order to grasp this "body politic in all its parts and as a whole," not only in times of crisis, it had to be tangibly constituted in its corporeal collectivity. The rising class, the bourgeoisie, developed the embodiment of the individual. Volney wrote in his "Health Catechism" of 1793: "Everyone is the supreme master, the complete owner of his body," and he structured his catechism around the body as the most elementary form of property.[34] The entire catalog of the bourgeois social norms subsequently flowed into the attitude toward this new form of property: questions about the regulation of the emotions and bodily needs, about behavior and the relation to the environment.

New medical insights contributed only indirectly to this creation of a new physical-moral economy of the body, yet they did arise in a close interaction with the basic social patterns. For example, Haller's discovery of "sensibility" and "sympathy" created a model that was very convincing to the profession, since the total integration and control of

the body was ensured by the "sensibility" of the nervous system. In
Haller's physiology the control of the body was now also physiological,
that is, it was natural, placed inside, because the sensibility of the nerves
and the sympathy of all its parts kept the body together. This scientific
theory reflected the changed placement of the body within the environment, the physiological theory provided a "naturalistic basis . . . for
[the] refined sensibility" of the individual.[35] As early as 1936 Norbert
Elias examined how the external disciplining of the body of the upper
classes, which at the beginning of the century still was accomplished
primarily by strict ceremonial rules of etiquette, shifted toward an inner
disciplining.[36] It included mental control, moderation of the passions,
but also restraint of movement and a calculated awareness of environmental influences as they affected "health." What one ate, how one
slept, how one rested, how one cleansed and dressed oneself, all this was
now—at least theoretically—arranged from the perspective of
hygiene.[37] "The study of disease was revealing the ways in which both
the physical and the cultural environment affected organisms so that the
interaction between life and its milieu was being conceptualized in
medical terms."[38] The "non-naturals" of classical tradition were revived
in a new guise, but their dimensions were thoroughly shifted, since the
relation between the described body and the managed environment
could now be scientifically measured, understood, and correspondingly
manipulated.[39] Traditional preventive behavior that ran in well-worn
tracks became a calculated attitude with a view toward exerting a
positive influence on and changing the factors that affected the body.
Prevention became an undertaking that was, in theory, feasible and
planable.

Using the essays about the body and health in the *Encyclopédie*, W.
Coleman has analyzed how this medical cosmology corresponded to the
individualism of the bourgeois class. The educated readers "shared and
perpetuated the new faith of the Enlightenment that one must change
man's way of thinking in order to change how he lives and acts. The
doctrine of the non-naturals as a guide to correct hygienic practice was
wholly consonant with this striking reorientation of Western thought
. . . Its use demanded adequate means, self-awareness, and the desire to
maintain or improve one's lot in life. Literacy, respect for the conclusions

of trained minds, and one's own experience—indeed the meticulous cultivation of that experience especially as it concerned the affairs of the body—these were essential to serious personal regimen."[40] The doctor should help in cases of illness, but the individual was now obliged to observe the "non-naturals" himself and arrange his life accordingly. A wealth of health manuals gave detailed instruction on how to do this. They established norms for healthful living within the family and under the supervision of women, who stood in the center of the health campaign as the extension of the doctors. The new rituals of a clean body and a clean home were rituals of demarcation, which had a personal as well as a political significance.[41] The new body assumed a central place in the self-image of the bourgeois classes. It was a "natural symbol," one in which the individual was to be embodied and by means of which he or she became visibly set apart from the "externally directed" nobility, as well as from the filth of the peasants and the disorder of the urban underclasses.

The relation between the macrocosm and the microcosm, in which man and woman had embodied themselves in regionally specific and often "bloody" ways, was replaced by the utopia of a human, disciplined body, around which a new kind of society could be constructed. In this body bourgeois sexuality became what blood had been to the nobility and the peasants, a change which Foucault repeatedly pointed out.[42]

Bakhtin called attention to this retreat into the body—one could almost describe it as the morphological dimension of somatic individualization—when he contrasted the closed body of the bourgeoisie to the "baroque" body. The body regions were rearranged into a new hierarchy: the backside and the lower body became taboo; orifices had to be kept closed; yawning must not permit a glimpse into the inside of the body; whatever protruded had to be drawn in or tightly laced up. Individual character was to reveal itself in the face, in the eyes. Corporeality was disciplined; it internalized itself and withdrew to the private sphere. The body aura was obliterated.[43] As early as 1942 Marc Bloch showed that human beings had an "aura" and that this aura and its effects on scrofula could become the object of historical investigation.[44] Somewhat later R. Mandrou examined how the sense perception of tongue, nose, and fingers gradually withdrew to the eyes, a restructuring of the cultural hierarchies of the senses which Elias had also noted.[45]

THE OFFENSIVE BODY

Alain Corbin has examined the way in which a somatic quality that was once regarded as "aura" and could even exert a healing power became an offensive olfactory emanation.[46] Starting from the change of the sense organs and the way they were experienced, he investigates the transformation of the body in Paris between 1740 and 1800. The personal aura became repulsive body odor. It was scientifically determined that the poor reeked, and that the odor of foreign "races," such as the Seljukes and the Samoyeds, clung to their bodies regardless of diet and hygienic habits. From the end of the eighteenth century the body was used in a new way for the purposes of social classification. Henceforth the body itself, not merely its clothing, its practiced and customary gestures, its ritual forms of expression, signaled the individual's social position.

The use of the "body" as an instrument of social classification created the basis for a divergence in the way the body was experienced that has remained potent into the twentieth century: foreign races, peasants, the poor, and women clung to the traditional perceptions of the body.[47] The Royal Academy of Medicine in Paris conducted an inquiry between 1776 and 1786. Responses sent from the provinces reveal that peasants and women shared the characteristics of the traditional body, which became the focus of criticism: the emanations of their bodies were uncontrollable, and the reactions of their bodies were unpredictable.[48] Both peasants and women became examples of defective health. A new concept of the individual, closed body that was intended to be "healthy," which corresponded to a concept of nature as fundamentally without defect, made the bodies of peasants and women appear pathological.

Situations of conflict brought out very clearly the contrast between the new body, with its utopian ideal that it was in its essence a "healthy" one, and the traditionally lived body, between the standardized body and the suffering body that clung precariously to life. The peasants resisted variolation precisely because they understood what its effect would be: "pus from one or two pustules cannot replace the abundant and necessary discharge of smallpox; the humors, resting largely in the body, give rise sooner or later to more or less dread illnesses."[49] In the final analysis, the enlightened reformer was not concerned with changing behavior but with creating a new body. As one country doctor wrote from the provinces, "it would be necessary, so to speak, to change the nature of the peasant . . . to make him into an absolutely different kind of person" (p. 104).

To recover and strengthen itself, the traditional body had to "flow": pus, blood, and sweat had to be drawn out. On this point peasants, women, and practicing doctors agreed. The new philanthropist saw a completely different reality: a body that should be preserved, improved, and must not dissipate itself—an economic unit. The conflict between traditional medicine, which constantly assisted the body in its self-opening, and the new medicine, which wanted to discipline the body, probably explains why the polemic for and against bleeding loomed so large at the end of the eighteenth century.[50]

Apparently women were the incarnation of some kind of bodily paradigm uniquely resistant to the new and differentiating conception of the inner body. "Medical policy," as well as a good deal of medical writing after 1770, focused primarily on the discovery, description, categorization, and administration of the inner female space from which the "body politic" had to emerge. Traditional knowledge about the processes at birth, which had been absorbed through practical experience, was now discredited through the medical training of midwives. Henceforth midwives were to acquire their knowledge and the legal qualification for their profession by learning the medical descriptions and practicing with mannequins.[51] This brought about a fundamental cultural transformation of the birth process: the act of delivering a woman became the birth of a child. Birth, at one time primarily a social, semi-public event among women, now became ideally a private event that had to be attended to in accordance with the logic of a physiological mechanism.[52] This reduction of birth to a bodily mechanism went hand in hand with a shift in the meaning of birth: what had been a "passage," a threshold experience with analogies between birth and death, became a productive process. Many of the factors involved in the creation of a gynecological medicine, which scholarly literature has interpreted as the enforcement of male power over the female body, reveal equally clearly the means that were involved in creating a new kind of corporeality.[53] The new "body" was defined through the process of isolating the female organs from the traditional undefined body: not only the "mother" (womb) and the woman who carried it were defined, but male and female bodies.

One more point is crucial in talking about the disempowerment of the body and the administrative-descriptive conception which took possession of it. This act of taking possession occurred progressively from the nineteenth to the late twentieth century, in the belief that it corresponded to the subjective need of the individual. Ute Frevert has spoken of the "politization of disease and health" in Prussia between 1770 and 1880. She documents the resistance of the lower classes not only to medical regulations, but also to the medical concept of the body. A circular from the Würzburg school commission in 1793 observed that it was difficult "to convince people who are in need of doctors and surgeons to be open to their (own) healing," and it lamented the difficulties "in eradicating harmful self-curing and the use of so-called home remedies."[54] The idea that health should be of service to the state fell on deaf ears among the sick lower classes; it was hard to convince them that medical policy was intended to protect the state from wasting an "instrument of the body politic."[55] The "catechization of health" became necessary to impart to the state and the burgher a new view of the body: "Whoever neglects the precious treasure of health offends all of society, of which he is a member. Society rightly demands of him that he sacrifice a part of his energies and time to her needs and for her benefit, who every day contributes so much to his need and benefit."[56]

And yet the new body was not the self-serving invention of the doctors. It arose as the need of a particular social class to embody itself in this body, and the force it exerted was at most a "gentle" one on the lower classes. The concept of "health" was politically very explosive: health as the goal of individual well-being concealed the context of the administrating and objectivizing of the "body politic," from which the concept itself had arisen.

The idea that all people by nature strive for good health has become so self-evident to academics in the late twentieth century that the history of this normative term "health" has long been excluded from scholarship. As long as I attributed such striving to the women in Eisenach, I simply could not do their complaints justice.

The self-evident, "natural" idea that everyone seeks good health has long restricted the range of scholarly inquiry. Jordanova has unraveled the ambiguities of *santé* in France around 1780 and the years following.[57] The Enlightenment wrote health onto its banner as a physical-moral category. The concept was politically so effective and so double-edged because the interest of the authorities and the national economy in a self-administered objectification of the self appeared in it as a subjective need of the individual or an act of philanthropy. The term always had a public face. *Santé* always meant "public personal hygiene," but the term also implied a theory of history by attributing the desire for good health to many generations for whom the realization of this desire was impossible. Political medicine cast this desire for a healthy body into a scientifically solid mold of norms and pathologies, thus creating a new image of humankind. By attributing this desire to humankind and grounding it in human nature, the human right to the "pursuit of happiness" (as laid down in the Constitution of the United States) took on concrete form as a right to health, and a new bodily dependence on unrealizable professional promises was born. *Santé, Gesundheit, health* became, in the course of one century, the basis for defining and diagnosing an ever-growing number of new pathologies, and for considering them so offensive that they cried out for treatment.

Kellert has described the difference between medically defined "health" and a person's knowledge of what he or she can put up with. He sees an enormous gap between the sociocultural perception of personal impairment and the medical definition of deviance from a normative health. Kellert offers numerous examples from so-called underdeveloped countries where people, despite showing "symptoms," did not think of themselves as sick and were not perceived as such by others. Other examples come from modern-day schools, where of one hundred children sent to school as "healthy" by their parents, nearly all were found to have "defective" tonsils or other "diseases" after a medical examination.[58] The personal desire for health thus led to an expropriation of health through the institutional mediation of the medical profession. Health, "as the organized concern for the well-being of others,"[59] is a synthesis of various influences: an icon of the Enlightenment, the demand of philanthropists, the legitimation of administrative reformers. Enlightened interest, the duty of charity, and scientifically grounded discipline merged in the "striving for health." The now "private" reality under the skin became a public affair. Nothing remained of the meaning-laden bodies of the women in Friaul. When I received my driver's license in California in 1985, I was asked as a matter of pure formality to donate my living heart to the California Organ Bank in case I should have an accident. Until that time I was to be responsible about my health; in a bookstore in Dallas I found about 130 manuals that would teach me "how to be an active partner in my own health promotion." For many years now the self-care-budget in the United States has been growing at three times the rate of all medical expenses combined. I am looking for Eisenach somewhere between seventeenth-century Friaul and twentieth-century Dallas.

THE POWER OF DEFINITIONS

Since the eighteenth century the anatomically and physiologically constructed body concept has been scientifically endowed with the appearance of being a natural phenomenon, while at the same time it has been made invisible as a social creation. What is so remarkable in this scientific creation of a seemingly "discovered" nature can be shown especially clearly in the example of the mythopoiesis of the modern female body. From Karl Figlio I have learned to distinguish the mutually reinforcing and interwoven mechanisms of this process.

Science, more than any other investigative and descriptive activity, creates and conceals the context from which it arises. As a formalized system of concepts, it combines elements which all have their own history and are expressed in language into a higher order of meta-language—"a collage whose persuasiveness is based on its assertion that what it expresses is natural." According to Figlio, this collage conceals its formative conditions in two ways: science naturalizes both experience and ideology, and it expresses this process in the language of abstract theses which covertly conveys an ideology.[60]

From the end of the eighteenth century on "nature" was created as an organizing category of thought. It was placed in opposition to "culture," thus representing the "wholly other" whose laws could be investigated. This dichotomous way of thinking in opposite categories of nature and culture is shot through with sexual references and metaphors in which woman is equated with nature. Woman becomes the symbol of a nature that can be discovered, deciphered, and illuminated by the light of reason.[61] Of course woman's close relationship to nature in the cultural imagination of the West has a thousand-year-old tradition, which Merchant has studied.[62] Moreover, the tradition of naturalizing things was in itself nothing new, since political positions and social orders were also described with naturalistic metaphors. The Scientific Revolution, however, produced a new concept: a nature that is passive, subdueable, inherently inert and obedient once its physical laws have been uncovered. Easlea has studied the emergence of this concept of nature.[63] It constituted a conceptual break with tradition, insofar as its now monistic essence no longer possessed any intentionality. Nature lay open to be appropriated and exploited. It was only through this process that the immanence of a "natural" and a "social" world was transformed into an antithetical proposition embodying a hierarchy and relationship of power and dominance.[64]

This concept of "nature," to which the body, particularly that of women, children, and "savages," was assigned, became central to the social-science thinking of the nineteenth century, and it imposed its inescapable grid on everything it embraced. Ever since the Enlightenment, science and medicine have used the nature they deal with, and which includes the inner body ("reproduction," "sexuality," and so on), to imply indirectly that whatever they conceptualize is immutably fixed. The means for conveying this idea are the forms of language, in which naturalistic statements are made about the physiological, mental, and social aspects of human beings.[65] The terms themselves create a link, a close relationship between statements about the inner body thus conceived and social definition.

The category "woman,"[66] therefore, is a product of nineteenth-century natural science, comparable to other categories with a naturalistic appearance, such as "family,"[67] "reproduction,"[68] "kinship,"[69] and "sexuality."[70] One of the great achievements of women's studies is that it uncovered and critiqued the ideological implication of this intellectual construct. "To unravel the ideological conflations that underlaid apparently empirical categories" is one of the central tasks of women's studies, according to Olivia Harris,[71] since "assumptions about nature and the natural are powerful metaphors that endow what are often quite transient states of affairs with an air of finality and eternity."[72] Women's studies have thus assumed a central role in the story that has uncovered how the naturalistic reality of the body was created as the object of investigation and treatment. At the same time they attest how much these concepts created by and borrowed from the sciences can be made into naturalized set pieces of one's own world view. The notions about corporeality seem deeply embodied in us, like petrified deposits of the modern age to which we belong.

The ahistoricity of women's bodies in the work of Shorter is almost a caricature.[73] What interests him in the past are objectively identifiable and statistically expandable symptoms of a concrete physical object, the female body: symptoms such as the tearing of the uterus, prolapse of the uterus, improper positioning of the fetus, and postpartum infections. The only reality he allows as a historian are these symptoms registered in medical terms. As Shorter sees it, contemporary conceptual patterns and images that were used to interpret the various ailments rested on a defective knowledge of what should have been evident from the beginning. For example, the image of the uterus as a moving creature, which suggests very complex inner experiences and external description,[74] "presupposed an enormous peasant ignorance of anatomy."[75] When women in labor showed concern for the white bed linen, which was both an economical as well as a symbolic precaution—white attracts "red" (the blood) from the body—they did so, Shorter argues, "only to spare the sheets!" (p. 56). Women, "who hitherto had been denied the platform of physical equality and thus the springboard to personal self-determination," owe to the progress of science their liberation from unspeakable and unappetizing clinical sufferings, which the author describes in great detail. Indeed the women's movement would not have been possible if women had not been able, through education, to discover their real bodies. Thus Shorter argues.

Ehrenreich and English take a different view of the relation between scientific conceptualization and the female body.[76] Progress could have "given" woman her real body, but it was systematically abused in order

to define woman in such a way that her second-class status, her usefulness as housewife and mother, and her need for dependence were natu-
ralistically inscribed in her body and justified through her anatomy and
physiology. On various levels these authors do not go far enough; they
fall short, in my view, of fully grasping what it is that they seek to
explain. First of all, these studies imply a remarkable intellectual
reversal. They vigorously attack the biologism which doctors, medical
science, and experts show toward women. But in their critique of the
concepts they examine, the very same "biologism" sneaks in through the
back door and reappears in their own concepts and categories, namely, in
the form of a naturalized idea of "woman" and in the collective category
of the "men" who define her. As Jordanova had already emphasized,
these studies do not offer an analysis of concepts in which an entire world
view is reflected; at best they are a critique of the "male interest," whose
ideology does not explain the essence of these concepts.[77]

Kniebiehler and Fouquet's work on women and medicine, a study
covering two thousand years, also starts from the premise that there is
such a thing as "solid knowledge" about the body, and goes on to
criticize that this growth of "rational knowledge" has gone on for too
long with male "ideology mixed in."[78] If only science could finally be
cleansed of these "irrational" elements, the uncovered essence of the
biological entity "woman" could at long last emerge. In a brilliant
textual analysis some fifteen years ago Kniebiehler identified the characteristics of the female body which had been described since the end of
the eighteenth century as the anatomical underside of social gender
characteristics.[79] But in this, as in later studies undertaken to uncover
reality-defining characteristics as expressed in the body, the characteristics are described as a misperception, devaluation, or colonization of a
consistently misinterpreted reality. Epistemologically these studies are
examples of a natural history of the female body. They fail to address the
body as experience, which up to the time of Storch was not medically
determined and for the patients in no way shaped by definitions. Studies
like that by Kniebiehler and Fouquet, which construct *one* tradition of
the defining-power of doctors and imply an unhistorical relationship
between the definers and the defined (even if the "content" of the
definitions changes), fail to see that both sides of that relationship as

well as the link connecting them are probably no more than a creation of the historian's mind.

Jordanova has linked the question concerning the essential transformation of the concept of nature in the eighteenth century to the question about the usability of the body as a natural symbol.[80] She turns the conventional perspective upside down. Instead of examining the relation between the anatomical-physiological construct and social ideology, she investigates how the concept of nature and the anatomical-physiological "woman" are interrelated. She outlines how the study of nature by the sciences supplied the very stereotypes through which the relationship between the sexes could be conceptualized and removed from "culture." Only "nature" that was examined in this way supplied the terms with which categorical clarity and demarcations could be created in the conflict-ridden social spheres. The exclusion of women from the construct of the bourgeois individual with all his sociohistorical facets is one such sphere. Only in this context did woman become a "two-legged womb,"[81] and pregnancy a mechanical process through which life was produced. "With the definition of life as a new guiding concept at the end of the eighteenth century, the mechanism whereby life was transmitted took on fresh significance. The capacity to engender seemed a special elusive force, made concrete through the female reproductive system."[82] Only now do we see the emergence of the conceptual context in which the fertile female body became the reproductive female body.[83] Only now, from the perspective of "reproduction," could the phases of a growing "belly," formerly experienced in a variety of ways, be arranged in accordance with the laws of production that applied to nature: "a nature which worked through laws, which was simple, economical and had no waste."[84]

A taxonomy whose purpose it was to describe anatomical-physiological developmental stages necessitated a hierarchic arrangement of each phenomenon observed in the organism. It made possible both a sexist social definition of woman on the basis of her "natural" being, as well as a new taxonomy of ethnic peoples, which expressed itself in racism. Both kinds of distinction, of "discrimination," are historically grounded in the sociogenesis of the modern body. In the late eighteenth and the nineteenth centuries a profound transformation occurred: in a process specific to each social class and occurring at different times and with varying speed, dozens of local conceptions of the body were scrapped, and in the crucible of medicine (which here represents both science and society), the new body was cast as from a foundry mold. How this mold shaped the ideas of an entirely new body, different from all the old scraps that went into its making, can be most clearly shown through the history of the female body. However, the belief in the truthfulness or scientific nature of this production of the body, which I have traced here through the production of "woman," has so skewed the perspective of many studies that they contribute little to an understanding of how this recasting occurred.[85]

A significant obstacle to a historical study of the body is created by a related prejudice that is embodied in most histories of the medical profession, and which Pomata has exposed. In her work on Bologna she has sketched a change in the nature of healers between the sixteenth and the eighteenth centuries, a change which I can explain only with the fact that the emergence of the "real" body was beginning. As long as this new body did not exist as a disembedded object, it could not be monopolized. Pomata describes for everyday life until the late seventeenth century the same thing Calvi found during the plague in Florence in 1620–1630: a multitude of groups, all of which I might call healers, practicing their trade side by side: *medici* with doctoral degrees, midwives, barbers, barber-surgeons, surgeons, bonesetters, pig-castraters, druggists and others who dealt in herbs and spices. The city administration made sure that each person stayed with his profession, partly to protect the populace and partly to protect the trades themselves. But it seems to me a gross mistake to see in these various healers, to whom Pomata adds the local saints, "specialists of the body" who as a group and each with his own specialty were already concerned with the same object—the "body"—like an early prototype of modern medical practices.[86] Pomata examines, from the perspective of social obligation, the relationships a sick person in Bologna could enter into during the earlier period of her study. She discovers that the choice of a healer was driven by a social logic whose dynamic was controlled by the sick person. Scholarship has generally interpreted the multilevel structure of the healing profession as a hierarchy of knowledge. But in an earlier study of

the same source Pomata showed that at least in Bologna it arose from the
cultural interpretation of the body.[87] She reveals an inner equivalence
between the organization of the healers and the conception of the body.
This body, with its complex relationship between the internal and the
external, with specific notions of hair, blood, and urine, of clean and
unclean, could in no way be monopolized by one trade, by one form of
knowledge. The real and symbolic multiformity of the body had its
counterpart in the multiformity of the social body of the healers. A
restructuring of the meanings of the body was thus a precondition and
consequence of the restructuring of the motives that determined which
healer would be consulted. Social historians of medicine have realized
the necessity of getting away from the narrow history of the medical
profession itself, of not restricting the historian's perspective by the
monopolistic claims of modern medicine. As the English medical historians Margaret Pelling and Charles Webster have demanded: "it is
important not to allow the special pleading of contemporary pressure
groups to lead the historian into undervaluing the activities of ar-
bitrarily defined sections of the medical community."[88] It seems necessary to supplement the historical critique of the naturalization of a
monolithic medical profession in charge of the body with a critique of
the parallel construction of a model of the body. Almost all studies
dealing with the emergence of medicine's monopoly of maintaining the
body's health can be used, if only implicitly, as sources to show the social
triumph of the new perception of the body. But in most studies on the
history of the medical profession this possibility is entirely overlooked.

BODY IMAGE AND SOCIETY

The new body that was gradually created beginning in the eighteenth
century was woven from the same materials of the social imagination
that went into the making of a new society.[89] Not only the language,
but also the perception of a period are shaped by its leitmotifs and
conceptual frameworks: "It is no doubt correct to take ideas out of their
medical isolation, and to examine them as stylistic elements side by side
with related ideas in other disciplines and spheres of life. The heuristic
power of such an approach is obvious and is far from having been

exhausted."[90] With this demand Temkin follows in the tradition of Sigerist, who as early as 1929 struggled along this path to find new insights into Harvey's concepts.[91] Starting from Wölfflin's ideas on art history, Sigerist arrived at characterizing Harvey's mode of perception as "baroque." In the same way art brought movement into architecture, and Galileo brought dynamic into physics, Harvey interpreted the flowing of the blood as circulation. Sixty years after Sigerist, the latest Harvey scholarship is returning to his work, seeing in William Harvey not so much the "discoverer" of blood circulation as one of the cocreators of the circulation concept, which established itself around 1750 not only in physiology, but also in economics, the natural sciences, and journalism.

Figlio prefers to speak of "concepts," and he examines the intrinsic equivalence of very disconnected spheres of reality as reflected in analogous conceptual frameworks. Using the physiology of the nervous system at the turn of the nineteenth century as an example, he perceives that this equivalence was created through the exchange of metaphors, the flow of "key-terms" that occurred between the scientific, social, and political languages.[92] Metaphors such as "constitution" and "organization" always establish bridges between the body and consciousness, between the biological, psychological, and social spheres. Jewson employs the term "medical cosmology"[93] to characterize the structural preconditions within which eighteenth- and nineteenth-century medical theory moved from the total person to a network of dependencies based on "microscopic particles."[94] A new school of English and American historians of science has subjected the traditions of their field to a searching criticism. Demanding "context-analysis," they work with methods of social anthropology in order to embed medical theories into the thematic landscape of a given period.[95] Shapin has pointed out that it would be unthinkable in anthropology to understand a period's conception of nature and body the way scientific history does: as individual "discoveries" that correspond to a "natural reality."[96] It goes without saying that the new body shows similarity to the social and cosmological reality.[97] Thus to me it seems arbitrary to derive corporeality from the social forms rather than social forms from corporeality. My body in need of treatment and the productive society surrounding me are cast from the same mold. The "development of a scientific fact" often proceeds, if under different names, in respect to the body, society, and nature.[98] All "facts" about my body carry a related imprint: its "reproductive capacity," its sexual "energy," even its "health"—all are concepts that would have been utterly foreign to Storch and his female patients. The term "reproduction" itself cannot appear in Storch at all,[99] nor a term that would have described something similar, since the eighteenth century had no word that embraced everything now subsumed in gynecology. The fact that Storch treats women does not make him a "gynecologist," since he is concerned with the entire life history of a woman (her bios), and does not treat a woman as an agent, a mechanism, a collection of cells that can reproduce life (zoé). For the same reason he has no term resembling our "sexuality."[100] Today women are concerned to ascribe to themselves a specific female sexuality, but not reproduction. A woman might refer to her reproductive organs, but she would hesitate to define herself by saying: "I have already reproduced myself three times." The women of Eisenach still thought of themselves in relation to *generatio*, which in popular parlance was something akin to "fruitfulness." Children were born from women; the womb had not yet become part of a reproductive apparatus.[101] Women were still delivered of child by other women; babies were not yet delivered by professionals, as would be the case a hundred years later. In traditional perception women gave children life; medicine was still far from assuming the protection of "life" in the womb as its mandate. It was medicine, demography, and political science which replaced the expressions of *generatio*—whether Latin or vernacular—with "reproduction." Prior to this new definition there simply was no term in which insemination, conception, pregnancy, and birth could have been subsumed. It would be a mistake to separate the scientific nomenclature of the nineteenth century, in which the inner landscape of the uterus was imprinted with the names of its discoverers, from the context of the functional terminology of demography and political economy. Reproduction emerged and was linked to the context of production as that term moved into the center of political economy around 1850. During these decades more and more necessities of life were transformed into the need for goods, and all goods were seen as the result of a process that was perceived as culturally disembedded and labeled "production."

Capital and work were the productive factors; the uterus as well as domestic work were newly defined as factors whereby labor force reproduced itself. *Homo oeconomicus* was equipped with a biological body that reflected this economic division of labor. Reproduction was inscribed upon a woman's body as her true "destiny," and the body she was given became the living proof of the natural origin of economic concepts. The equipping of women with a reproductive apparatus led to a cultural disembodiment of the processes of *generatio,* analogous to the "disembedding" of the productive economy which accompanied the end of a culture of subsistence and self-sufficiency.

The emergence of "sexuality" reflected on the level of the body a new view of the physical universe, very similar to the way in which reproduction reflected a new view of a society that was economic. Sexuality cannot be found in Eisenach. Lust and desire are present in many manifestations, yet in the shadow of Galen's doctrine they assume only a marginal place. For Storch, as for most doctors still oriented toward Galen, lust was not a medical problem. It interested the doctor only if it got too "hot."[102] Only immoderate lust was addressed in the medical category of "excesses." This category included such other things as an inordinate weakness for wine, Brunswick beer, and Eichsfeld sausage, overeating, and other kinds of immoderation. Our modern "sexuality" took shape with and after the Marquis de Sade. With de Sade sexuality became visible, describable, dissectable. Only here did the history of attitudes toward lust reach the stage Foucault has called an epistemological faultline. With this transformation, sexuality became one of the many layers which together composed the anatomized body as a multilayered text.[103]

It was much later that Freud conceptualized "libido" as a psychic energy, and he did so with concepts and terms adopted, in part verbatim, from an article by Helmholtz.[104] He linked the body to the new mythology of energy, which was assuming a central place in the sciences in the wake of discoveries in physics. Just as "reproduction" had embedded the body of women into the context of labor force, and as earlier notions about the waste of bodily strength through ejaculation during intercourse had embedded it in a "spermatic economy,"[105] physics manifested itself within the body as "sexuality." For hundreds of years, right up to the mid-nineteenth century, the cosmos had been seen as an

interplay of a disymmetrical complementarity between body and movement, force and matter. "Energy," the final reality, the "stuff" whereby
everything maintains itself, emerged as a theme after 1870. Matter was
reduced to the principle of the conservation of energy. Energy and
sexuality were only two ways of expressing one theme: the genderless
monism of a final, single matter. "Sexuality" redefined and reinterpreted
lust as profoundly as reproduction had transformed *generatio*. The power
of words and of the contexts from which they arise reveals itself in the
fact that we are unable to entertain conceptualizations different from
those inherent in the words and their contexts.

In the end the striving to maintain health undermined the self-
evident nature of life. Pain and illness, once a form of punishment, the
yoke of fate, a trial, or a burden, were turned into symptoms of disease
within the body. In medical theory toward the end of the eighteenth
century the body waned as a source that imparted meaning to suffering.
Figlio has remarked: "nosology was the central point around which
medical thought was conceptually organised. It was a taxonomy of
disease, and in that sense, it isolated and categorised disease as something
essentially foreign to the living organism. It turned the attention of the
physician away from the period in the life history of an individual,
which one might call 'being ill,' and directed it toward a foreign entity
separable from the patient himself." After tracing the developments in
physiological and pathological theory between the late-eighteenth and
the mid-nineteenth centuries, Figlio continues: "Disease, once the state
of a person, became first the qualitative alteration of the vital properties,
then the quantitative deviation of a quantitative measure. In this posi-
tivistic tradition, physiology and pathology became the establishment
of norm and deviations of physico-chemical parameters."[106] Jewson
traces the steps in the "disappearance of the sick" from medical cosmology during the transition from medicine at the sickbed to the hospital
medicine of the nineteenth century, and from there to modern laboratory medicine.[107] He describes how the theories and techniques of
physics penetrated into the study of living organisms during the last
stage, contemporaneous with the entrance of physical energy into sexol-
ogy. In the course of this transformation "being ill" loses its former
meaning as a personal event in a human existence and becomes a

deficiency in relation to a medically described norm, which for the most part cannot be experienced by the senses.[108] As a way of mediating this new body, a body in need of therapy and diagnosis and experienced as the seat of diseases, there gradually arose a new medical theory and practice focused on normalization. Disease becomes the bread and butter of doctors. In the words of Tristram Engelhardt, the leading thinker of the new medical-philosophical scholarship in the United States, "disease is a mode of analyzing phenomena for the purpose of intervention, of diagnosis, prognosis and therapy."[109]

The Body in History

Beyond the large field of the history of medicine, historians can find stimulating ideas in mythology, the study of semantic fields, iconography, folklore, and art history. Even in these fields the focus is rarely on the phenomenon I am seeking: the reality-generating experience of the body that is unique and specific to a given historical period. Yet the very different perspectives of these disciplines promise direct access to expressions of the body that are not ordered through the grid of a remote medical description.

MYTHOLOGY AND HISTORY

The movement of mythological patterns and themes across time stands in contrast to the genesis of modern terms. The traditional justification for seeing woman as a lesser being and the fourfold classification of humoral characteristics belong into this category. The reception of ideas in history has been studied mostly as the story of learned systems recorded in writing, with the goal of "showing the lasting influence that classical ideas . . . have exerted on Western medicine across centuries."[110] The emphasis in such studies has been on the reciprocal influence of such systems and their receptivity to written currents of thought from other cultural spheres—for example, from Islamic culture. Throughout his life, G. E. R. Lloyd has resisted the tendency of his fellow historians of medicine to link such crosscurrents of tradition with the names of Hippocrates or Galen, Aristotle or Soranus.[111] He shows that the patterns we name after later teachers are clearly visible in early archaic Greece, and that the scientific traditions of Greek urban culture continuously assimilated elements from popular culture, which they in turn enriched.[112] Lloyd's interest in the reciprocal influence of popular beliefs and embryonic science in the fifth century B.C. has led him, for example, to a study of the gynecological writings of the Hippocratic Corpus. He notes that as late as 1983 most of these had not been translated and that critical editions and commentaries were not available for many of them. I couldn't help but think of my own source when I read Lloyd's complaint: "it would be difficult to find any other field of Hippocratic studies where such rich sources of evidence have been, for so long, so unexploited." Lloyd's analysis of Hippocratic gynecology allows him to probe the barriers that exist between men and women. Like me, he has no access to what was said by women themselves, or even healers among them. After finishing my own commentary on Storch, I was encouraged and consoled by Lloyd's profession of scholarly modesty in the last volume of his work: "What these men have to say about their own relationships both with their women patients and with women healers of various kinds represents, to be sure, just one side of those questions . . . Yet the evidence can, with discretion, be used to provide the basis of some observations on what the authors themselves sometimes recognize to be complex issues. How far were women, when sick, treated differently from men? To what extent did the diagnosis and treatment of gynaecological conditions in particular reflect assumptions concerning the inferiority of women?"[113]

Lloyd is not interested primarily in the treatment of women as depicted in the Hippocratic Corpus. Rather, his attention is focused on the question of how the unwritten tradition was assimilated to medical practice, how it was critically sifted and used, how unsuitable elements were discarded and eliminated. He found the gynecological tracts especially useful in trying to answer these questions, since there was one thing that very clearly differentiated the treatment of women from the treatment of other patients: "a certain distance or reserve between the male doctor and the female patient" fostered the "desire on the part of the doctor to enlist the assistance both of the patient herself and of the women who attend her" (p. 75). Both Lloyd and I found in the biology or complaints of female patients, though mediated through a male doctor, a privileged access to the dialogue between popular belief and learned interpretation of the embodiment of suffering.

The question that arose for me in reading Lloyd's work concerns the parallelism of two ways in which traditions relating to the body were passed on: in popular tradition, which was limited to oral communication and gestures, and which was recorded only in the notes of what the doctor understood about the women's complaints; and in the history of learned traditions. In examining my source I continually stumbled upon motifs (both in the doctor's opinion as well as in his account of the women's beliefs) that were at the same time clear echoes and yet fleeting shadows of ideas about humors, fluxes, and the openings of the flesh, ideas that had already appeared in classic works of archaic Greece. Is there something here that has preserved itself? What importance shall I assign to it?

There are two reasons why Lloyd is not of much help to me on these issues: first, because he restricts himself to an exegesis of classical texts, and second, because I have found in a different line of inquiry a deeper insight into the gulf between the two modes of transmission. Laín Entralgo has argued that what changed in Greece between the fifth and the fourth centuries B.C. on the part of the doctor was not so much the patterns in which the body was conceived but the importance of the doctor's word.[114] Before the fifth century there was no writing, hence the body was not described.[115] The body could only be talked about. "Nothing as yet can be 'looked up' with the eye, everything must be 'called up,'" as Walter J. Ong said in his foreword to Laín Entralgo's work.[116] The perception of reality under conditions of a preliterate orality bears no comparison to a descriptive mode of perception. The alphabet "introduces a new state of mind—the alphabetic mind, if the expression be allowed."[117] Without a concept of memory as the storehouse of retrievable sentences that can be quoted verbatim, reality does not solidify into the sort of descriptive terms that have become so self-evident to us. There remains something fluid and incomprehensible about the perception of the body, which stands in sharp contrast to the clarity of the demarcation that developed in Classical Greece. Until the fifth century (and for many centuries thereafter) the eye not only sent out rays with which it saw, the eye also "breathed in" what it perceived. Breathing, smell, and sight were still all of the same stuff: the breath.[118] There is no comparison between the mode of oral transmission—and not only its content—and the mode of transmission in a textual tradition. Only the intensive literary culture of the fourth century made possible the emergence of a corpus of body descriptions, a way of speaking of the body described in this way, and the development of an iatric discourse whose stages Entralgo has traced.

These reflections were important to me in making a distinction between the two modes in which a motif, such as that of the humoral characteristics, could be transmitted. One mode can be investigated as a critical study of literature, the second demands methods and tools which the historian has to devise for himself. Yvonne Verdier reports that only fifteen years ago the women of Minot, a village in Burgundy, were convinced that their menstrual blood interrupted the fermentation of wine, dissolved uncooked sauces, and spoiled honey. The bees shunned a menstruating woman precisely as they do in Pliny's *Naturalis Historia* (11b, 28c 13).[119] The question whether we are dealing with the survival of ideas received from a Hellenistic writer, or whether Verdier today, like Pliny in his time, should be seen as a witness who records the persistence of an unwritten motif, is important to me as an historian, since I encountered similar things in Storch.

Storch begins nearly every report on a patient with a note about her humoral constitution. But Storch was an avowed student of Georg Ernst Stahl, a firm opponent of the traditional doctrine of the humors—as a chemist even more than as a doctor. I must therefore exercise the greatest caution in regarding Storch's characterization of his patients with the humoral schemata as a medical-diagnostic procedure. When Storch speaks of a woman as a phlegmatic, his usage is not far removed from our own. And yet, in using this old formula, dragged along like so much baggage which does not at all fit into his own doctrine, Storch was perceiving something which the word today no longer expresses. To him, and to the women, warm/cold, dry/moist were qualities linked to the blood's composition—and for the women probably in a different way than for him. For the women more likely speak of thick and thin, sharp and mild flows, or they connote these qualities when they adjust their language to that of the doctor. But both doctor and patient speak of basic elements that shape body experience. It is tempting to reduce the statements of the doctor and the women to the reception of the same classical texts, which among the women, perhaps generations earlier, had been received with less or a different kind of understanding than they encountered in the learned tradition of the doctor. But I cannot exclude the possibility that the variant interpretations which the doctor and his patient had about the difference between heat and heat treatment, or between "drawing out" and "expulsion," represent two currents of tradition that are not comparable: in other words, that the different way in which the women experienced the body stemmed from their being deeply rooted in an older level of motifs that had been handed down orally and holistically.

The question about the possibility that body sensation, body perception, and body symbolism have two very different histories on two very different levels has been raised also by Sandra Ott.[120] She gathered her experiences in Sainte-Engrâce on the northern slope of the Pyrenees among a population of ancient Basque shepherds. In this village conception is understood in an analogy to cheesemaking: the semen of the man causes the woman's blood to curdle, just as rennet curdles milk. The precise description of this image is strikingly similar to the text of Aristotle in *De Generatione Animalium,* Book II, 739b.21–22. The same cheese analogy is known from at least one village on the same northern slope during the Middle Ages.[121] According to a confession recorded by the Inquisition, the priest in that village tied an herb around his neck during intercourse; Beatrice, the noble owner of the sheep pen, regarded that same herb as the antidote to another herb used by the shepherds to curdle milk. The image is ancient: "Remember [O Lord] that you made me from clay . . . Did you not pour me out as milk and curdle me like cheese?" we read in Job 10.10. It also appears in Hildegard von Bingen,[122] except that here it was also the physical incarnation of the love between man and woman that was depicted in the image of cheesemaking.[123] Sandra Ott therefore cannot answer the question whether the analogy among her shepherds goes back to an Aristotelian text, or whether Aristotle was the anthropologist's precursor in reporting an unwritten tradition.

The implications of all this were clear: no matter how useful the history of the reception of scientific themes across time might be, I had to become open to the idea that patterns and motifs I encountered among Storch's women patients reached the doctor along a path that stretched back for hundreds and thousands of years, and that they were not modes of thinking derived from medicine. The work of Mikhail Bakhtin suggests the complexity of the interaction between such patterns that have long existed within learned doctrine and their counterparts that are fundamental to popular cosmology. The materiality of the baroque body that Bakhtin found in Rabelais—its elements of air, water, earth, and fire, its continuing transformation, the relation between the interior of the body, its orifices, and the external world—are like echoes of a tradition in which Pliny, Isidor of Seville, the Hippocratic cosmos, and images of Aristotle flow together. And yet Bakhtin's textual analysis shows that this body of the people in the sixteenth century was not directly built up from these writings. Many of Rabelais' images "remain an enigma. This enigma can be solved only by means of a deep study of Rabelais' popular sources . . . Rabelais' images are completely at home within the thousand-year-old development of popular culture." According to Bakhtin, the *ordo* of the Middle Ages contributed substantially to the emergence of a dualistic world, one that manifests itself most clearly in laughter, a laughter that has nothing to do with the laughter of modernity. In Cervantes too this other world is still evident in Sancho Panza, a direct descendant of the pot-bellied and fertile demons depicted on ancient Greek vases. But Cervantes shows us this demon through the eyes of Don Quixote; he tries to tame his wildness and put it at the service of a universal and deep utopia of popular culture. Not so Rabelais. According to Bakhtin, all acts in the drama of world history "were performed before the chorus of a laughing people."[124] This chorus of the people, resounding from all their pores, found its eminent chorus-master in Rabelais.

There is no hint of a carnival in Storch's record and nothing of the lustiness of Rabelais, the medical professor from Montpellier. In Storch's practice everything is very puritanical and bourgeois. And yet the body which the women conjure up with their words and which the doctor treats, resembles the body of Pantagruel more than that of a modern person. Despite the small-town, provincial manner in which our ambitious Protestant doctor recorded his perceptions of the body and published them for the benefit of his younger colleagues, he was paradoxically a distant relative of Rabelais, the "priest of Meudon." Storch too is a witness to an orally transmitted popular concept of the body. Like a stream of dense lava reaching into the time of Storch, this popular body retained its identity much more so than the phenomena historians like to call "longue durée." When it came to interpreting my source, these two sides of the history of the body again and again raised a heuristic problem: on which of these two levels should a statement be interpreted? In her study of the *Chirurgia* of Mondeville, Pouchelle was very conscious of facing the same problem. Images and themes in her text seemed peculiar to the Middle Ages; yet during a later ethnological survey she finds them in a rural area of Normandy: "This convergence disturbed me. It was not possible to see these images, which despite the triumph of medicine still shape our lives, as merely the antiquated dust of a vanished time. On the contrary, their vividness forces us to understand corporeality as that sphere in which we can observe the "longue durée" that so fascinates the historians of *mentalitées*."[125] It seems that the motifs and images of the body unfold in two kinds of time, a historical and a transhistorical time, and that the body, especially at work—when laboring[126] or suffering[127]—is a bridge between these two realms of time.

THE HISTORY OF METAPHORS

Sometimes it seems that two different scholarly disciplines carefully restrict themselves to reading the same text on two different levels: history in search of facts, and literary studies in search of metaphors. By contrasting two works that influenced my heuristic method, I hope to justify the restrictions I imposed upon myself in interpreting Storch's metaphors.

M.-Ch. Pouchelle has shown how metaphor, as a way of rendering the "lived body," embeds the body into the environment of its age, unlike the objectifying and isolating description of the body as an object. She examines images and motifs of the "longue durée" across a period of sev-

eral centuries and ends chronologically about one hundred years before
the transformation of classical medical doctrine, an event on which
MacLean has focused his attention (more about him later). Though these
two scholars have very different ideas about the meaning that lies hidden
when people speak of the body, both have succeeded in building a bridge
across disciplines and opening up new methodological territory.

Pouchelle examines the *Chirurgia* of Henri de Mondeville and finds in
this text, which strives so hard for a realistic naturalism, a continuous
correspondence between the conception of the body and the conception
of the world. Both conceptions are mediated through the metaphorical
dimensions of the words. As etymology tells us, the essence of metaphor
is to transport one reality (as though in a vessel) into another reality
(meta-phora). A metaphor unites in a single word disparate realms of reality, making them appear as one. Mondeville, who as a surgeon made
every effort to describe the elements of the body "such as they are," cannot but evoke a cosmology. The body he describes reveals itself as a mirror of medieval society. The anatomical description tells of the structure
of the social and political order, of the place of humankind in God's *ordo*
of the world, of humankind's closeness to the world of animals, plants,
and minerals. Thanks to her methodological approach, Pouchelle goes
far beyond any previous studies about microcosm-macrocosm.[128] Instead of arriving at the usual parallel or analogy of world image and body
image, she lays hold of an incredibly rich imaginary incarnation of the
world *in* the body. The vehicle of this incarnation are metaphors, which
express a *similitudo* between things. To begin with, Pouchelle arranges
the metaphors that express similarities between parts of the body (inner
metaphors) and those that originate in the world and are applied to the
body, according to motif groups that are inherent in the text and thus
Mondeville's own. To reconstruct the contemporary associations and the
cast of symbols to which they belong, she draws on other texts of the
Latin Middle Ages as reference. Finally she confronts Mondeville's
images with modern texts that examine the "anthropological structures
of the imaginary," the basic motifs of our thinking and imagination.
Her method involves also a very personal introspection. Having eluci-
dated the historical text with the help of her own psychoanalytic experience, she relates it to the images of the unconscious taking shape in her

own body. The historical analysis of hidden meanings and psychoanalytical exposure intersect. Because of this, Mondeville, surgeon to Philip the Fair, attests the "persistence of certain forms of representation, the rootedness of certain images in a bodily morphology, an essentially identical moment of the imagination beyond space and time."[129] Pouchelle's method is an attempt to close the distance between body and world, the distance between two things that are today isolated, and to eliminate entirely the gulf that others try to bridge with words such as "correspondence" and "similarity." According to Pouchelle, the reality of engrained images of the modern unconscious and the metaphors of the Middle Ages, which incarnated a cosmos, are made of the same material. What once joined "outside" and "inside" in a unified image of the world is identical to that which the historian discovers in her inner self.

Ian MacLean has a very different attitude toward his material, textual commentaries from the sixteenth and seventeenth centuries.[130] And this material also speaks very differently about reality. Here language is no longer primarily the "glue of the universe," an embodiment of interconnections through analogies. Beginning in the late sixteenth century, this metaphorical language was subjected to a critical scrutiny, from which gradually arose the new, discriminating language of science, and the attempt to describe the world with precise definitions.[131] Henceforth things were to be separated, the relating and equating of things to the surrounding world was to be precluded. MacLean thus examines a different language, a language in transition, which is a precondition for the creation of a purely physical body. He takes this language at its word and no more. He does not trace the implicit and hidden suggestions that can be contained in a language about the body, even though he too examines layers of language. He starts from the *loci communi* that were received from the classical heritage and traces their critique and transformation in the sphere of the learned tradition of the Renaissance. MacLean restricts himself to a closed corpus drawn from the learned Latin of the Renaissance. These *loci communi* concern woman, ideas about gender differences, and the link between gender-difference and other conceptual differentiations in the contemporary mental cosmology. All these aspects together make up what MacLean calls "the notion of women," the cultural concept and "discourse" about "woman"

and "femininity" in this period. Whereas Pouchelle deliberately shied
away from following the spread of an image or a theme from one written
source to another,[132] MacLean turns the history of reception upside
down. Instead of constructing vertical lines of development, he looks for
horizontal references in texts from contemporary scholastic theology,
medicine, ethics, politics, and jurisprudence, with all their mutual
cross-references, in order to record with great precision the decline
and persistence of the classical concepts. While Pouchelle goes deeply
into the implied imaginary realms, MacLean concentrates emphatically
on the explicit statements read literally in the clear light of learned
exegesis.

The body that emerges from these two studies is very different, but
not because the authors examine different historical periods. Using the
woman's inner body as an example, I will show briefly what this
difference is. In Pouchelle, the "womb" is a space, an ambiguous shell
showing all the similarities to other cavities in the "belly." Its crucial
characteristic is innerness; the woman's womb seems like an archetype of
the mysterious and the hidden. Pouchelle's analysis of the metaphors
that refer to the materiality of the inner body penetrates to the symbolic
equivalence of material and immaterial dimensions: "the kinship, virtually a blood-kinship, between the feminine element and the interior
habitable space."[133] The relation of the sexes is embodied in the body—
inside vs. outside—and in the world—closed, domestic space vs.
external sphere, unbounded space, the forest. But this relation is itself a
mirror of other equivalences of soul and body, humankind and cosmos.
By using the method she does, Pouchelle uncovers not just a single
dimension or even something purely material; instead, she brings to
light forms of embodiment. In contrast, MacLean's analysis, based on a
literal reading of statements, succeeds in showing clearly—though
without emphasizing it specifically—the contraction of woman from an
inverse embodiment to a functionally different body. Despite the tenacious persistence of classical conceptual frameworks even after the sixteenth century, woman gradually emerged as the anatomically different
body. The inverse equivalence of man and woman very slowly gave way
to a concept of physiological difference in which woman was newly seen
and "upgraded" as a being physiologically predestined for motherhood.

Gender was given an anatomically precise place. In learned discourse of earlier times the visible and invisible "private parts" of woman had been "seen," despite their seemingly obvious morphology, as being just the same as the male parts, only turned inside. Now a "sexual functional view" discovered them in their "true" anatomical morphology. [134] The previous cosmological interpretation of gender relations, the difference between man and woman, in which gender relations was part of a dual view of the world and in which "anatomy" was interpreted accordingly, gave way, seemingly in the direction of greater scientific accuracy, to a new designation of the sexes derived from anatomy itself. The bodies of man and woman were placed on opposite ends of a polarity; they were constructed as disconnected entities; the parallelism *in* them was abolished and with it all ideas about a reciprocal embodiment. We shall see that one hundred and fifty years later this transformation had not yet reached Eisenach, or had met there resistance from a different living tradition. The aim of the medical authors examined by MacLean was to describe the bodies of man and woman as mere bodies, that is, "such as they are," which is why the inside was turned inside out, examined, and described. Gradually and haltingly, a "real" body emerged from the previous cosmos of embodiment. At the same time there remained clinging to it what MacLean would probably regard as "ideology," which flowed into this naturalistic construction as a distorting, more or less obsolete bias.

PHENOMENOLOGICAL AND PSYCHOLOGICAL INTERPRETATIONS

The object of Pouchelle's study—the body of the past as embodied in metaphors—has also become in a special way the focus of psychological investigation. I have already mentioned hints in that direction in Pouchelle's work. It would be a great loss for historians if they failed to take seriously the contributions to the transformation of body metaphors that have come from the phenomenological psychologists of the school of van den Berg. [135] In this "metabletic" analysis the question of where and how the heart and the womb, for example, are experienced becomes more important than the question of how they are visualized. The new impulses the historian can get from these authors concerns their methodology. These authors are clinical psychologists, trained to examine the statements of their contemporaries for their experiential content, to ask what it means to call someone a "halfhearted person," and what happens when "the heart sinks into the boots." What does it really mean when someone acts in "cold blood" and "breaks hearts"? Trained in clinical encounters, the psychologist then goes to work to examine the metaphorical meaning of Harvey's "discovery" of the divided heart. He sheds new light on the reason why all scientists (from the time dissection of the heart began in Greece[136] until the seventeenth century) denied that the septum dividing the right and left ventricles was impervious to blood. Contrary to all the evidence, they could neither see nor imagine a divided heart. In similar fashion the "heart polyp," which the anatomists of the seventeenth century "saw," described, and illustrated, became quite believably a proliferous, branching thing that grew from the heart, which it then enveloped and suffocated.[137]

More difficult, harder to understand for me as a historian, and yet very insightful are the phenomenological studies from the Jungian school, which have been appearing in the Eranos Yearbooks. The analysts of this school trained by James Hillmann include several whose interests are historically oriented. It is true that their investigations look for historically specific manifestations of how people imagined what are in the final analysis always the same archetypes, and that this gives rise to what I would call a "natural history of the invisible body," a critique that also applies to Pouchelle. Nevertheless, these studies do guide us onto paths that would otherwise remain closed. Examples of this kind of work are Berry's search for the always newly reemerging figure of the nymph Echo,[138] and Sardello's clinical evidence that the inhabitants of Dallas feel a compulsion to imagine the city as a metaphor of self-perception.[139] As someone with no experience in the routine of a clinical psychologist, I found it a particularly stimulating experience to follow the thoughts of Romanyshyn, an experienced clinician with historical training. In the textual commentary to Harvey, he presents the heart either as a cipher for courage and then again as a model of the pump.[140]

These scholarly initiatives, which are concerned with a scientific analysis of the body as an object of perception, go back (as their bibliographies indicate) to a change in German medicine in the later 1920s, as we can see clearly in Zaner's work. [141] Hartmann has written a historiographical account of this change. [142] With an eye toward their medical practice, strongly influenced by the reception of Freudian thought, and basing themselves on direct experience at the sickbed, Viktor von Weizsäcker, V. E. von Gebsattel, and others tried to free themselves from the "scientific image of man" that made the patient into a case and to discover and treat the complete person as a suffering subject. Disease was to be seen as a mental and psychic disturbance of the relation to one's environment and fellow human beings. Writing at a high literary level and in the hope of reforming the practice of medicine, these men focused their attention on the doctor's relation to the individual life story. Their analyses were based on the ways in which the suffering, the dying, the tortured, or the crippled perceived the "I," perceived their own body. "The subject of medical anthropology is the human being as nature, that is within the realm of biological-vitalistic causes and purposes. But to the extent that the human being entertains ideas, realizing values within himself, medical anthropology also deals with him in the totality of his existence." [143] "The human being is the place where nature and spirit meet." [144] Despite this attempt to see in the individual the unique realization of naturally predetermined elements, an acquaintance with this school of thought expands the vision of any historian concerned with bodies that have long since vanished. Weizsäcker urged the modern doctor not to let the bio-logy (life story), which is at the center of Storch's practice, disappear behind the factual nosography in which doctor and patient today collaborate. [145] Plügge, who places himself within that same tradition, deals primarily with the corporeal-spatial self-experience: with health and its disruptions, with the question of how the skin is today becoming the experienced surface, or how pain makes the body its staging ground. [146] The reflections of these doctors brought me closer to the women in Eisenach. In their works I found patients of my own generation who expressed experiences that seemed very similar to those I read in Storch, but which I myself cannot articulate because my scientific education has deprived me of the necessary words. [147] Upon closer examination, however, I had to ask myself a critical question even in relation to anthropological medicine:

Did it in the end also contribute to creating the patient with body and soul, in other words, to making him the subject of treatment and the object of examination, in the way Armstrong and Arney have tried to show for postwar medicine in the United States?[148]

Crucial to my understanding of Storch was the work of Zur Lippe, which is difficult to place between conceptual history and art history on the one hand and historical psychology on the other.[149] Whereas Plessner, for example—but also many of the people he refers to—makes fundamental statements about the experience of the body, Lippe stimulates the reader to historical thinking. In his doctoral dissertation under Theodor Adorno he examined the geometrization of space in the seventeenth century as expressed in new body disciplines: a new art of fencing and military drill, and a new dance. Their point of reference was, as never before, a Cartesian system of coordinates existing in space. This system is concretely expressed in the sequence of rooms in a baroque palace or the layout of a French garden. It seems that in the process a reduction of the spatial experience to visual dimensionality was anticipated at court, that space was deprived of its reality perceivable through nose, ear, and touch, and was assigned a new, geometrical disciplining function. Parallel with the homogenization of space as a segment from an infinite matrix of three directions, the reality under the skin was also for the first time perceived as inner "space"—no longer as the site of a metaphorical heart chamber, or as a womb-barrel, or as intestines-cooking pot, but as an extension, beyond a skin that has become merely a boundary, of an orderly cosmos into the new private sphere. It is thus only with hesitation and for want of other words that I speak of the Storchean body as "inner space." The female body implied in Storch's accounts is not a visible object which takes up space and within which its organs are located. The blood embodied in the women is more like an orientational surge, creating space as it flows. Just as my own body is no pathway to the past, no such pathway leads through the inner reaches of my space. In my own experience bodies are located in space, and the Cartesian coordinates locate the body in space and space in the body. Zur Lippe has shown that this perception is the result of a "two-fold change in the anthropology of the modern world-image." The naturalization of the body and of space go hand in hand. Zur Lippe speaks here of the "effort . . . to read the meaning and the laws of human existence from external 'nature,'" which is only a formal inversion, since in fact "the image of nature is modeled after the socially conditioned idea of human beings, which in turn, through circular reasoning, is deduced from the image of nature."[150]

THE BODY IN THE MIRROR OF REALITY

The body I "have" is like a text. I can see it; I can imagine it. But perhaps I can do so less clearly than the much younger women I taught in California. From childhood on they are surrounded in the classroom by anatomical charts, each in a different color. One chart shows the skeleton in black as the framework of bones, another the nerves or the muscles in vivid colors, while others depict the digestive, endocrinal, urinary, and reproductive systems. As these separate textual layers are absorbed by the children, it has been observed more than once that variant body images of Italian, African, or Scandinavian origin, which had persisted in America for two or three generations, disappear within a homogenous model.[151] In this way even "being a woman" or "being black" can become the purpose of special courses. The course descriptions explicitly offer the opportunity to learn about one's own body through a self-reflective comparison with teaching models, and to practice the "experience" of this body under psychological guidance. Just as the native English language can become an "acquired foreign language" for an African-American, the woman's body is today offered as the subject matter of college courses. The prenatal training of a pregnant woman at San Francisco General Hospital includes instruction for the first and most important lessons she will have to teach her newborn before it even reaches her breast.

This acquisition of the body through descriptions, drawings, instructions, and exercises is in stark contrast to the historical generation of a host of meaningful perceptions of reality, as whose center each person experiences himself, and which he or she experiences as his or her own embodiment. "Center" here does not imply any economic-political position that enables one to create a "definition," but the epistemological place that each and every one assumes in such a context. Meaning and importance are attributed to these perceptions not through descriptions (with an implied appeal that the individual identify with them), but through metaphors.

The difference between these two diametrically opposed modes of establishing reality becomes clear when I contrast the anatomical models of health handbooks to the still-remembered experiences that Yvonne Verdier has examined.[152] As I have already pointed out, in Minot menstrual blood was seen as a substance that would spoil or rot the salting tub, bacon, brine, mayonnaise, and wine, while it could not harm dried or cooked food in the home. The linkage of these things bespeaks a deeper order with roots beyond the material substance and embracing the entire world. Through the example of pig-slaughtering, Verdier shows the coherence of the peasant division of labor between man and woman and the symbolic interpretation of the artisanal, domestic, animalistic, and cosmic spheres—for there was even a connection between the pig to be slaughtered and the position of the moon. The "blood" of women, whose proximity can cause wine to turn, is only one element in a context of things that are linked through their meaning. "Blood" is not "defined" as something that does something; rather it acquires this power through the metaphorical connection of elements and things that belong together because they are culturally associated and whose connection has been confirmed by practical experience. The web of meanings thus created, or which has always been "there," is so complex that it can never be fashioned from only one description, one view, one perspective. What characterizes this world are the implied analogies, the metaphorical equivalences between things; what characterizes a described world is the isolation of the object, of the body as such. In Minot the nature of the women's body lies in the eye of the beholder, but the images the observer forms are an echo, mediated through traditions and practices, of culture embodied in the self. The body is a mirror of reality as well as the source of the mirror. In the California classroom with its medical textbooks, there was one eye and one method that defined and described the body. That body becomes real because we live in a world in which textbooks create reality. Here the image and the experience of the body are strangely one-dimensional, and this may have something to do with the fact that only an outside eye has grasped the body. Verdier unfolds the implied cosmos of Minot only occasionally through descriptions of the village; for the most part she relies on ten years of conversations with the women. The manner in which something is said reflects the manner in which something is done: "façons de dire, façons de faire." Saying, doing, and being are interwoven: "doing"—cooking the wedding feast, washing the newborn and the dead, sewing the wedding dress—as well as things "done"—the menu, the linen, the fabric, the cut of the dress, the alphabet stitched in red—incorporate the mental and thus the real landscape of the mind, a landscape that is so uniquely portrayed in a village like Minot.

Because of its inherent power, menstrual blood periodically restricts the movement of women in Minot. The meaning of blood draws boundaries around the things women may touch, but these boundaries seem in some way "osmotic," unlike the boundaries that are set up by a normative prohibition or definition. It would be a mistake to confuse such cultural restrictions with the discrimination produced by the medical definition of the female body. In Minot the body as such is never actually present: it always lies "between" things and manifests itself in actions. It is perceived as an aura; it is present like a smell or a sound, not an object with clearly outlined contours. It is as inseparable from gestures and facial expressions as it is from the visible and invisible substances that flow from it. This is why a demarcation between the inner and the outer is not possible, nor is a measuring of the body. Depending on where in the village or the house and in whose company the body appears, it seems to take on different dimensions. Men and women shrink and expand again, depending on whether a girl is learning embroidery, herding sheep, or disappearing into the kitchen.

Finally the body is most intimately established through the way it is dressed and undressed. This is the argument of two recent works in art history, which have influenced my methodology. Both studies are surprising, in that both succeed in bringing to light for the first time two different and apparently critical phenomena in painting: the history of Western dress and an examination of the genitalia of Christ.

Anne Hollander studies the meaning of the body through costume.

She begins with a periodization of her material: the cloths of antiquity, which could be worn as a toga or a mantle, and today as a sari or dhoti; the baglike garments of the Early Middle Ages, with sleeves and openings for the extremities, worn as a frock, a dalmatic, or a doublet; and the tailored clothes, use of which began to spread in the thirteenth century. It was only with the appearance of tailored clothes that the sartor, the tailor, took his place beside the spinners and weavers. Only from the High Middle Ages on was the tailor's art called upon to create body-shaping garments by cutting and sewing sleeves, bodices, and pants. Hollander's attention focuses on this last, characteristically western-European phase in the history of costume, with special emphasis on the relationship between costume (at court and in the theater) and painting as the vehicle that conveyed the epoch-specific normative shaping of the person. [153]

Hollander shows that the nakedness of the body is historically experienced as a relationship to the clothes which are considered proper in a given period and which the naked person lacks: "nakedness is not universally experienced and perceived any more than clothes are." The experience of the naked body has a history that becomes metaphorically visible through its costume. These material metaphors embody the self-image of each period. Only if the naked flesh fits into the clothes of its period does the inner eye see it with satisfaction, and the customary way of looking in a given period, especially in the late Middle Ages, was conveyed through painting. The elements emphasized in the female body change over time: now it is the fullness of the belly, now the heaviness of the breast or the curvature of arm, shoulder, and thigh, in which the feeling of an age seems embodied. But at no time before the late modern period did the Western imagination create that sharply delineated and fully articulated female body which, through modern anatomical-medical description, has become characteristic of our time, a body for which the bones are the frame and the skin the outermost boundary. This modern body, a "resilient and bony body," "a compact and unified visual image," mirrors a reality of the flesh that never before could be experienced. [154]

Leo Steinberg starts his study from a discovery he made. Art historians have overlooked a striking and clearly iconographic motif in

Renaissance painting both north and south of the Alps: in depictions of Christ the *ostentatio genitalium* is as ostensive as the *ostentatio vulnerum*. [155] In hundreds of paintings he examined, the focus was on Christ's genitalia, and the scene was intended to "reveal" them. Lovingly Mary takes hold of the penis, and the Christ Child responds by reaching for her chin, an expression of bridal love throughout the Middle Ages. The shepherds gaze admiringly upon this nakedness of the Lord, grandmother Anna looks at it with gentle eyes. The frequency and stylization of this denuding of the flesh is for Steinberg an argument that we should interpret these pictures as primary texts for a statement about the incarnation of God that was unique to the Counter-Reformation. This *ostentatio* represents a step in the development of the dogma of the reality of Christ's body. From the twelfth century on this dogma had been emphasizing new elements with the doctrine of transubstantiation, the bodily ascension of Mary, and the many miracles of bleeding hosts. Steinberg deals at length with the question how such an important motif, even if it was limited to one hundred and fifty years, could hitherto have been overlooked by iconographic scholarship.

Steinberg's book was doubly important for me. First, Steinberg confirmed a belief I had already gained in years of conversations with Ruth and Lenz Kriss-Rettenbeck: from the Middle Ages on Christian art, especially folk art and the expression of popular piety, should be seen as privileged sources for the study of body perception. Second, my disembodied notion of what constitutes religion prevented me, and several generations before me, from perceiving the vanished body.

TWO

Johann Storch and Women's Complaints

The Biography of a Pedant

My only witness to body perception in the eighteenth century is a narrow-minded, well-read pedant, who never forgot anything and who lived for his profession and found in it a path of social advancement. Only once did he get as far as Wolfenbüttel, to visit a patron who was suffering from gout; other than that he rarely got beyond Eisenach and Gotha. As town physician and later as court *medicus,* he was in the service of the small-town ducal residence throughout his life. His livelihood, his reputation, his privileges, and his position remained in the shadow of the duke.

But he relied heavily on his skill, his persistent efforts to continue his education, and the publication of his writings. He was a devout Lutheran, placing the imponderables of his practice under "God's guidance and care." Although sharply opposed to all devilish nonsense that produced superstitious cures, he firmly believed in bodily emanations, which he knew from his female patients, that were miraculous and not fully accessible to reason. He attributed his thriving practice to his diligence, and yet he knew that the success of a cure was never predictable, was never entirely thanks to his own doing. Though not without superstition, he was a sensible Lutheran, rooted in the traditional body perceptions of his female patients, yet at the same time knowledgeable about the medical theories of the time. From an early age he was a marginal figure. Though he had access to the medical faculty of his territorial university, to the old-established burghers, to circles of the regional nobility, and to high officials, it was always as a "client." And yet he pursued his advancement tenaciously, and at times petulantly. His practice was for him also research, the source of his diaries and thus his ticket of admission into the world of learned natural science.

Let us take a closer look at this man. His autobiography, published posthumously by his brother, can serve as our guide.[1] Johann Storch was born in 1681 in Ruhla, the son of a local healer and tailor who worked "empirically" and dealt with medicines and herbs. His father already had taken over this profession from his father. The village in which Storch grew up contained six hundred houses, a large village and densely settled owing to the local craft of knife-grinding; it was three hours south of Eisenach. "The boundary between Gotha and Eisenach runs right through the village. It is formed by a stream called Erbstrom, and in 1702 the Lords Commissioners from Saxon Gotha and Eisenach regulated it and marked it with wooden border-posts," we read in his autobiography.[2] Storch stuck to this border throughout his life, geographically and socially. Even if he later occasionally went as far as Seesen, Brunswick, Dresden, and Freiburg, he could make a living only in Eisenach and Gotha. He was dependent on the physical imponderables of the Saxon-Ernestine house. When the Eisenach line became extinct in 1741 and the residence was relocated to Weimar, Storch moved to Gotha, where he enjoyed patronage at the court.

In his memoirs Storch notes an early interest in the local plants and minerals. Whatever was needed in his father's unofficial *Officin* (apothecary) grew in the well-wooded landscape around Ruhla: arnica, gentian, veronica, and so on.[3] Minerals could be studied in the abandoned iron mine with its dilapidated drifts and shafts; the water in the well of the forester's house on the Eisenach side was rich in *Vitriolum martis,* which later became, theoretically justified, one of the most important ingredients in his preparations. Between the mountains of Ruhla lay "the most wonderful meadow lands with the purest and brightest springs," and the waters from the surrounding area were later also a fixed ingredient in his treatments for cleansing the inside.

His parents decided to send their son off to the *studium medicum,* so that in a time of growing restrictions on healing without training and licence, the father's practice, which was becoming illegal, could be carried on unchallenged. Since the middle of the century pressure had been mounting to extend the reach of medical ordinances into the countryside and to regulate the healers.[4] Jena—the territorial university of Jena had been part of the Duchy of Saxony-Eisenach since 1690—was probably closer to Storch's home than the University of Halle (founded 1694), the Academia Fredericiana. At that time the medical school of the Academia Fredericiana was quickly establishing itself as a leading place of study. Like Leiden in the Netherlands, it even attracted students from abroad.[5] Storch enrolled at the University of Jena in 1698. The gymnasium in Eisenach, and in particular a young theologian who had enjoyed free board at his parents' house in return for tutoring their son, had introduced him to the rudiments of Latin. It is easy to determine what teachings young Storch would have been exposed to in Jena. The first *ordinarius* (full professor), Wolfgang Wedel, Professor of Anatomy and Physiology, was a follower of the "mechanical doctrine."[6] Based on its principles, he taught a system that must have been quite remote from the student's own experience: the body was made up of tubes in which moved fluids composed of minute particles. The student may have been more familiar with the idea that the heavenly constellations and diabolical powers could have effects in the body via extremely fine liquids that formed the nervous system.[7] Wedel taught also the *Fundamenta Medicinae* of Friedrich Hoffmann, which recommended a quite empirical and skeptical approach to the actual practice of medicine. Wedel's own writings dealt with much that was of practical usefulness for a doctor—classifications of medicines and diseases, for example—and he also lectured on "women's diseases." As late as 1721 Storch still used his notes from a course *de morbis mulierum* to pronounce a fatal prognosis for a woman who had just given birth, since Wedel taught him that it was a bad, indeed a fatal, sign, "quando puerperae nudae velint videri," if women in childbed want to be seen naked (6:49).[8]

Slevogt, the other *ordinarius,* was a cautious follower of Stahl's physiology, and, as the biographers tell us, he introduced Storch to Stahl's doctrine. In actual fact, though, there were probably no significant differences between the theories taught in Jena at the end of the century. Stahl had not yet fully developed his theory, and access to information was not easy for the young student. "At that time . . . we could do no more than get our hands on several successively published disputations," Storch writes about the difficulties of obtaining in Jena information about Stahl's theory.[9] Eventually Storch ran out of funds. He was unable to continue his studies beyond his second year and had to leave the university. His biographer Börner also tells us that Storch had learned how to perform the "art of dissection" with "skill and success" in Jena's anatomical theater. In the course of the eighteenth century this skill became increasingly important as a status symbol of a learned, scientific doctor.[10] Storch retained his enthusiasm for anatomy, and it probably established a mental bond between him and the scientific medical research of his time, even though as an interest it was largely disconnected from his practical work.

After leaving Jena, Storch joined a colleague who was socially more privileged and enjoyed patronage, and who began to practice in Eisenach as a *medicus*. Two years later, in the summer of 1701, he submitted in Erfurt his inaugural disputation on "The Proper Selecting of Remedies," and was granted the licentiate. He lacked the necessary funds to obtain his doctorate, however.[11] Storch's course of study was typical of the late seventeenth century: practical work, university study, and a kind of apprenticeship complemented each other, and the licentiate by no means concluded a formal course of studies. The ways in which academic *medici* were trained, examined, and licensed were still as varied as the ways in which other healers acquired knowledge and legitimacy. Even after the promulgation of the Territorial Medical Ordinances, in the late seventeenth century a bewildering array of paths to the *medicus* remained, with knowledge, patronage, practical experience, and skill as contributing factors. To be sure, university studies—whatever that meant beyond mere enrollment—were a prerequisite for becoming a *medicus,* and especially for taking on a position in a city or even a medical office. But the university was not an examining authority. It bestowed titles—the licentiate or the doctorate—on the basis of a disputation, which was often written by the professor and had to be publicly defended by the student.

Titles too could be bought. What we could call "knowledge" was subjected to examination only after examining bodies had been established, some within the universities, some in opposition to university traditions, such as *collegia medica* on the level of the territorial states.[12] At the same time one could acquire legitimacy through a special privilege from the territorial ruler, who licensed all sorts of "healers." This practice persisted into the late nineteenth century. A large-scale study of the biographies of university graduates, done only for the medical students in Halle, reveals great discrepancies in the courses of training pursued by students. Somewhere along the line the student had to show that he had been enrolled at the university; at some point he had to acquire the licentiate or the doctorate. But these things by no means necessarily preceded practical work as an apothecary, a healer, or a surgeon. The doctorate bestowed a title; it did not constitute any sort of proof of ability. Qualifications could often be acquired outside the university: the path to becoming a *medicus* led through the jurisdictional thicket of the corporatively oriented medical faculties, and the practice-oriented administration and licensing by cities or territorial states. In regard to the licensing of doctors, the Medical Ordinance of Gotha from the year 1695, which was also valid in much the same way for Eisenach, stipulated that doctors had to produce "credentials regarding their skill and ability from universities or from learned doctors."[13] The lack of uniformity in the training that produced learned doctors is important, since it tells us something about the conditions that shaped a person's self-image, about the tensions between the academic self-image and a craftlike, practical competence.

In the summer of 1701 Storch was twenty-one years old. What opportunities existed for a young *medicus* with a university licentiate? Theoretically, he could settle in the region served by his university without any further examination or licence.[14] But in the cities the freedom of setting oneself up was restricted by practical considerations. The city *physici,* if they existed, guarded their own territory; elsewhere one needed licenses, the patronage of a professor, letters of recommendation, marriage connections, or money to buy one's way in. Since Storch had none of these, he remained in his home town. He worked with his father, and even after he had married and set up his own "economy," he was willing "to make do with a lucrative village." After all, he was known here, and the net of privileges cast by the territorial ruler and the cities did not reach this far, since a rural practice did not bring wealth or status. His autobiography reveals that the process of establishing oneself as a *medicus* depended on a number of factors. Patients made a practice; in order to survive, one had to be introduced. Storch began to practice in Weimar in 1702 with permission from the territorial lord, "but owing to a lack of patients [I] could not subsist for long."[15] One also had to become integrated into a network of existing positions and the men who held them. Finally, a license from the town *physicus,* the council, or the duke was a prerequisite. However, there was in Eisenach, a personal physician with a licence who could not succeed because he lacked enough clients. Three factors accounted for a successful practice in theory: personal initiative together with a licentiate or a doctorate degree; a reputation among clients; and permission from the city authorities—a privilege. The way in which a university-educated doctor set himself up was still very much in line with the traditional conditions of trade as set by the old established burghers, or the granting of privileges that was characteristic of absolutist rule.

The breakthrough for Storch came only several years later. His mother-in-law wished to have her only daughter's "support and company" back in Eisenach, and the patronage of her confessor paved the way for Storch. The chief court preacher used his influence at court, and in January 1708 Storch was granted a high ducal decree "to act as a town *medicus* in Eisenach." The decree contained only the permission to open a practice there; it did not hold out any prospects of an office. Storch moved to Eisenach that very month. Since 1672 the town had been the residence of the independent duchy or principality of Saxony-Eisenach, and because of the presence of the court and its favorable location, it was a bustling and economically rising city. Approaching the city from Ruhla, from the south, Storch must have had a view of the city as a chronicler described it in 1777: "The city of Eisenach is located . . . in a pleasant valley, the most beautiful part of which extends lengthwise from east to west; toward the north, however, it spreads out into fertile plains, which are covered with meadows and fields and through which different streams flow. The city itself is situated on dry ground along a gentle slope that rises imperceptibly from the north toward the southeast, and which offers splendid views to those who inhabit the highest areas."[16]

Circumstances would prove favorable for Storch. His arrival coincided with the rise of the residential city and the development of the export trade in knives, for which Eisenach was a center. The establishment of the court resulted in a flourishing economic life in the city, circulating money, goods, and contracts. But the presence of the court was also the reason for the decline of the legislative and executive powers of the old burgher upper class. The same years saw the waning power of the council and of the organs of town government, which became mere recipients of orders from the princely government.[17] The power of the guilds and corporations was undermined through a system of princely privileges to workshops, the first factories outside the town. Eisenach was the small-town capital of a tiny absolutist principality, dozens of which existed in the area of Saxony-Thuringia. In the early seventeenth century Eisenach was being ever more densely settled, its population and the number of its houses steadily rising. In 1700 the losses of the Thirty Years' War had just been made up as the city stood at 7000 inhabitants; around 1740 the population was 9000.[18] The building activity of the court attracted artisans. Tax exemptions and a supply of free or subsidized building timber from the princely forests supported civilian house construction. An entire street was uniformly planned, the castle was rebuilt, an orphanage and a prison were erected, and a hunting lodge was constructed. Finally, the proper adornment of a fine residence included paving some streets and one of the two market squares.

Eisenach, like most of the small towns in this period a farming town with extensive fields and meadows, was favorably situated along the road that connected the fair towns of Leipzig and Frankfurt on the Main, a road increasingly well traveled. The town was also part of the network of the Imperial Thurn and Taxis Post Stations, with a post office in the middle of the city, so that "one can send letters not only throughout the entire Roman Empire, but also to all outside places."[19] Markets were held on Wednesdays and Saturdays, and by law all artisans had to set up stalls at these markets. The markets served also the town's grocers and apothecaries, as well as the peasants who brought their grain to town. Four times a year supraregional fairs were held in the city, and outside merchants were allowed to attend them for a fee. The inhabitants' livelihood and their partaking in the economic upswing depended on privileges and various properties: fields around the city; the use of orchards and vegetable gardens; a share of the large municipal sheep-raising on two pasturages outside the town; and ownership of the raw materials for the most important trade, the working of local or imported sheep wool. Textile work was the largest craft in the city. There were also a few masters who were engaged in the putting-out system by giving spinning work to the lower class in the city and to workers in the countryside. The brewing trade, the right to brew and sell beer, was monopolized by the so-called *Brauhöfer,* the old established upper class of the town. The city's trade was divided between long-distance and wholesale trade reserved for the town patriciate, and the many small grocers, spice vendors, and street hawkers; the latter, however, damaged the local craft industry with their illegal imports.[20] The frequent complaints of local merchants and craftsmen about illegal competition from transient traders—Jews, Italians, "ointment-sellers," and pill-hawkers, who had to pay fees of safe conduct for their stay in the town—attest to the purchasing power of the burghers and the lively traffic that flowed into Eisenach as a central town on the road linking the fairs. As far as one can estimate from the secondary literature, the town offered a good setting for a medical practice: more than 1700 "taxable" burghers with their wives and children; the court with its officials, grooms, maids, footmen, and other domestic personnel and servants; the "militia"; and finally the transient merchants.

The arrival of court and the princely government resulted in social restructuring. In the old division, with its three taxable burgher classes, the upper class, which staffed the city council, was composed of wealthy merchants, guild masters, and the *Brauhöfer,* among whom were the remnants of the old patrician families. The new sumptuary regulations of the Police Ordinance of 1704 divided the burghers into four classes; below the burghers stood the propertyless, politically disenfranchised *Schutzgenossen.* The first class now included, along with the "princely councillors," "noble persons," and "superintendents," also the "doctores" and the "licentiates."[21] The social structure of the residential town was determined entirely by the court. The diminished social status of officeholders, council members, and burghers reflected the fact that political and social power had become centralized around the court and the princely government. The same is true for those offices that had previously fallen under communal jurisdiction, such as that of the town *physicus*.

As we have seen, Storch needed a princely decree to set himself up as a *medicus*. Small residential cities of the early eighteenth century had none of the collective municipal organs of residential doctors which had emerged in some major trading cities and imperial cities from the sixteenth century on, and which strove to control the licensing of legal healers. As a result, the court had authority over the process of licensing. A study of the nearby duchy of Anhalt-Bernburg and other small residences in Saxony has shown that "public health" depended entirely on the resident ruler. He controlled the establishment of practices by the *medici,* who frequently served as his personal physicians; he appointed town and state *physici,* if such offices existed; and he determined the membership of the medical board.[22] "In the small-town-absolutist regions, one cannot overemphasize the importance of a ruler's interest and commitment in determining the effectiveness of up-to-date medical legislation and its usefulness to the population."[23] In larger cities there may have been some wrangling on this issue between the territorial ruler and the city. In university towns the privileges of the medical faculties, with rights to licensing and visitation, were also important. Eisenach had no such counterweights: no corporative organization of the resident doctors, no medical faculty, and a weakened council. The University of Jena does not seem to have exercised any authority here. This may have had something to do with the fact that until 1690 Jena had been the residence of a lateral branch and an independent principality. The pharmacy in town rested on a princely privilege. The Medical Ordinances of Eisenach, passed in imitation of the Ordinances of Saxony-Weimar and Gotha,[24] emphasized the legal status of the personal physician as a municipal medical officer.[25] Thus Eisenach did not have any kind of professional association for Storch to join, or toward which he could have oriented himself in his professional ambitions. But we do find rampant competition among the *medici* for influence and clients. At the time of Storch's arrival, in 1710, about a half-dozen *medici* stood at the pinnacle of the medical hierarchy in Eisenach: these were the

personal *medici,* the court *medici,* and the town *physicus.* Below them
ranked the doctors who held licentiates or doctorates and who practiced
on their own without any special post or patronage. Then came the
surgeons, barbers, barber-surgeons, midwives and other helpers, traveling surgeons, "empiricists," "oculists," "healers of the stone-evil," herb
hawkers, and so on.

Judging from Storch's autobiography, the self-image of the academic
medici who worked in Eisenach during the first half of the century was
oriented neither toward a professional collectivity nor toward "health
policy." The autobiography is silent on all questions regarding health
"policy," even for the period after 1720, when Storch was town *physicus.*
But Storch complains at great length about his colleagues, laments the
squabbles at court, and voices fears that his influence may be undermined by the "envy" and "selfishness" of the competing *medici.* The
major threat came not from below, from the "quacks" and other non-
academic healers, but from members of his own group, whose advancement seems to have depended entirely on the imponderables of the
princely household. In this sense Storch's autobiography is not the work
of someone with a professional self-consciousness, but of a man who
stood in the prince's service, even though he had an outside practice.
Although rank, age, length of residence, and experience could be
important factors in the success of a career, their role was overshadowed
by the all-important court patronage. Storch earned that patronage by
successfully treating the Duke's gout and the Duchess' illness: "a special
coincidence in the year 1731 brought about that I assumed treatment of
Her Highness, the ruling Lady Duchess, who had been given up on.
With divine blessing the treatment was successful, so that within a few
weeks Her Highness could be seen at table once again," he writes, and
hastens to mention his colleague's envy.[26]

An important role in Storch's autobiography is played by various
"well-disposed patrons" who interceded for him at court. His practice,
however, the basis of his income in the first years, especially before the
steady side income from his post as town *physicus* after 1720, was in the
hands of non-noble patients. The fact that he was lucky enough to avoid
"blame" and "defamation" was important to his success, as was the fact
that satisfied patients spread the word about his healing arts. Patients

made a practice successful—not the doctor. Of course Storch was not without skill. At the very beginning—"his practical fortune was thoroughly dependent on the first patients and treatments" (p. 19)—he was sought out by a forty-year-old maid, who suffered desperately from dropsy; since Storch cured her and she went on to live for many more years, word of his skill got around. According to his records, his patients in the first years were primarily burgher artisans and the poorer members of the town's lower class: only slowly did he reach the women of the court and through them the large group of servants. From an early period on he based his practice on the Stahlian method, which he used very skillfully as a lever for his advancement, since it distinguished him both from the *empirici* and from the mechanically oriented *medici*. Storch himself listed the following as factors for the success of his practice: "divine providence" and his skill in "women's cures," to which his own wife was walking testimony, for, as he dryly remarked, "divine dispensation has given me a woman from whom I could learn more than from hundreds of other patients. For up to her sixty-first year she was laid up fifteen times with this disease [pleuritic fever], eight times she survived illness in childbed, twice she had cold fever and jaundice, she often suffered from hemorrhoids, ten years she spent complaining about stones, not to mention other inherited hysterical misfortunes" (p. 16). His skill during several raging fever epidemics and "red dysentery" in the city consolidated his clientele. When his one-and-a-half-year-old son died, "I remained at that time without patients for fourteen days, and was not a little concerned that my practice might go under" (p. 19).

   Storch advanced along with his practice. There were setbacks, since he initially dispensed privately, that is, he handed out medicines himself, thus violating the privilege of the pharmacy. Legally this was a question of power, since the line between a "pure" doctor and an apothecary who did not practice medicine was fluid in the early eighteenth century. The monopoly of the pharmacy in Eisenach was a question of princely fiscal policy, not one of "public health service." After a few years Storch was given the post of *miliz-medicus* (militia physician); at first this was a post without salary, later it brought in 48 reichsthaler a year. After having been initially passed over—following unfair treatment which he complains of bitterly—he was given, around

1720, a salary as court *medicus* (without a formal post). In 1720 he was also appointed to the post of town *physicus,* which brought his total salary to 200 reichsthaler—provided it was paid. He moved to the center of town, where he had bought a residence and, at moderate cost, had turned it into one of "the finest-looking houses" (p. 23). But his social position was always precarious. It was his constant fear that the "professional envy" of his colleagues might undermine his reputation. When he began to publish, he was accused of having damaged the city with his accounts of the fever epidemics. After quarrels and threats that he would leave town, he was finally given a "high princely appointment as personal *medicus,*" along with the prospect of a salary, in order to keep him in Eisenach. The title imposed the obligation that he make a personal appearance at court twice a day, as well as the burdensome restriction that he could not travel away from town for more than two or three hours. However, the squabbling between the actual personal *medicus,* his *substitutus,* and other attending court *medici* does not seem to have ended. A *medicus* who had just moved to Eisenach from Weimar, and whose cures were more effective, caused Storch "the greatest distress," until he finally managed to obtain, in 1735, a decree, "drafted, written in fair copy, and sealed," which elevated him to the rank of "counselor and personal *medicus,*" inclusive of a salary to go along with the new title.

After the duke's unexpected death in 1741, Storch was freed from "the wearisome work and attendance at court," and through the mediation of a patron he found service as personal physician to the duke of Saxony-Gotha, with a fixed salary of 365 reichsthaler. Apparently his practice in the city, built up over thirty years, and the position of town *physicus* seem to have mattered little to the now sixty-year-old Storch when balanced against the income and service at court. Storch also became town and state *physicus* in Gotha and a member of that city's *collegium medicum.* Several years earlier he had been inducted into the Leopoldina, and now he finally received a title as *Hofrat* (court counselor). A look at his children confirms his successful career: one son was a doctor with a doctoral degree (Storch had been able to pay for both medical studies and doctorate) and a personal *medicus* of the Duke of Saxony-Meiningen; one daughter was married to a doctor who served at the court in Schwarzburg-Rudolstadt; the other daughters were the wives, respectively, of a princely steward, a princely master of the horse, a princely counselor, and a princely architect. Thus, without exception the next generation was engaged in princely services, rather than in town offices or artisanal or mercantile pursuits. Future research may explain the social position of the youngest son, "Johann Gottfried," of whom it is said: "he has learned the art of riding" (p. 28).

The Protocols of the Town Physicus

Pain is in the body. It leaves no trace for the historian, unless complaints about it are recorded. Years ago Jean-Pierre Peter wrote that the archives supply the historian with silent bodies.[27] The words set down by doctors, administrators, and pastors create an appearance of objectivity. Roy Porter insists that we are still completely ignorant when it comes to discovering how peasants, artisans, or the educated understood their illness and their desire for well-being.[28] He was reflecting on the sources we use. As soon as we shift our view from the doctor (who is usually an educated person) to the patient, it is difficult to find any sources at all. Porter has turned to autobiographies, letters, and articles in "moral weeklies."[29] Françoise Loux and Philippe Richard examine proverbs.[30] What is striking in reading Porter is the wealth of words used in describing the state of health: Pepys trying to expel the *Dantzicker Girkins,* which lie as "matter" in his body, with a sweating treatment, or Miss Hallam of Islington, a pastor's daughter, dying one hundred and twenty years later of a convulsion in her bowels brought on by a clap of thunder the previous Monday morning. The words of the patients and the terms of the doctors were thus still interacting. Only the professionalization of medical terminology, which went hand in hand with the making of the new body, produced two heterogeneous modes of speech and perception and silenced the patient. We have grown up with this now traditional dichotomy. Our perception of the body is based on the gulf between objective condition and subjective experience, and we tend to regard every statement by a doctor as a professional pronouncement arising from a medical framework of definition. But prior to the nineteenth century this boundary between diagnostic vocabulary and the feelings of the patient was blurred and permeable, if it existed at all.

There is no question that Storch's patient histories differ from the *observationes medicae,* the case studies of the seventeenth century. As Storch himself polemically remarked, the latter were created "ex prae-conceptis opinionibus, and were hatched more in the studies than at the sickbeds."[31] He was right. The focus of attention in these Latin texts was primarily on remedies and theories. Many authors were explicitly concerned with collecting scientific oddities.[32] Authors took little or no interest in the course of a disease. The Latin is rigid; a single case was used to prove a preconceived theory. Nor do Storch's diaries belong to the genre of German tracts that were sold and hawked at fairs from the late sixteenth century on: herbal books, recipe chapbooks, plague-prevention tracts, instructions for uroscopy, books on midwifery, calendars, and classics like the *Secreta* of Albertus Magnus.[33] Finally, it would be a mistake to place Storch among the German medical case histories and guides of the later eighteenth century. Here the style has changed; the people are instructed and lectured to in a condescending manner on how to "treat" and "cure" themselves and how to feel.

Storch was not alone in the kind of writing he did. A new medical genre appeared around the turn of the eighteenth century: detailed patient histories from preclinical medical practice that were written up in German. Since the authors made no directly relevant anatomical or physiological discoveries, and since their cases are full of details which historians have so far considered irrelevant, this genre has been under-utilized by scholars.[34] As German literature this type of preclinical patient history is unique, and within the genre Storch seems to me a true master.[35] He is part of the first generation in which learned medical knowledge was recorded in German at all. To the end of his life he was constantly quoting the latest Latin publications of many colleagues. Even though he translated Stahl's lectures into German, whenever he wanted to assume an air of learnedness he used Latin; indeed, he often had to use it if he wanted to get published. His diaries are shot through with Latin quotes and technical terms. He often specifies the meaning of a German word with a Latin synonym or uses a Latin euphemism. And in this world of learning—in which the medical profession still used Latin as the accepted language in education, publications, examinations, and academic conferences—Storch published the first German case descriptions in his *Medicinische Jahrgänge.* The transition from the rigid, classical, foreign Latin to the record of his patients' complaints captured in the vernacular entailed also a transformation of their disease from a state into a process.

Storch did not write as a scholar for other scholars, but as a practical doctor for "young, future practitioners." He did not wish to "present to the world" an "especially learned work," but wanted to publish his record of "unembellished notes for the day-to-day usefulness of younger colleagues."[36] The purpose of his writing dictated the language he used: German. Not that the Latin language would have been incapable of describing medical histories, or too clumsy. The case histories of the neo-Hippocratic tradition of the seventeenth century show that the classical language as such presented no obstacle. But it was a foreign language and simply could not convey the patients' words, even if a doctor used it skillfully for framing his observations in the pattern of a Latin amanuensis. Storch wrote down what he heard from patients. He broke a thousand-year-old framework: he wanted to take the patient at his word. As the Württemberg personal physician Lentilius wrote in the preface to the third *Jahrgang* of his protegé: "Certain expressions in the description of diseases and their circumstances, certain emphatic *Locutiones proverbiales,* which cannot be expressed to native Germans as well and intelligibly in Latin," forced the author to break with the tradition of Latin, because, as he adds, "one cannot express in Latin how the sick complain, how they describe what it is they feel."[37]

In Lentilius we have an older colleague who described Storch's achievement as well as the dangers of the new approach: "selfish apothecaries, know-it-all surgeons and barber-surgeons, especially discharged military surgeons . . . superstitious midwives, greedy druggists and confectioners, depraved pedlers, ragged and seedy craftsmen," who "utilize the German medical books as suits their fancy," could now read the doctor and do their own quackery. Despite all this, the doctor had new ears for what his patients were saying.[38] For Latin marked not only social distance and kept the patient at a proper distance, it also separated the body as described by the doctor from the words of the patients' complaints.[39] A patient history written in Latin made it unnecessary to record in concrete detail the chaotic sensations that were bred in the inner body. The unsuitability of Latin for expressing experienced reality is reflected also in other writings of the Stahl school, particularly in learned treatises that used the traditional scholarly language. In his *Tractatus de haemorrhoidibus* (1722), Michael Alberti suddenly switches languages: "expressiones patientum: it twitches, rips, tugs, pulls, stretches, driving against each other back and forth, like knives, needles." In another passage, while discussing the *Motus haemorrhoidalis interni speciali,* he helplessly departs from the Latin: "spasmodice contractiones: ut exprimant: it was just as though someone were gripping them inside with two hands, thus holding back their breath," but then switches back and continues in Latin.[40] Pain simply could not express itself in a foreign language.

As far as I know, the patient's own recounting of his or her suffering held a unique place among Stahl's followers. Writing down these stories was Storch's life work. "Observations which are meant to be useful must have above all this prerequisite, that they are composed by honest and diligent *medici* who do not mix in the least bit of *figmentum* [invention]: if one can expect this from them . . . one must not fear from it any fraud and misleading to the detriment of other patients. But in order that an observer should not deceive himself and others, let him consider this the best and surest way: he should keep certain *diaria,* and should occupy himself at least every day, if not every hour, in recording conditions observed in his patients . . . If he is inclined to make *reflectiones* about one occurrence or another . . . I advise that he carry out his intention during the time when everything is fresh in his mind."[41]

Storch himself adhered to this maxim. Most of his publications[42] are derived from the records of his personal, reflective observations from his practice in Eisenach, from the "continuously kept *diario,* in which every day I faithfully and diligently noted down what I had encountered in my practice."[43] Storch published *Diseases of Women* when he was in his sixties. Along with his *Diseases of Children* and the detailed account of his own dropsy, it represents in a sense the compilation of the sum of his experiences. These are the ambitious publications of a man who was now a scholar, an aging doctor, and who could look back on forty years of practical work. In his earlier writings—the *Medicinische Jahrgänge,* for example—the author's tone had been more cautious, humbler. Storch had been afraid of compromising himself and anxious about "presenting

himself on the stage of medicine."[44] In those writings he was more
interested in thinking about his cases as a researcher and turning them
into theoretical problems. Having lived his life faithful to the maxim
"that I do not engage in the least *allotria* or *oeconomica* and also avoid all
wasteful *conversationes,* and thus rarely spend a quarter-hour at leisure,
but rather devote all hours free from practice to these *studia activa,*"[45]
and having received the recognition of the scholarly world—admission
into the Leopoldina, the academy of scientists—Storch wrote the *Diseases of Women* as a man who surveyed his cases for publication with self-
confidence, peace of mind, and learnedness.

The actual case studies make up seven hefty volumes of the eight-
volume work, subdivided according to the "natural state" of the women:
maids, women who miscarry, women in labor, and so on. Each volume
embraces approximately the period from 1721, when Storch was made
town *physicus,* to 1740, when he stopped practicing in Eisenach. There
are about 1816 individual cases, in which a total of some 1650 different
women were treated.[46] Each history begins with a brief characterization
of the woman, the time of her first consultation, her complaints, her
medication, and so on. For example:

> "A young artisan's wife, eight months pregnant, complained on May 20,
> 1732 about heat and surging in her blood, and about intense pain in all
> her limbs. I prescribed Pulv. antispasm. 6 doses, whereupon these surges
> and pains subsided.   (3: 615, case 179)

The structure of the cases is uniformly the same, especially with regard
to the rigid pattern of the woman's complaints and the response in terms
of the prescribed medication. At the same time, however, the stories
show a great diversity. The guidelines for each volume are the women as
cases, which is why the individual histories are very different in content
and length. If a woman visited him for the first time in 1721, and then
consulted him repeatedly over many years, Storch listed all these encounters in her case successively after the first entry in 1721. Each
volume thus blends the woman's personal chronology and a chronology
of his practice. This structure, together with a certain lack of clarity in
the cross-referencing,[47] defeats any attempt to translate the source back
into a horizontal situation, to examine how many women Storch saw in a

given period (one month, one year).[48] *Diseases of Women* allows only a rough quantitative estimate of the extent to which Storch's practice was a "women's practice." And for a sociohistorical study we lack additional concrete information on income, fees for medication, and gifts.[49] It was not Storch's intent, after all, to record his practice as such but the cases of sick women he had encountered in Eisenach. We shall see later that these are not "patient histories" in the modern sense; they are simply what a learned doctor around 1750 recorded as cases he thought worth describing. For many cases Storch added the observations of other doctors which he took from the literature and discussed the advantages and shortcomings of his treatment. The source comprises three interwoven parts: Storch's own cases with his personal reflections; case histories drawn from the medical literature; and Storch's own more narrowly "medical" discussion, in which he took issue with the *mechanici,* the "innovators."

The *observationes* of colleagues which Storch gathered from the literature show that he read widely and collected diligently. Naturally he knew and cited the main works of G. E. Stahl and his acknowledged followers, for example, M. Alberti and J. Juncker in Halle, G. Nenter in Strasbourg. But he also knew many of the inaugural disputations that were presented to these men and dealt with medical problems, for example, the "Disputatio de osculo morbisco et mortifero" published by Alberti in Halle in 1746 (8:45), or the "Disputatio de lethifera praematura formosorum deformatione" (Halle, 1735) (6:210). He quoted and discussed—in part positively, in part critically—Stahl's opponent Friedrich Hoffmann. He also relied, sometimes word for word, on the medical journals of his time: the *Breslauer Sammlungen,* a German-language collection of individual patient histories (published between 1718 and 1736), to which many practical doctors from the region contributed; the *Büchnerische Sammlungen;* and the *Commercium litterarium,* an academic journal from Nürnberg edited by followers of Stahlianism. He made use of the publications of the Academy of Natural Scientists, the *Ephemerides* and *Miscellanea,* reading not only contemporary issues but working his way back to the seventeenth century. The important medicolegal literature—for example, M. Alberti, J. B. Carpzow, H. F. Teichmeyer—appears in excerpts, as do the main works of the surgeons, for example, Lorenz Heister's *Observationes anatomica.* He introduced cases from the *medicina consultatoria, medicina practica, exercitationes practica,* and *observationes* of the better-known seventeenth-century physicians. He drew on N. Ettmüller, Th. Bartholin, Corn. Bontekoe, Corn. Stalpart, W. Rolfink, D. Sennert, W. Wedel, and others, and used the classic sixteenth-century collections of men like Fernel, Forestus, Platter, Schenk von Grafenberg, and Hildanus. Moreover, he had read and excerpted the main authors among the French works on midwifery, men like Mauriceau, de la Motte, and the *Louise Bourgeois.* I did not find any citations of the English scientists, such as Harvey or Boyle, and the Italian anatomists are missing also.

Storch was an obsessive compiler, but the criteria he used for his collecting were not those of a dogmatic follower of Stahl. They were also not the kind of criteria that would have made it possible to corroborate any kind of theory, nor were they oriented toward groups of diseases or "symptoms" in the narrower sense. Storch compiled a collection of all the individual "histories" accessible to him and related to his cases in Eisenach. The relation between these various cases was rooted in the infinite possibilities of the body. For Storch the practitioner, the essence of the body was the unlimited multitude of stories it could tell. But he was not collecting things for a princely curio gallery: Storch was collecting *bio-logies.* His way of thinking, oriented toward details and analogies, drove him to gather stories, for the body which he pursued all his life apparently had no norm, it was never complete.

As medical literature, Storch's patient histories stand at a watershed. Each case is made up of individual stories, many of which sound like tales from old miracle books and the contemporary sensationalist literature. What turns the stories into a "case" (casus), and thus of interest to younger colleagues, is the fact that the doctor strung them together in a patient history. The organizing principle for the stories was the event witnessed in a specific time and place either in Eisenach or elsewhere: the passing of pins in urine; bristly hair in the private parts; ailments brought on by a baptismal feast. The organizing principle for the patient history was the status of the women: maids, pregnant women, and so on. Hence alongside the very detailed narrative reports about the women of Eisenach there existed stories that had been observed elsewhere. But a case in Eisenach and a case cited from literature never add up to *one* body that can be abstractly comprehended. In the summer of 1721 there was girl in Eisenach who "got scared at the time when her menses were flowing, whereupon they immediately stagnated." Storch notes the development and treatment of the problem and ponders its cause. He concludes the case with a counterexample from the *observationes medico-chirurgicorum Thesauro* by Professor Walther of Leipzig, who had reported that a sixteen-year-old girl with the same stagnation "had been freed from the *obstruction* and cured within a few days by the scare and subsequent anger when a boy hit her in the back with a snowball" (2:111). Insofar as historiography has even examined such texts, it has always tried to interpret the observations of the past within the logic of contemporary medical "theory." But as we have seen, the latter presupposes the rationality of a constituted, modern body. And such a body does not seem to have existed for Storch, much less for the women he treated. How else are we to understand the tireless efforts to find additional true stories of embodiment? It is this perception that gave rise to the proliferation of details and minute observations, even in the "scientific" part of the source; this holds true for the Eisenach stories as well as for the examples Storch cited. Two neighbors in Eisenach quarreled over seating rank at a baptismal banquet; the flow of the new mother dried up (8:56); a noble lady ran to the fountain in her undershirt when she "suffered a fit of apoplexy" during the night, and the "sergeants who were coming to report to her husband surprised her along the way," so that she could "pass only with the greatest embarrassment" (8:56); a greyhound lapped up the blood in a bloodletting bowl, so another bowl was quickly filled with blood drawn from a steward so that the pregnant woman might think it her own and "not be terrified by the bad omen and thus harm her fruit" (3:406); in 1703 in Emleben (near Gotha), Storch had "seen and talked to" a peasant, "who fell into a deep melancholy every time his wife was pregnant and did not say a single word" (3:90). Apparently around 1750 all these stories were a legitimate form of "scientific" discourse about the body of women, thus it was worth the trouble for Storch to search out other examples. Among them was the "misfortune" of a prominent cleric in Nürnberg. Doctor Wurffbain, in the *Miszellen* of the Scientific Society, reported that he "suffered toothaches whenever his wife was pregnant until she felt the movement of the child" (3:374). Then there was a case that had occurred a hundred years before. A *Hof-Frauenzimmer* (court-lady) "was standing in front of a mirror with a bunch of pins in her mouth when she was startled by a prince who approached from behind and slapped her on the back, whereupon all the pins fell into her throat. However, she felt no pain from the pins, and on the third day she passed all of them through her urine" (2:538). This mid-seventeenth-century observation by the scholar Bierling was confirmed by his contemporary, the anatomist Stalpart, who dealt with it in his *observationum variorum centuria* and "attested . . . ex *Epist. Langii* that it had been five pins" (ibid.).[50]

Storch does not merely compile. On the contrary, he cites meticulously. He is careful to provide the details that vouch for the truthfulness of his examples: the medical qualifications of the author of the report (no mere empiricist, no teller of fairy-tales), the place of the observation, the time, the social status of the "patient," possibly the age, and all other details considered important. A desire for the greatest possible authenticity is expressed in the verbs, which are meant to render the event or observation truthful: such and such "has seen it," "indicated," "confirmed," has "truly seen," has "related as certain," has "known" a woman, and so on. Even when they were quite marvelous, the stories were believable because they were attested by the eyewitness testimony of qualified observers. The eyewitness account could go back some time, and it might have reached Storch very indirectly through a chain of several people. These stories of the body were more believable for Storch than "evidence" from the "atlas of anatomy"—which was being slowly uncovered through dissection—that these stories were anatomically and physiologically impossible. The eyewitness account of a phenomenon of the living body was more convincing to Storch than a fact uncovered in a dead body. But we must not forget that anatomical discoveries, like all of medicine up to the end of the eighteenth century, were still compatible with the miraculous that was slow to disappear.

Storch was no obscurantist, nor can he be understood as a dogmatic Stahlian. He was, for example, not uncritical concerning magical practices. He considered the belief that menstrual blood could do powerful things a mere "fabrication" and complained that these things were spread "not by upright medici, but by swindlers, ignoramuses, liars, and other such people" (2:44). But when, as town *physicus,* Storch was asked to attest to the harmlessness of a widow's menstrual blood, which she had transformed into blood sausage and fed to her lover to arouse his lust, he was unable to declare with complete certainty that it was indeed harmless. The final decision of his life, however, pointed toward the future and in the direction from which such certainty would come. Storch "accurately recorded" the development of his dropsy "in his orderly diary from day to day with his own hand and with his usual tirelessness and diligence." His account stops only shortly before his "blessed passing." His brother reported: "Thereupon I myself carried out . . . the *exenteration,* as he had committed me to do the day before his passing, out of brotherly affection and to soothe the feelings of his family who was present at the time; it is hoped that this dissection report . . . has sufficiently attested the examination and description of the corrupted viscera and thus the cause of the disease."[51]

THREE

Medical Practice in Eisenach

What we know about the elements of a medical practice in the early eighteenth century is fragmentary. Nevertheless, some fixed markers have existed within this nearly unexplored field, basic facts that are mentioned again and again in the literature as beacons of certainty. Following Jewson or Waddington, I started from the assumption that the self-image of the medical practitioners in the eighteenth century was shaped by their relation to their upper-class patients, toward whom they stood in some sort of client dependence.[1] The ineffectiveness of therapies, speculative healing, and the orientation toward the symptoms of the sick—all this is said to have tied the doctors to the goodwill and patronage of the upper class, since the absence of a professionalization of the practitioners meant that there was no counterweight to these dependencies. Grouping the *medici* socially with the nobility and the gentry emphasizes the distance of the doctor from the "lower classes." Doctors' fees, the consciousness of social status, and the geographic distribution of academic doctors in the ancien régime have been offered as reasons for the distance between learned medicine and the poorer, illiterate sick.[2]

Learned medicine, which is seen as having been largely useless if not downright harmful, is said to have had no contact with the lower social strata. Both are seen as largely separated and unconnected worlds. Furthermore, the literature suggests that there were definable types of doctors—the *medici,* the surgeons, the apothecaries, and so on, as the Medical Ordinances defined them—who, as specialized practitioners, formed a closed group of legitimate healers, and who can be opposed to the illegitimate "quacks," "charlatans," and so on. The healers, trained either at the university or in an apprenticeship, are distinguished from the untrained practitioners—two directly antagonistic groups of healers who competed against each other. Statistical analyses of the distribution of doctors in the countryside have shown that learned doctors rarely set up practice there, which is one reason for the assumption that the rural population had almost no access to medicine.[3] Was the province a "medical wasteland"? All these assumptions are based on the drawing of certain boundaries: a boundary between learned and popular medicine; a boundary between the upper classes and popular culture; a boundary between academic and "magical," "superstitious," or ignorant practices; a boundary between the noble and learned and the poor sick; a boundary between city and countryside. Boundaries of knowledge, of space, of money—precisely the boundaries of our own world.

Dockès examined how the economists of the seventeenth and eighteenth centuries treated space.[4] His book helped me to think differently about the drawing of boundaries in the ancien régime. Space was seen more as concrete landscape than as a segment from a homogeneous dimension. A commodity that was carried across a boundary changed its meaning, not only because it was measured differently, but because a different context imparted a different value to it. The drawing of a boundary was not so much the creation of a dividing line as the perception of an area in which two different spaces intersected. This insight was important to my interpretation in different ways: it taught me not to be misled by our modern concept of "overstepping the bounds of one's competence" when analyzing the encounter between doctor and patient in Storch; it also helped me to interpret the seeming boundlessness of the body in relation to contemporary notions of boundaries.

In this chapter I try to describe the forms of encounter that were possible between a doctor and his patients in Eisenach around 1720. Insofar as my source permits, I will describe the structure of the relationships that women entered into with a doctor. What were the elements of the encounter, how did they proceed, how long did a treatment last, what did it include? But first I must emphasize once again that my source, the diary of a *single* doctor, reveals only a tiny slice of all the healing relationships in Eisenach that were considered meaningful and were sought out. Our source is like a silhouette: the outlines of Storch's practice are clear, and it is only by inference that I can fill in the blank spaces in the background. Within these blank spaces the women, their husbands, mothers, patrons, or teachers, chose Storch as a healer. He was only one possible point of approach among a multitude of possible paths for obtaining advice, medications, and "relief." Although there is much to suggest that Storch had a thriving practice that was well established in the area, he had no monopoly on healing. He was not an authority who excluded other options, not even with those patients who displayed an "enduring faith" in him.

If I try to examine the text in search of the blank spaces that are only hinted at or not mentioned at all—spaces in which Storch was not active, in which he was not called upon as a healer—there opens up a network of people who offered advice within the circle of the sick: the mother, relatives, female neighbors, corn-cutters or urine-examiners, traveling tooth extractors, pill hawkers, barbers, illegitimate but resident practitioners, military surgeons of a regiment that happened to be stationed in town, barber-surgeons, and on up the scale to the practicing *medici* of Eisenach and neighboring cities in their specific ranking. The letter of the law in the Medical Ordinances established clear differences between these people, but the sick followed a different logic in making their choice. I can only try to describe the options available to Storch's female patients and to embed his practice within that environment; the source does not permit a detailed description of the world of healing in Eisenach at this time.[5]

The ailing women and their closest female relatives are at the outer edge of the circle in whose center I must locate Storch's practice, and they are at the center of the circle at whose outer edge Storch's practice may have been situated. These women frequently knew what was "wrong" with them and tried to obtain the necessary remedies of their own, without recourse to a legitimate healer. Self-diagnosis and self-therapy run through Storch's cases like a red thread of everyday practice and are present even during his visits. It is the red thread of bleeding, purging, of substances that promote the menses, of the many home remedies that seem part of everyday life. A maidservant "has nearly a half-pint of blood drawn from her arm because of an insufficient flow of the *mensium*" (2:283). Another maidservant, seized with a violent toothache around Christmas, self-prescribed a bleeding at the hand and had a vein opened (2:480). A maid took "wormseed and senna leaves for purging" right at the time when her menses were flowing (2:220, case 51). A mother bought purgative powders for her nursing daughter who was suffering from "heart-anxiety" (7:236, case 108). A servant-girl, "on the advice of her family," took a strong dose of crushed bay leaves "to promote the menses" (2:180, case 40); a woman cooked some juniper juice for herself to achieve the same effect. A girl who was planning to attend a dance at the parish fair and did not want to be held back by her menses, ate constipating things (2:92); a noble girl felt a heaviness in the stomach after eating white cabbage and took an emetic.

If mishaps occurred, the women knew what was good for them:

> The wife of a carter, pregnant in the eighth month, "took a hard fall on her stomach on Sept. 22, 1726. On the advice of some women, she was soon bled from the arm." (3:427, case 84)

> A soldier's wife, pregnant in the seventh month, felt "swooning combined with faintness" and had three ounces of blood drawn. (3:626, case 187)

> On September 9, 1722, a poor woman, thirty years of age, experienced a sudden, violent nosebleed in the seventh month of her pregnancy. Against the nosebleed, "she is using every remedy she can think of or which has been suggested to her." (3:217, case 32)

These are only a few incidences which show women counteracting a mishap or ailment on their own initiative, restoring their well-being or simply doing what was considered necessary on a regular basis to maintain it. Most of the remedies they reached for evacuated, cleansed, or strengthened the body. The arsenal of home remedies against nosebleed, fever, milk stagnation, sore breast, nausea, and so on, would fill pages. The mothers and women of the neighborhood most often advised in such cases and procured the remedies. In fact, if there was such a thing as two groups of healers, the mothers seem to have been the real opponents who meddled in the trade of the *medicus,* since their presence extended right into the sickroom, even if the doctor was there. They tried to impose their ideas, which came from a culture of self-treatment. They quarreled with the doctor about closed or opened curtains in the room of a woman in childbed, about saffron soup or about the diagnosis, and they circulated womb-cleansing powders and heart-strengthening waters that showed good results. Let us look at one case:

> A pastor's wife from the country, well into her thirties, developed a fever after a strenuous and difficult birth. Storch was consulted; he left behind a prescription and advised a thin diet, ideally water. The mother, however, "thinks that harm is being done to her daughter with the thin diet, and since the husband must pay for it, she set it aside and tries to strengthen her daughter with wine and beer." (6:97, case 21)

The mother resorted to a logic in which criteria of social status were mixed with notions about the inner body: the daughter should be given what befitted her station and what was good for and strengthened her. The mother's assessment carried more weight than the council of the doctor, who was only a guest in the realm of self-treatment.

Self-treatment included an investigation of the causes of pain. Women frequently tried to find out for themselves what ailed them before requesting a prescription from the doctor. Here too we meet mothers, neighborhood women, girlfriends, sisters, or relatives. Two examples:

> In March 1728 a young woman, about thirty years of age, experienced "strong pains in her abdomen and an urge toward giving birth." She consulted her mother and felt "compelled . . . to have a woman take a look if something strange might by going on "in her private parts, which Storch, whom she later consulted through her mother, was never allowed to see or touch. His prescription was based entirely on the mother's report about the "strange" thing a woman had found. (4/1:162, case 36)

> A peasant woman from Berck felt a "hard lump" on one side of her uterus. She decides to have "a cousin of hers, a smith, examine and feel the lump." This relative advised her to place softening compresses onto the painful area. When these failed to bring relief, she asked him to lance her side. (3:320)

In countless cases the women sought advice in the circle of healers closest to them: from the barber, the surgeon, an "empiricist," the midwife. A servant-girl got a scare in the summer of 1722 when she was caught in a downpour; as a result her menses stopped. She sought advice and treatment from a *chirurgus*, who bled and "purged" her without authorization, that is to say, without medical supervision (2:149, case 29). After a different woman had suffered an abortion, the midwife advised bleeding and the barber opened the vein (4/2:75, case 11). A young nursing woman, who was ill with "melancholy thoughts," called in a *practicum,* who was a "relative" of hers, and got advice on how to promote the menses (7:264, case 130). These "lower" healers in Eisenach also included the women of the neighborhood and traveling specialists known for certain diseases or special skills. In one part of town there was a woman, the widow of a pastor, who "presumed to advise pregnant women and those in childbed, and treated them with heat remedies from a book of recipes" (3:426). Time and again this widow crossed Storch's practice; she dispensed advice and remedies in her local circle. In one of the neighboring villages lived a "female quack" who had a regular "practice" for pregnant women and women in child-bed; she was famous for her reliably effective purgative prescriptions (6:406, case 156). Traveling healers stopped off in Eisenach; for example, the "Turkish woman doctor" who spent some time there in 1726 and was able to attract clients even from court circles. She based her treatment on uroscopy, and Storch had to go to quite a bit of trouble to obtain permission from the reluctant duke to chase her out of town. Toward the end Storch himself had been treating a servant-girl who took her urine to the Turkish doctor, accepted her treatment, and died (2:268, case 64). A case of melancholy in the form of "pensive thoughts" manifested itself in the daughter of a simple man of the middle class. For months she worried "that she has taken the Holy Eucharist in a state of unworthiness, and equally that her prayer is not effective and she does not have the consolation that it is being heard" (2:278, case 65). The menses were coming only "in a few drops." Storch was consulted, but his remedies did not really work; they neither dispelled the melancholy nor got the menses flowing. The parents became convinced that "witch-craft" had to be behind the whole thing, and they procured remedies from the executioner. A woman in childbed whose milk had stopped for four weeks (7:40) did the same.

Obviously a unique and very complex logic determined the healing relationships that were entered into in Eisenach, and this logic was by no means determined solely by the cost of the treatment. All the cases I have cited were at one time or another in Storch's practice, whether before, during, or after receiving advice, treatment, and care from one of the other practitioners, most of whom were illegal quacks from the perspective of the Medical Ordinances. The boundary between these unauthorized or only partially authorized healers, who nevertheless treated a great many ailments, and the authorized *medici* was fluid, and the sick seem to have had their own way of negating or very selectively confirming this boundary, which was officially rigid but in reality permeable. We can thus draw some preliminary conclusions:

This boundary was not primarily one of social status, since even noble women treated themselves, used the advice of women friends, and called in quacks, even though the sequence and frequency with which these steps were taken were different among aristocratic women.

It was not geographical, since "nonlocal" women and women from the countryside consulted Storch as well as other healers.

It was not clearly linked to the severity of the disease, such that an academic doctor was consulted if the pains worsened.

It can not be differentiated using criteria of "internal" and "external" treatment, in the sense that the doctor had a monopoly of internal remedies, since the women bled themselves, took expulsive remedies and purgatives on their own initiative, on the advice of an empiricist, at the suggestion of a surgeon or barber, or as part of a treatment by Storch.

In order to understand the driving forces behind the range of choices open to the sick, we must first take a look at the doctor's practice itself. In the twenty-two years of his diary, which he digested into his *Diseases of Women*, Storch lists about 1650 women. Of the 1816 numbered cases he describes, probably half record treatments where he attended to the woman with a single prescription only. Many other women, however, looked him up again and again during the course of their lives at specific moments—in times of an acute threat, during pregnancy, childbirth, and confinement, or even for seemingly trivial causes. Still other women kept up a continuous relationship with him, which developed over many years in the continuous exchange of messages.[6] These were very different forms of encounter between a woman and the doctor, and the impulses behind them must have had different motivations.

Who are these women who came face to face with the doctor, who made up his practice? The first picture we get is extraordinarily confused. There were very young girls, for example, an eight-year-old "girl," who, "pale and green in the face," was to be treated by him for "fatigue" on July 28, 1722 (2:140, case 24), or a six-year-old girl who was also "pale" and showed up for "stomachaches" (2:467, case 130). But most of Storch's female patients were older women in the "middle years," between twenty and "well into their thirties": pregnant women, women giving birth, in confinement, or nursing, all of whom needed something from him. Occasionally, and not unusually, women older than that appeared, women who were over forty and still getting pregnant. "Unmarried women" turned up who were not getting pregnant but complained that they never even had the monthlies; instead, as one of these women said, "from the child-bearing years on [she] has had the evil thing" (8:604, case 196). Even old women of sixty and seventy desired something from Storch's practice, although they showed up in distinctly smaller numbers. Among them was probably his oldest female patient, a robust woman of seventy who sought him out in August 1740 to get advice about her "frequent nosebleed" and the "monthly blood," which she still felt occasionally, though not regularly (8:628, case 210).

Through the moral and humoral categories of the doctor's glasses we see brief excerpts of a multitude of women's lives, not only in regard to their age but also in regard to their social status, their living circumstances, and the conditions of their bodies. Storch described—to take examples from volume 8—gaunt, corpulent, fat, robust, well-shaped, as well as soft and sensitive women. There were women endowed with a "resilient nature," and those with a "delicate constitution"; many women had an "angry temper," a "fiery temper," or were "headstrong," but there were also those who were "well-mannered," of "quiet and decent deportment," of "cheerful countenance." Some women were crooked of body—for example, a "person lame in her back" or a woman "with somewhat rickety ribs." Storch gives us a glimpse of table and bed, of stomach and lust. There was a woman whose marriage to an old gentleman had put her in a position where she could indulge a little in wine and good food, while another noblewoman had "to live frugally, against her habit," because her husband, an officer, was paid a low salary.

Another woman had "unexpectedly been reduced to poverty" and could allow herself very little. The forty-year-old wife of a "drunken and rash military surgeon" was tormented by her husband, while the young wife of a cavalryman "gave the same [sexual] services to the officers as she did to her nusband." In the case of a young woman who was married in the fall of 1737, we are told that the consummation occurred eight days before the monthlies (3:703, case 263), while in another case, word was sent "in a despondent mood" about the sixteen-year-old daughter of a distinguished man because her "monthlies" failed to appear.

The women of the stories come from all social strata of Eisenach: noble women and ladies of the court, wives of merchants and artisans, servants and chambermaids, peasant women and pastors' wives from the countryside, daughters of schoolmasters, wives of court councilors and of the burgomaster, wives of court employees (footmen, chancery clerks, coachmen, gardners), wives of tenants, soldiers, and officers, girls from the orphanage, beggars, and impoverished widows.[7] Some of the women were clearly anomalies: the wives of emigrants from Salzburg, who passed through Eisenach in 1732 and had to be taken care of in the city hall; a gypsy woman who made her childbed in "cool and rainy weather on a little straw and rubbish"; an "imprisoned woman" who, on June 2, 1738, complained about "stirrings of fever"; and a Jewish woman from Hessia, "well-shaped and twenty-four-years old."

Most of the women recorded in the diary lived in Eisenach. But we also hear of women from the surrounding villages and from "outside" towns. Occasionally we find information about distances: a peasant woman from a village two miles away sent a message concerning a hemorrhage (4/1:127, case 27); a noble lady seven miles distant inquired about the nightly discharge of a "mola" (4/1:164, case 38); a poor woman sent an urgent request over a distance of three hours on foot (3:217, case 32). Some peasant women visiting the market looked up Storch in person; a maidservant who had been sent into town stopped by; a young "woman" who was in Eisenach visiting a female relative appeared at Storch's house. A mother came from Jena with her twelve- or thirteen-year-old daughter to accuse a "robust literato" of violating her daughter and to have her examined by a professional (3:375, case 111). Women who were passing through town appeared in Storch's practice, like the millineress from Hanau. It was said of her that, although she "is used to traveling a lot, she leads a blameless life and while passing through . . . [lodges] here with a respectable lady." Even distant places are mentioned, for example, Zell in the Thuringian Forest, from which place the forty-year-old wife of a hammersmith requested a prescription through her husband, "because the monthly time has stopped."

Thus, from the welter of information a dense network of encounters slowly emerges.[8] From the perspective of my source the doctor stood in the center of this network, which spread from its core of Eisenach into the surrounding countryside, occasionally extending beyond the borders of the duchy and taking in women who were far away, for example, women from Eisenach who had moved away or were traveling and reported to their *medico* by letter. The network drew its patients from an area larger than that served by a modern general practitioner. This far-flung network was created by the unique form of the women's wishes and the form of the doctor's possible responses, and both were grounded in the contemporary conception of the body.

But the doctor and the women by no means always met face to face. On the contrary: the majority of these meetings went through inter-mediate channels—letters, oral reports, messages, requests, and the written or oral answers of the doctor carried back by the intermediaries. In a great many of the case histories Storch did not see the patient, at least not during the critical stages. There are stories in which he never saw the patient and yet had close contact and took care of her for years—sometimes to meet her by chance years later. The doctor's visit with the patient and the patient's visit to the doctor's house were only one facet of his practice;[9] alongside and of equal importance stood the messages carried by intermediaries. The greater the distance the greater the importance of a written and oral mediation of the meeting.[10] A great variety of people who acted as intermediaries can be identified: a mes-senger, a friend, a relative who happened to be on his way to Eisenach, the pastor with some business in Eisenach, the husband traveling to the fair in Leipzig, the servant who was being sent to the market. But mediation was not just a function of location; it was part of the way in which the doctor and the women related. The channels of mediation were grounded in social circumstances, forms of language, and social distances: noblewomen wrote letters or sent a servant; a mother sought advice for her daughter; a peasant sent his maidservant with a message; the wife of a sergeworker, in childbed with fever, sent her husband or a child. The women, whether from Eisenach or the surrounding area, sent news and messages.

Here are some examples: The mother of a twenty-year-old "person" who had "marched" to Hungary with a soldier in the previous summer and now lived in unclear circumstances, came to ask for a "prescription for a dropsic swelling" (3:714, case 266); a nineteen-year-old peasant girl appeared in Storch's house, but she was accompanied by "an old woman who spoke for her" (3:542, case 127); a maidservant had her "concern disclosed" "*per tertiam*" (through a third party) (3:543, case 127); a father wrote from outside the town to ask what should be done for his twenty-year-old daughter, "one of whose breasts shrunk two years ago" (2:424, case 114); a peasant from a remote estate came in person to show the urine of his twenty-two-year-old daughter who had had no flow of the menses for half a year (3:560, case 139); once a year a country pastor's wife sent her urine along with a report about the flow in her golden vein and her blood (8:379, case 95). A messenger reported that a hard-working maid "has a bleeding," but neither the messenger nor Storch saw the girl. Four days later Storch received a second *relation* which corrected the first report (2:223, case 53).

While a woman was in childbed or giving birth, the midwives brought news, picked up prescriptions, reported on the woman's condition. Noblewomen in particular wrote personally; they described their condition to the doctor and inquired, reported, complained. A noble widow wrote every year from her estate twelve miles away. She reported about the effect of the vine harvest and the new wine on her inside, about riding in the coach, which "greatly agitated" the "flow in the golden vein [hemorrhoidal vein]" and caused her "to feel surges in her blood" (8:342, case 83). It is striking how often men were also involved in transmitting very precise details. The husband of a Jewish woman suffering from a rash came to report and "asked for a prescription" (3:684, case 242). A "young peasant lad" brought the urine of a twenty-four-year-old girl who "has not been well since St. Michael's" (3:502, case 113). An "unmarried male person" requested, on behalf of a young woman, a prescription against the white flow and obstruction of the menses, which Storch gave him without hesitation (3:503). In the case of a seriously ill woman confined to her bed, "the husband has sent word that the body of his wife has opened with a discharge of much . . . matter and winds" (8:226, case 56). The husband of a twenty-six-year-old woman reported that, at the beginning of a recent pregnancy she "had sweated profusely. This sweating . . . was still continuing in her hands, which would easily get cold. She has no appetite, and a glass of wine easily induces a soaring heat" (4/1:173, case 43). The letters from aristocratic or bourgeois fathers and husbands, which Storch inserts into his text, show an extraordinary descriptive precision, an interest in minute details, and a careful recording of the sick person's sensations— "scratchy-sounding cough," "rumbling in the body," "pain and pulling in all the limbs"—as well as the writer's feelings: "Yesterday, she was— Praise be to God!—very well, and today even better" (2:183, case 63).

These lengthy messages, which we hear so directly and painfully across the gap of time, form the core of the "encounters" between the doctor and the women, and constitute the main material of the source. The reports, letters, messages, news, and notifications capture the women's complaints. Storch recorded them very carefully. They can be clearly identified within his case histories by the grammar ("she has sent word") and the manner of reporting (she "sensed," "felt," "experienced"). They are the material to which he added his own reflections but essentially took over unchanged. He was the recipient of a complaint and the recorder of subsequent complaints ("she had someone report 'today,'" "reported yesterday," and so on). Even when Storch saw the woman with whom he was talking—in which case our source says that she "told" him—in most instances he did not touch her for the purpose of examination. Here too he acted on the basis of what the patient said and what he could find out in further conversation. The importance of words and the public nature of the complaint stand in sharp contrast to the unimportance of a medical examination and what one can almost call a taboo against touching. The careful, word-for-word recording of a complaint and all the aspects of the story are inversely related to the distance the doctor assumed to what is, in the modern sense, the real object of the stories: women's bodies. This distance did not arise from a prohibition of coming into contact with the messiness of the body. Rather, it was a distance in which the body, despite the openness of its innermost flows, laid claim to an element of the unfathomable. The words of the sick and the signs displayed by their bodies spoke sufficiently of the inner condition. Even when Storch went to see a sick woman, his visit was an extension of the written or oral message. His treatment was based on the words of the sick; he rarely diagnosed something that could not also be delivered by messengers, openly and visibly: blood drawn from a patient, which provided clues about the woman's inner condition by the way in which it settled; urine that was examined for quality, color, consistency, and sedimentation; the fluids drawn out by a blister-inducing plaster, how much there was and of what kind and quality; the "mola" a mother brought on a plate to have looked at, and which he examined and cut up with his penknife. His diagnosis—if this word is even appropriate—took as its clues the words of the patient and the matter released from the inside of the body. The distance Storch had to assume toward the women's bodies was so great that he usually made a careful note when he had stepped across it. In the case of a fifty-year-old Hof-Frauenzimmer (court-lady) he recorded the following:

> "Anno 1726, on May 17th, she showed me with great embarrassment her left breast and on it a hard knot covered with blue veins. It had appeared three years before at a time when her monthly cleansing failed to come, had grown bigger and was now causing her pain and burning." (8:350, case 85)

Or:

> A young woman, twenty years of age, "bashful" and with "quiet manners," "had to force herself on October 2, 1734, to show me her painful left breast exposed." (2:521, case 160)

When it was possible for him to do what would have been quite natural for any midwife, he writes: "since she now no longer refused to have this area [a hernia] touched" (8:224, case 56); or: "as she was leaving, she uncovered with great modesty and embarrassment a lump on her right side" (8:520, case 166); or: "thus she decided to have the injury looked at more closely" (8:580, case 180); or: "since she was expected to die, she agreed to have her naked body looked at and touched" (4/1:17, case 5). This distance had little to do with barriers of social class, since even the poorest women as well as the "strumpet" with a bad thigh he visited in prison did not have to let Storch see their bodies unless they themselves expected some benefit from it. In a few cases Storch wanted to investigate his finding more closely but was unable to do so against the will of the patients. A young woman who was suffering from a stagnation of her monthlies and was taking diuretic remedies, and whom he suspected of a secret pregnancy and abortion, never had to undress; only when Storch surprised her at home "scantily dressed" did he catch a glimpse of the outline of a big belly. This supported his suspicion, but he was never able to confirm it through a hands-on examination (3:577, case 154).

This distance of the doctor's gaze to women's bodies is in striking contrast to the publicness of bodily phenomena we today carefully conceal. Touching, feeling, and examining seem to have been in a mental realm different from knowing, hearing, and telling. The body was surrounded by a kind of personal sphere that could be physically penetrated only in legitimate relationships—and Storch did not belong to the circle of those who were allowed to touch without special permission. Touching was culturally permitted along the boundaries of gender: women examined other women; the midwife examined and reported to Storch what she felt; a mother proceeded to feel her daughter's swelling in the body. Men who were relatives were not excluded: the husband or a cousin were allowed to touch. But Storch needed the permission of the patient or a mandate from the authorities. If he suspected syphilis, and in cases of "contagious" sores, boils, or spots, he summoned and visited patients in his capacity as town *physicus* (7:248, for example); in cases where a wet nurse had bad milk or breasts covered with sores, the authoritative order broke the sphere of what was beyond touch. Wet nurses had to consent to being examined, since their breasts and milk were no longer their own. In this instance the authorities' claim to supervision legitimated a culturally illegitimate procedure. On the other hand, general knowledge and public expression concerning blood flow, pus, urine, and coughed-up matter do not seem to have been in any way disgraceful. Incidental comments in the text shed light on the public nature of the inside. A noble lady who lived seven miles from Eisenach had a "good friend" report orally "what sort of complaints she was again feeling from the white flow" (8:417, case 109). Another noble lady, nearly fifty years old, had a very strong menses for eight days during the absence of her husband. News about this bleeding, which reached him in a tavern in a loud and dramatic story, gave him an opportunity "to show the guests how much he esteemed his wife." With three postal horses, Storch and the intoxicated nobleman set out that very night to hasten to the bleeding wife (8:532, case 168).

Storch's stories are full of neighbors who knew about the flows, bleeding, the color of urine, the sliminess of the blood drawn—about everything that emanated from the body. A woman tavernkeeper came to fetch a prescription for a shoemaker's young wife and told Storch about the "white flow" she was "concealing out of bashfulness" (8:558, case 173); female neighbors present during the doctor's visit could report details from the past; the chambermaids reported on the urine of their lady; a messenger brought details about an aborted pregnancy, "which had a thick, tough skin, and in the middle a thing with black-brown skin" (4/1:234, case 76); a mother I have already mentioned brought at noontime "a large lump" in a bowl (4/1:266, case 92). In the case of a poor shoemaker's daughter, whose first bleeding failed to come, we hear that prayers were said for her in Church for over six weeks— undoubtedly not with explicit reference to all the details, but with an implicit openness of what it was about. Whenever Storch wanted to know more than was directly accessible to him, he found ways and means through female neighbors, women friends, and servants, who "revealed" what they knew about the state of the patient's body. Given the very different modern taboos about the unappetizing aspects of personal secretions and excretions and their culturally sanctioned revelation in the objective realm of medical treatment, I am helpless in the face of the discrepancy in Eisenach between, on the one hand, the culturally sanctioned social sharing of knowledge and the openness concerning the details of ailments and excretions and, on the other hand, the taboo against touching the body. This prohibition against examinatory contact by the doctor existed even after a patient's death. Only in the rarest of cases was Storch able to prevail upon the relatives to permit an "opening." It almost seems as if the integrity of the person, which could be breached only in the context of personal relations with relatives, friends, and neighbors, was still incorporated in the dead body.

The contrast between the distance of the *medicus* to the body as such and his attentive nearness to the transmitted complaints was the basis for a kind of practice that could bridge great geographical and social distances. The meeting between the doctor and his woman patient was established by the latter's articulating a complaint and the former listening and responding to that specific complaint rather than to objectified symptoms. What, then, was the content of the messages, which we must distinguish strictly from the conditions about which Storch was summoned and consulted? The women complained with a rich vocabulary, and the imagery of their complaints speaks of a wealth of word-creations for the inner experience of pain, a wealth now lost to us. [11]

Suffering in Eisenach had to be verbalized before a *medicus* could deal with it. The doctor, after all, acquired his knowledge of the patient predominantly through his or her words. There were no laboratory results to establish a disease as an objectified condition; even uroscopy was only an aid in interpreting the spoken word. [12] The doctor did not work from his findings but from the expression of suffering in the patient's complaint. And that complaint concerned pain or fear.

Töllner has emphasized that pain emerged in medicine as the "guardian and keeper of life" only around the mid-eighteenth century. Until then, pain was "nothing other than the suffering of the soul from the defectiveness of the world." Pain was not conceivable as a symptom, "the soul felt the injury to the body directly as pain, because body and soul, though terminologically distinct, were still imagined as one reality and could therefore not be separated." Even J. B. Helmont saw no link between the cause of pain and the experience of pain: "Nothing can be afflicted with pain except the soul itself." [13] Whether pain was seen as Hippocratic disharmony, as a Platonic deficiency in the mode of existence, as a Manichaean mistake of the demiurge, or as a result of the Christian fall from grace, these perceptions were based on the notion that pain expressed the broken state of nature. Pain could thus be endured or overcome, at best it could be alleviated, calmed, soothed, but fighting it would have been meaningless. A sufferer could defy pain, try to deny it, submit to it, but he could not escape it. It was only with Leibniz that the Cartesian idea of pain as a message from the body to the consciousness became a part of medical thinking: pain turned from a flaw of nature into a protector of life. Storch was still not thinking about combating pain, just as he was not concerned to make his patients healthy. *Medici* "patch up the sick" (8:469). The body manifested itself to him in its pains. He could not get rid of pain any more than he could get rid of the body.

A pain, an ache in the body, did not inevitably seek out a specific word, did not lead to only one of many possible formulations. A sharp pain in the chest, which today we might call "heart failure" or "heart trouble," in the context of Eisenach was articulated with other words and thus in an entirely different dimension. "Heart trouble" today is different from what was conveyed in eighteenth-century Eisenach by the expressions "heavy heart," "bleeding heart," "anxiety of the breast," "heart-throbbing," "heart-trembling," "storm in the breast." Medical history has examined the history and structure of the terminology of disease in different periods in relation to the theoretical framework of this terminology, but we know next to nothing about the language in which a disease was dealt with, not on an academic but on a personal level. This gap in the existing scholarship is the legacy of the development in which power over the correct word became concentrated on one side only, that of medicine. Today we can only stutter or keep silent in the face of the normative nomenclature of medical language.[14] Today I would have to say, "I have a cardiac insufficiency," thus classifying myself as the bearer of a disfunction. However, the interpretation of chest pain as a disfunction is culturally determined and only one among many possible means of expression. If I want to speak more loosely I can say "my old pump is not working," using an image that could not have been articulated prior to Harvey. The language of pain and the articulation of suffering, as cultural achievements in enduring pain, are historical phenomena. They are all the more revealing the less medicalized a society is, and the less they are therefore devalued by a medical context. The language of pain conveys an entire world view. As long as there was no classificatory landscape of the inner processes of the body, the pain that was to be described, which lurked invisible inside the body and could not be grasped objectively, had to be expressed in relation to a third phenomenon. The premedicalized language of pain was necessarily metaphorical. To be more than groans, this language had to use images which, through the use of analogies, made a statement about something that could not be expressed as such. Metaphors contain comparisons. They express one thing through another and thus speak implicitly of the "meaning" imparted to a sensation. The subconscious, culturally determined choice of images allows a unique insight into how a different age experienced pain. A metaphoric language reveals layers of perception precisely through its mediated structure, since it can speak only in a contextual relation. "Cardiac insufficiency" speaks about a purely physical, universal, and isolatable phenomenon. The "attack of heart-trembling" and the "painful tearing in the heart" of which a fifty-year-old court-lady spoke in March 1720, and which she had suffered as a result of "frantic exertion and fear" while fleeing Saxony before the advancing Swedes in 1706 (8:114, case 25), obviously mean something very different from cardiac insufficiency.

How can I bring order into the multitude of words for pain? It is clear that an arrangement into groups based on any kind of medical classification is meaningless, since it would subvert what the women of Eisenach themselves meant. A rough division suggests itself if I separate complaints expressing an inner sensation from those manifesting themselves in something visible on the outside, and if I finally group together those complaints expressing other causal chains.

The chapbooks of remedies and the vernacular pharmacopoeias of the seventeenth century arranged their prescriptions from head to foot, a tradition that reached back into the Middle Ages. [15] This arrangement imitates the experience of the sick person, who also thought that the entire body "must be at the command" of a pain that manifested itself in a very specific way depending on the bodily part affected. From head to foot the women of Eisenach complained of the following ailments (taken from volume 8):

> Slight headache, darkness of the eyes, a feeling that their hair was falling out or sight was fading or hearing was disappearing, a tearing in the jaw, a dizzy and dull headache, heavy tongue and speech, toothache, nosebleed, a flux in the ear, hiccups, a sore throat, a rising in the throat and

constriction of the same, contraction of the throat, withdrawing of the gum, bilious vomiting, choking, hoarseness and coughing, phlegm dripping from the head into the throat, neck pains, tightness of throat, sweating of the head, gloominess of thoughts, sadness.

Searing pain in the limbs, numbness in the arm, trembling, tingling in the limbs, numb hands, cramped hands, crushed limbs, heaviness in the arm, stirring in the arm, apoplexy in the right arm, tearing fluxes in the limbs, fright in the limbs, painful gout.

A rising of the blood toward the breast, shortness of breath, a tight shortness of breath, choking in the breast, stinging pains around the breast, anxiety, fearfulness, a wooden stake in the heart, squeezing in the pit of the heart, heart anxiety, a pain in the breast that felt as though something was eating inside, anxiousness, throbbing of the heart, burning under the breastbone.

Painful womb colic, womb fear, womb anxiety, womb trouble, cramps, a cold womb that was open too wide, a knot in the womb, a closed-in wind turning toward the womb, a womb cramp manifesting itself mostly in the mouth and in the tongue and rendering the latter useless for speaking.

A swollen body, a thick belly and rumbling, upward rising wind, downward moving wind, stagnating wind, stomach cramps, a rising from the stomach, rattling in the body, griping in the body, a feeling as if everything was turning about in the body, a fluttering sensation in the lower body, a body full of wind and water, burning in the stomach, constipation, burning pain in the side, pain around the area of the liver, pleurisy, spleen fear, pain in the soft part of the belly like a cold stone, fits of the evil thing, stone colic, raging pain in the hip, urge to urinate, knots on the buttocks, lameness in the back, sensitive pains in the back, loins, and hips, stoppage of urine, pressing of feces.

Feet and knees that are stiff and lame, sensitive pain in the shin, heat in the feet, swollen legs, swollen varicose veins, pains in the foot as though the blood itself was trying to force its way out, cold feet, a bad foot.

To these terms for the inner sensations in specific body regions should be added those words that describe conditions that were not specifically localized: boiling up or surging, heat, cold, shuddering, feebleness, sweating, anxiousness, swooning, dizziness, nausea, feeling ill, shaking, fright, cramps, twitching. In addition to describing what they were feeling, the women also complained about things they could observe, smell, or feel on their bodies: nettle rashes, scabies, redness, feverish rashes, burning sores, knots in the breast, chapped hands, reddish rash on the forehead, scaly rashes, swelling, soreness, an oozing dampness, ulcers, bleeding from the womb, coughing up of blood, vomiting of blood, flux from the ear, a bloody discharge from the golden vein. Finally there are the many words for matter discharged by the body: clotted lumps of blood, watery but sharp blood, foul-colored blood, melancholic blood, blood that pulled like twine, black filth, black and slimy blood, water and black diarrhea, bloody excretion, reddish water, a mess of foul phlegm, brown urine with grit in it, a discharge of greenish moisture, a lump of a skinny thing, a smelly discharge, a nasty and foul-odored discharge that smelled like milk.

Many of the complaints expressed something else as well: an observation about something that was *not,* something that failed to appear, a flaw or a deficiency: the milk was stopped up, the monthly blood was stagnant, the flow of a woman in childbed was stopped up, the wetness under the breast dried up, the knots on the legs disappeared, the body did not open itself, the golden vein became blind, a flow in the ear vanished. This was followed by descriptions of the effects of these deficiencies. Finally, and almost inseparably, we must also include complaints about anger, fright, sorrow, excitement, agitation, sadness, and fear. The source reveals an intimate link between these four aspects of the complaints. The women complained about one part of the body or another, about something that was happening in the entire body, something that appeared on the body, and something that threatened them with its absence.

What did the women want from the doctor with these complaints, and how did the doctor respond to them? What was the immediately apparent impulse behind these various reports? What was the doctor supposed to do? In a modern practice the aim of a doctor-patient interrelationship is predetermined, at least on the surface: the doctor is expected to make a diagnosis and to treat and cure the diagnosed illness. The women in Eisenach wanted neither of these things. The circumstances leading to a complaint and the queries linked to them were as manifold and specific as the doctor's responses.

There was a whole spectrum of what the sick and their families wanted. Some women asked explicitly for advice. A sergemaker's twenty-two-year-old daughter, "in *obstructionem mensium,* with a headache, tiredness, and a pale color" (2:564, case 184), did not want a prescription from the apothecary. All she sought was advice; in fact, she wanted to have her home remedy, melissa tea, confirmed. The gaunt wife of an artisan went out to gather wood "with a pregnant belly" and fell down with her gathered load. She did not look Storch up because of this mishap, but to seek "advice from me about nausea and other complaints stemming from her pregnancy" (4/2:19, case 3); she too wanted to hear only that the "small spoonfuls of cinnamon-water" she was taking were good for her. Other women inquired about a treatment with medicinal water because they were planning to take a trip. Among those seeking advice were women who had not come earlier during serious crises. One such woman was the "choleric" wife of a tailor, who had given birth many times and had to carry "at least five" of her children to the grave. In May 1730 she appeared in the sixth month of another pregnancy to ask Storch "whether bleeding might not be of benefit to her" (3:576, case 152). With the noblewomen with whom Storch maintained constant contact, such queries were embedded in the exchange of medicines and complaints, letters and visits. The poorer women apparently decided to consult the doctor only at a specific point in time. At that moment the doctor was probably consulted as an expert, an authority, but an authority who was to confirm the pattern of their home remedies and treatments. Even in cases of serious illness, the request occasionally was for nothing more than a formal *consilium,* a written, learned opinion about the cause of the disease, the prognosis, possibly of the kinds of remedies to be used and how they were supposed to work. The parents of a seventeen-year-old girl with a cough were thus told that, "for certain medical reasons," "such a cough was not yet to be seen as a consumptive lung-cough, but a stomach . . . cough." They were then informed how they were to arrange the treatment and to administer "gently purging and opening remedies" (2:104, case 13). In the case of a thirty-three-year-old lady who was laid up with dropsy, Storch was "asked by her father to look at her in his presence but not treat her" (8:63, case 12). Here too Storch was consulted as an authority, and in both cases he was then given an *ordre* to write out prescriptions. But his *consilium* was integrated into a pattern of consultations by other practitioners, the "ordinary" *medici,* who were engaged in continuous treatment and whose knowledge Storch was only to enlarge upon and supplement. In cases where a *consilium* was requested, Storch was being asked for his learned medical knowledge—the *consilia* are full of physiological reflections; in most other cases where advice was sought his recommendations were integrated into the usual practice of self-diagnosis and self-treatment.

Advice was followed by a remedy. Just as the complaint was the central element for the patient, the slip of paper prescribing the remedy for the apothecary was the doctor's pawn. In the vast majority of all case histories the women asked for these slips. They wanted a "prescription." They usually did not say what the remedy should contain, but they often knew precisely which effects they expected from the prescription. Sometimes they knew this hoped-for effect more precisely than the doctor, who could not always get from the women's reports a precise idea about their condition. A noble lady requested "a sudorific, without reporting any other circumstances" (8:570), and Storch prescribed. A thirty-six-year-old woman, "conditionis honoratoris," who felt "fairly weak" after an aborted pregnancy, "very much wanted to attend . . . a wedding feast, and so asked for a prescription of some strengthening remedies" (4/1:153, case 34); Storch prescribed. A thirty-year-old woman, who suspected "an ill condition of the womb" in herself, asked for "womb-cleansing" and a few days later also for a purgation; Storch prescribed (4/2:155, case 35). A choleric lady had been badly frightened when "one of her horses" fell down, and she asked for a remedy; once again Storch had something to prescribe (8:323, case 80). The forty-year-old wife of a court employee reported that her menses had "hitherto showed themselves little and irregularly, and now one period had stayed away entirely," and she requested an expulsive prescription (8:184, case 43). Another woman, around thirty, complained of "stoppage of her monthly time for fourteen days, without being able to give the cause," and asked for a prescription (8:150, case 31). A thirty-four-year-old woman felt nauseous and "requested a prescription" (8:209, case 50). Without speaking with the doctor, the women requested remedies to reduce the sharpness of their milk, drops to cure gas, a "purgative which could also be called a womb-cleanser" (6:779), or something as a "precaution against blood-vomiting" (8:368)—and Storch wrote out prescriptions. A woman's complaint frequently contained the answer she expected from the doctor. It was combined with a clear request that the doctor prescribe a home remedy or the desired remedy from the apothecary. The doctor's prescription was thus often a confirmation of the patient's own assessment. The doctor became a roundabout route, an authority used not to choose a remedy but to confirm a remedy, its use, and possibly also its effectiveness.

Women who wanted to induce abortions used and manipulated the doctor in this way. A maidservant, for example, tried to obtain purgatives to cleanse her inside:

> "In April 1722 a strong, otherwise well-looking, sanguine maidservant asked for a prescription for my purgative essence for her lord, who usually consulted a different *medicus,* saying that on a former occasion he had felt well afterward . . . I believed her pretext and prescribed the purgative." Three months later she requested for herself a "prescription of a somewhat strong *purgation,*" and now Storch realized "that her stomach had been upset by something other than food and drink." To keep her from procuring something stronger elsewhere, Storch then gave her only a "mild *species.*"   (3:199, case 28)

The blanks in our source, forms of routine self-treatment within a web of familial and neighborly healing relationships, were at the center of the doctor's practice. Medical and lay activities overlapped not only in cases of less alarming pains such as stomachaches, gas, or a bad womb; the more complex forms of medical practice also moved between these two poles. In many instances of what appear to have been serious illnesses, the women reported their condition and the doctor sent a prescription; if necessary he repeated it a second or third time upon a renewed request. Take, as one example, the wife of an oilmaker. She was well over thirty years of age, her husband beat her, and she had to lift heavy sacks. On May 6, 1734, she suffered an abortion with a great deal of "bloody water." The next day she was in pain, someone was sent to the doctor to ask for a prescription against these "after-pains," and he wrote one out. Storch records: "what happened afterward I cannot report, since I was given no further news" (4/1:239, case 72). The case was closed, Storch never saw the patient, but that was obviously not desirable or necessary for him to supply what was requested.

Very often the doctor was in the service of his clients' ideas of the body, and this was by no means limited to the well-to-do and courtly patients. Well over half of Storch's cases were those in which the doctor was asked for a prescription only once, and in these cases he was urged to prescribe precisely what the woman already knew and possibly had available at home. The doctor was thus asked to serve his patients' ideas of their bodies: the women sought comfort in the symbolic act of the doctor's interpretation by means of his prescription. It often seemed to me that what was actually going on in this practice was this kind of ritualistic confirmation.

The picture of Storch's practice and the possible relations between the sick person seeking advice and the doctor becomes even more complex. On the one hand, Storch offered personal visits in addition to his prescriptions and, on the other, other healers, some legitimate and some unauthorized, offered services very similar to his. The sick thus had not only a choice of healers but also a choice of what they requested from them: advice, prescriptions, continuous treatment, visits—an incredible density and variety of possibilities. This broad range of options was available to the poorer women of Eisenach as well. For the richer burgher women and noblewomen the options were more extensive, but they were not substantially different. The poorer women went back and forth between the legitimate *medici* and *chirurgi* and the illegal healers, thus manipulating the boundary drawn by the Medical Ordinances. The same thing occurred in the higher social strata of Eisenach, as women ranked the access of the *medici* as *medicus ordinarius* or *vicarius,* consulted other doctors, brought in additional opinions—and even help from "quacks" if they could not obtain the desired effect on the legitimate side of the boundary. This drawing on and using healers to confirm and deal with one's own ideas about the body seems to correspond to the characteristics attributed to the body at the time.

One social difference did exist. The higher up and wealthier a woman was, the easier it was for her to keep a single *medicus* continuously as her personal physician. She could then ask for the whole register of his services, and could use *her doctor* as a clearinghouse for dealing with all spheres of her life in which she chose her own remedies, as well as those instances when her own knowledge was exhausted.

Let us take a concrete look at these options:

A young girl, between eighteen and twenty years old, sent a report in early August 1724 that "for some time now" she has had her menses "very little and pale-colored and has felt tired and nauseous when it occurred." She was forced to keep to her bed. Storch sent a prescription, and "cannot report how the remedy worked . . . since at that time a young *medicus* was tending to the patient." (2:248, case 57)

This girl appeared only once; afterward she seems to have switched to another doctor. More convoluted was the case of

the wife of a sergemaker, over thirty years of age and past the midpoint in her pregnancy. She got her monthly flow "in the form of a reddish, festering matter." She decided to have herself bled, but since she suffered persistent pains, "she requested a prescription," which Storch sent. Several days later she suffered an abortion, but for three days the afterbirth failed to follow. During this time she tried to promote the discharge of the afterbirth with home remedies and with the help of "a military surgeon who was given to quackery." "Since it [the afterbirth] now seemed corrupted . . . I had to give another prescription." After the woman had taken Storch's remedy "the afterbirth was expelled." (4/2:10, case 2)

The sergemaker's wife did not ask Storch for advice, a visit, a prognosis, or the like. She used him to get access to internal remedies, while her trusted helper seems to have been the military surgeon. In another case,

the thirty-year-old wife of a fisherman sent word on October 24, 1737, about "shivering" and an "intolerable pain below one of her shoulders." Storch suspected something consumptive and sent a powder. The next day she sent word that "heat and thirst were very great," but that the "shooting pains" had eased. Five days later Storch was called for a "visita-tion," and it turned out that the woman had aborted a seven-month-old child during the night, "of whose pregnancy I had not been told anything before then." During the following weeks, in which the condition of the desperately ill woman worsened, there was a daily exchange of messenges and several visits. A "close woman neighbor" later "disclosed" to Storch that the woman had in the meantime also procured inner remedies from a "quack." (4/2:225, case 64)

Here Storch was asked to visit because the woman's condition was obviously deteriorating, and the request came only seven days after the initial decision to obtain a prescription from him. At that point the woman (or her family) decided that it was necessary to see the doctor, perhaps because the treatment of the less respectable healer who had been consulted first had caused the abortion—or had failed to prevent it.

In the case of a pastor's daughter, the actions followed a different pattern:

> The girl was twenty-one years old. Around St. Michael's Day 1737, she was frightened "by a dog which barked loudly at her just at the time when her menses were flowing." Her menses were stopped up during the entire winter. In January she took the remedies of a young *medicus* who was a relative of hers. Once, in March, she complained to Storch about a host of "troubles": "heart-throbbing, tiredness, bad color, strong and uncommon sweating, with a strongly itching scorbutic blister." Storch gave prescriptions for a cleansing tea, a purgative, and an expulsive essence. Prior to the girl's death in November, Storch was asked on two more occasions, once every three months, for a prescription on the basis of reports about her condition.   (2:559, case 181)

In this case the family probably relied during the entire time on the prescriptions from the *medicus* who was a relative. But why was Storch, almost regularly every three months, asked for additional remedies?

> A woman who at the beginning of her case in 1720 was forty-seven years old and who belonged to Eisenach's upper burgher class had contact with Storch over seventeen years. During five of these years she repeatedly suffered from strong and sudden bleedings. The diary reveals that Storch, in a case where the complaint seems ("objectively"!) to stay the same, at times sent up to twenty prescriptions in one month, with the doctor and the patient exchanging reports and prescriptions for remedies on a daily basis. This happened especially at the beginning of her treatment. In the following year she obtained prescriptions only in intervals of several months. During one year, when she was "in a tolerable condition, so that she had no need for a prescription," Storch was not consulted at all. During a crisis the following year he had to visit her once and gave a prescription. When her husband died and she "thereupon" developed "a troublesome cough," she again solicited a prescription.   (8:177, case 42)

In this case periods of intensive contact alternate with times in which the same problem was reported merely as "a passing complaint," and with times in which the patient procured remedies and treated herself with advice from an "old matron." Storch was here almost something like a *medicus ordinarius,* a personal physician. But unlike aristocratic women, who during the same time would have requested more frequent and continuous visits and prescriptions, this woman had begun to live with her bleeding, or she helped herself differently in the long pauses between being bled and purged.

The case of a peasant woman may serve as an example of how a woman cleverly manipulated the services available to her.

> She appeared in Storch's house in March 1737 and had him examine her left breast. She wanted from him, not from a surgeon, advice on what should be done. "Since she has had it [a knot in her breast] looked at several times, she was resolved to have it cut out." She asked Storch for a prognosis about the outcome of the procedure and agreed to "entrust" herself to his "supervision and treatment." Storch gave her remedies for inner loosening and purging and asked her to return to Eisenach to have the excision performed in his presence as soon as her next monthly period was over. The next time she came with a barber-surgeon from her neighborhood, "who wanted to know how to perform the procedure." The woman and the surgeon had Storch tell them in detail how the excision was to be performed and how the bleeding could be stopped, and they assured themselves that there was no danger to the woman's life. They postponed the surgery, but in fact the woman had the lump cut out in her "own dwelling" in order to "lower the costs." They had obtained such thorough instructions that he "accomplished [the excision] successfully by himself, without the presence of a *medicus.*" When the woman had strong pains in her left arm on the fifth day, the surgeon himself went to Storch in Eisenach to get "additional advice" and a prescription.   (7:212, case 91)

This woman, who appeared only this one time, must have procured what she needed in her own circles and from this trusted barber-surgeon. But once the lump in her breast had grown to the size of a "small chicken egg," she was alarmed and went to Eisenach to Storch, whom she regarded as an authority, to get advice which she would take back to her realm of self-treatment. During the session of instruction in Storch's house, the two systems of healing met in a dialogue that was very profitable for the woman though less so for Storch.

Under the mantle of their lords' protection, servants were often given treatment which they otherwise surely would not or could not have sought out so frequently. During house calls, Storch frequently also treated the domestics of his patients. Two examples:

In early August 1740, around noon before lunch, a woman cook in a noble household poured a pot of boiling water over her chest. Storch happened to be visiting the household. He "had her step in front of the fire with her upper body uncovered," advised against the home remedies she had been using and prescribed ointments. He tended to her continuously for a week. When the pain worsened, and the wounds "gave off matter and were in need of cleansing," Storch had to call in the wife of a surgeon, since the young cook "would not tolerate any male person." (7:296, case 176)

A day laborer's wife in the Gotha village of Craul am Hainiche gave birth to triplets in the beginning of January 1732. Fourteen days later she complained about "feverish heat with a subsiding of her milk." Storch gave her a prescription which the lords of Hopfgarten had requested as they passed on her complaints.

A few cases involving noblewomen show clearly the various healers working side-by-side or at cross-purposes, since in these instances the various people called in did not come from the hushed-up world of unauthorized healers but from the official hierarchy of the *medici,* to which Storch himself belonged. Subtle gradations of nearness or distance to the body of the patient created intricate quarrels among the doctors competing for trust. The distance between the doctor and the bodies of the women, which we have seen as a fundamental element of the medical practice in the multifarious ways in which doctor-patient encounters were mediated, could, in the case of a noble lady, be dissolved as she gradually extended her permission to a physician to draw closer; this process culminated in the exclusion of other healers. Storch recorded a decisive moment in the case of a young woman who had consulted both him and another *medicus:* she "displayed a lasting trust whenever I wished to help her with good advice and prescriptions when she was ill" (4/1:267, case 93). To be admitted to "confidence" in a mutual story that became increasingly close and extended over time meant gradually to gain insight into the inner space of the body. Let us look at a case in which Storch successfully negotiated this choreography of "opening":

An elderly lady, sixty-nine at the beginning of the story, had known Storch for some time from a distance, since she "entrusted [to him] nearly all her domestics," and Storch ate at her table. "Nevertheless, she did not

wish to reveal anything to me during the lifetime of her regular *medicus.*"
At table she mentioned nothing of her complaints, her "secret troubles."
Only behind the closed doors of her study, where she would withdraw after
the meal along with her trusted doctor, would she entrust herself and her
complaints to the *medicus.* The old doctor died, and in the course of the next
two years Storch moved closer to her and upward on the ladder. At first he
merely duplicated the remedies of the late doctor and supervised the lady
when she decided to bleed herself. Slowly, hesitantly, she let Storch
slightly modify one remedy or another. In December, during a "flux and
breast fever," and "since she perceived danger to herself," she asked that he
visit her. When his remedies worked well, she "decided henceforth to show
stronger trust." He promised improvement "if she would only follow his
prescription." A more stable relationship was thus established through a
promise. Slowly the lady became "more open-hearted." After more than
half a year, when she was again afflicted by her "usual colic pains," she
lifted her dress at the side: "she decided to have the problem looked at more
closely." Storch comforted her with a positive prognosis, and "thereupon
she allowed me to prescribe remedies for her as I saw fit." That same year he
also succeeded in weaning her from some of the self-treatments to which
she had grown accustomed, though even this was a slow, hesitant process
in which she carefully weighed his opinion and her own experiences. In the
following years Storch was the only one consulted; he had to be ready to
visit and became part of her daily routine. When he moved to Gotha in the
spring of 1724, "she was very anxious on his taking leave . . . that she
would now in her old age have to entrust herself to another, younger
medicus." During the summer he still took care of her from Gotha, since she
only very slowly opened herself to another doctor, whom, during the
winter, she gradually came to trust.   (8:578, case 180)

If a doctor moved up into a stable relationship of trust, this step
demanded from him all the services he was able to provide: the intense
exchange of messages and prescriptions, continuous visits, availability
upon request. He was called at night, during the day, once, twice, or
three times a day. With aristocratic ladies who lived for part of the year
or even permanently on their estates or in the surrounding villages, this
demand was quite strenuous. "Trust" was exchanged for the doctor's
presence whenever it was needed.

A lady in her mid-twenties who kept him as *medicus ordinarius* sent to ask
about "swooning and shuddering." When the prescription he sent back

not only failed to help but a "paroxysm" developed in addition, Storch had to "set out at eleven at night to travel a mile over country." Two days later he had to return. The swooning had lessened, but the lady complained of "a cold spot on her head and cold feet." Toward evening of the same day, on which the woman had eaten "a considerable portion of sauerkraut and pork" for lunch, the swooning threatened to return. "She requested another night visit in very cold weather"— it was in February 1731. (3:513, case 120)

Nevertheless, a woman's trust, that is, her decision to admit a doctor continuously into her own space and to demand his presence upon request—a trust which in poorer circles probably was established within networks of relatives and other healers familiar in the neighborhood— was only a fragile protection against the admittance of others. We find gradations of trust in times of crisis. One of Storch's patients had long been laid up with an illness. Though she was supplied with a steady stream of prescriptions, the pains persisted. Eventually "her patience gave out, and she was carried away to using all kinds of empirical remedies" (8:290). The alternation between inclusion and exclusion was usually indicated in the source by the laconic remark: "therefore she used another *medicus.*" But it was not a change in the forms I have described, for they existed side by side. Storch treated the patient, but had to "confer" with the former *medicus* and "request prescriptions from him"; a few days later he found his remedies combined with remedies and a bleeding prescribed by the doctor of the patient's sister. A few days after that an old out-of-town *practicus* was in Eisenach; "he had been called here for a noble patient," and Storch had to bring him along "for a visit" (8:198, case 48). In the case of this lady of about fifty the various consultations involved at least the following people: her sister, three *medici,* "someone" who "advised her to eat cubebs to strengthen her stomach," and the patient herself, who tried some of the prescriptions her sister had obtained from yet another person at some earlier time.

Storch worked in a variety of roles: as a "borrowed" *medicus;* as a *vicarius;* as a *medicus* consultant who was supposed to "treat" *collegialiter* with the *ordinarius;* as an *ordinarius* sharing the work with an invisible *medicus* who was present through his powders and essences; as an *ordinarius* who, even when treating aristocratic patients, had to share space with barbers, barber-surgeons, and surgeons, some of whom were present, some of whom worked in the interstices of his meetings with the patients. Once when he was out in the countryside overnight, a *practicus* who had been living in town for thirteen years and another old *practicus* were called in, and "these two I met in the process of giving out prescriptions" (8:431). From January to May 1736 Storck attended a lady he had known since 1720 as an *ordinarius,* treating her in several visits each day. Storch worked alongside other healers and diagnostic information: a colleague of equal rank (though this man spoiled his "reputation"), a letter from a "famous and experienced *practicus,*" instructions from the *consilium* of an out-of-town *physicus* to whom the lady's urine had been sent, a "famous *practicus*" who was there when Storch was not, a "known quack" who sent his "herbal tea," and a midwife who visited (8:167, esp. 169, case 41). In this seeming chaos we see an exact gradation of access, over which the patient decided: a woman, the midwife, who was allowed to touch and examine her; Storch as *ordinarius,* who was responsible for the flow of the medications she obtained; a local *medicus,* who was initially consulted only for his opinion. Later the *medicus* also sent prescriptions. Finally he was summoned to support Storch, but in the end he was dismissed since his drops proved ineffective. Storch, however, as a long-time doctor of "confidence," remained in her trust, his position weakened by the *consilium* of an out-of-town *physicus* who had been consulted without his knowledge and strengthened by the *consilium* and visit of a famous practitioner. Finally an unknown "quack" was brought in marginally; "tea"—but no internal medications—were procured from him.

The logic of this permeable space around the body of the sick—whose entrances and intermediate levels were guarded by the sick and their immediate environment, in which inclusion and exclusion, penetration, "opening" and closing existed—was apparently grounded in the conception of the "space" from which the complaint was reported. The patient's decision was embodied in the very center, the landscape beneath the skin, the invisible sphere of the body's interior. And as we have seen, there were many ways to obtain advice, treatment, and care for this inner space, to manipulate it by introducing and evacuating substances. No external knowledge, no title or exam—that is, no "professional" attributes—was important enough to be accepted fully as a counterweight to an *inner* conception. It was here, in the interior of the self, in the understanding of its processes and flows, that the decision on what constituted healing was made. Not rank and a learned reputation, but a female patient helped Storch when another patient's confidence began to waiver:

> "Around that time this woman, who had had many clysters for her hernia, helped me in treating a man who was laid up in the neighborhood through her example. She helped persuade this man to continue the needed clysters. This did more than all other encouragement; for patients . . . are always doubtful whether what (their *medici*) are saying is correct." (8:237, case 56)

FOUR

The Perception of the Body

I happened upon Storch's *Diseases of Women* by accident, at a time when my own work on the perception of parturition in the eighteenth century was already well advanced. Reading Storch, I soon realized that my own assumptions, and what I considered self-evident, could not do justice to his text. At first I read and collected cases from Storch's compendium with incomprehension. Only through a long and arduous process of reflecting on the compiled registers of all the cases did I begin to sense the importance of Storch's terms and ordering criteria. For time and again I caught myself ordering "things" according to my own anatomico-physiological grid, or according to criteria that were familiar to me from the history of eighteenth-century science. The temptation was great to interpret Storch's notions through Stahl's doctrines, and thus to dissolve them within a doctrine to which the doctors around Halle supposedly adhered. The more deeply I read my way into the source, the more impossible it seemed to accomplish such a reductionism. The most important elements in Storch's ideas about the body were those he had in common with his women patients; thus they were not influenced by Stahl, vitalism, and Halle.

As time went by it seemed less and less meaningful to me to order my information according to "things," such as the frequency of eclampsia or ruptured perinea, or according to social status and the meager social indicators. It proved impossible to trace these stories back to "real" illnesses, since many of the "diseases," such as the insatiable need of a nun from Eichsfeld to be butchered, make little sense within modern medical concepts. Where was the dividing line between the real and the unreal? Was there even such a dividing line in Eisenach?

Gradually the outlines of a perception that the doctor and at least most of the women had in common emerged, a perception of the "body" foreign to me. The doctor's description of this "body" became the central focus of my attention. And at that point, my own certainties became an obstacle. I found myself unable to infer directly from the source to a "real corporeality," since the latter was always only implicitly hinted at.

I therefore decided to create a construct to help my reflections. I called it "orientational patterns of perception guiding the doctor's practice." Why this complex label? What the source describes and wants to describe for young *practici* are exemplary practical procedures. In each case the doctor described his perception of and prescriptions for a woman. In doing so he invariably referred in each case to her "body," even though he rarely ever actually saw it, and if he did then it was, except for face and hands, through the multilayered clothing of the time.

Yet Storch's reflections were guided by a conception of the body that was accessible to me only insofar as it informed his practice. If I wanted to adhere faithfully and closely to my source, I could hazard only to say: "I know the notions orienting the doctor's practice"—without knowing to what extent this statement contained the totality of the body he experienced.

In order to depict this intuitively grasped body conception, I had no choice but to probe it for describable elements, to break it down into meaning clusters. I could also have spoken of meaning bundles, focal points, or image elements. In contrast to my own objectified criteria, with the help of which everything or nothing in the text could be ordered without revealing a contemporary meaning, many of these focal points proved heuristically very productive. In nearly all cases they could also be closely related to conceptual patterns, themes, and motifs that were familiar to me from the scholarly literature.

A dialectical dialogue between contemporary sources, "themes" discussed in the secondary literature, and my own material allowed me to reduce the number of these orientational notions to a dozen. At the same time, the fact that I could relate these meaning clusters to each other created a much more precise, clearer, and more solid picture of the conception mirrored in the sources, which initially I could grasp only intuitively.

What is directly mirrored in the source are the doctor's conceptions.

The women's conceptions of their own bodies are mirrored only indirectly through Storch's report. In my commentary on the different orientational notions I try to address the differences that emerged between the doctor's practice-guiding conceptions and the notions of how personal suffering was embodied, which are reflected in the women's complaints. A few very clear differences appeared time and again, like the one between the doctor who tries to entice the stagnant blood to open up, and the women who want to expel it. I found no reason to suspect contemporary gender differences behind these divergent attitudes. Storch's wish to "cleanse" the women with borax, instead of "promoting" them with saffron as they themselves wanted, shows that Stahl's theory influenced not only Storch's thinking but also his concrete perception of the body. I was surprised to discover how close the "body" of Storch was to that of the women when it came to actual practice. Storch's diaries have often struck me as a twenty-five-year struggle to force his own body concept, which was repeatedly confirmed as he listened to the women's complaints, into the scheme of Stahl's categories.

Metamorphosis within the Body

The body in Eisenach is opaque. It is a place of hidden activities. As long as a person was alive, his body could not be opened, his inside could not be deciphered, could not be seen. People could speculate about its inside only with the help of signs that appeared on the body or emanated from it. All this was self-evident before our anatomical certainties became common knowledge.

Vesalius' anatomical illustrations and Harvey's experiments on the living body were known to the educated practitioner of the early eighteenth-century—even if Storch did not know about the latter. But this knowledge, gained by examining dead or dying bodies, was transferred very slowly into the conceptual world of the practitioner.[1] In practice the dead body did not yet cast its shadow on the living body.[2] The dissecting knife could reveal the deadly devastation of an organ, and the anatomist could explain the damage as the result of a disease, but this did not explain the way a disease affected the living body. When Storch occasionally "opened" a deceased patient, whom he had never "inspected" or touched while she was alive, he was investigating her body, not the ailments through which he had known her during her lifetime.[3]

Anatomy, the body dissected into its component parts, did not correspond to the composition of the living body. Even if by Storch's time the dead body had for decades been depicted as geometricized interior space, the living body remained a realm into which physiological theories and general concepts were projected, in which a pre-Cartesian world view was refracted and reflected. As long as modern etiology and the modern visualization of the body interior had not prevailed, the only limits to the imagined processes inside were those drawn by the culture's conception of the world. Despite the geometricization of the Baroque, the disciplining of the dancer, the fencer, or the soldier when loading his musket, the inner body remained a world apart.[4] Thus, in Eisenach at least, the body of a living person could bring forth whatever seemed plausible to the prevailing notions of the time. What seems physiologically fixed to a twentieth-century person, could appear within very different explanatory frameworks in the cosmology of an early-eighteenth-century doctor.

In early-eighteenth-century Eisenach the inside of the body was a sphere of surprising changeability. The possible transformations within this sphere of incessant metamorphosis seem unlimited. Storch, who could not "view" the inside any more than could his contemporaries, speculated on rules about inner processes, which he inferred above all from the body's emanations. No body could have been descriptively grasped in its hidden interior as a universal and universally valid entity, for only the diversity of individual stories could be recorded. These stories resisted any attempt at generalization, since they appeared only as experienced processes. The inside could be grasped only as the place of an experienced but invisible flowing. Thus the external flows were aids to understanding the inside. The doctor and the women interpreted them as signs of inner movements. The doctor recognized a similarity, an analogy, or a difference between fluids that issued forth; he claimed that this allowed him an insight into what was going on within.

> The wife of a princely footman, twenty years of age, lay sick after first childbirth with "cold sweat," "heat," and a feverish rash. Over the course of several days she suffered repeatedly from loose bowels and complained

about the "drying up of the milk." She had frequent diarrhea "that looked whitish like milk"; later the diarrhea came out "white, like curdled cheese."   (6:606, case 281)

In this case Storch thought that the discharge, "white, like curdled cheese," "originated in the regurgitated milk." To substantiate his theory he listed a number of other authors who had observed that women's milk could take irregular paths, *vias extraordinarias* (608). Apparently milk could pass from the breasts to the stomach and there be excreted as white milk. It was also documented that milk could move inside to other locations, again without changing its substance. Storch cites several examples from the literature: milk was repelled from the breasts "but issued forth from the mouth with the spittle";[5] a young girl had plasters placed onto her swollen breasts, whereupon "the menses broke out, which in color, smell, and taste resembled milk" (3:225, case 32). The discharge from the "genital members" could be viewed as milk. We are also told about an incision for bleeding from which "pure milk" had been drawn, and of the discharge of milk instead of urine (2:323). The transformation was also documented in a different sequence: a nursing woman took elderberry juice as a purgative, whereupon her child "fell into a sweat, which in color and taste was like the elderberry juice" (7:132). What shows itself on the body's surface can be observed and examined, and it speaks of an inner process through "smell, color, and taste," through its "likeness" with analogous matter.

Storch's conception of the inner metamorphosis allowed him to assume that milk was not a substance that could be engendered only at *one* location inside the body and be excreted from only one body opening (the breasts). Milk could emerge from various openings and could resemble other excretions. Since milk appeared "on the outside," it must have strayed along "erroneous paths" on the inside.

Let us look at another case:

The young wife of a tanner, who had developed an "oozing sore" on one of her legs while still unmarried, was pregnant. During the pregnancy this oozing on her legs disappeared. After the birth she ran a fever in childbed and developed an inflammation in her breast. When "the latter subsided, she said she got a red and itchy rash" and a "stopped-up belly." Storch gave her prescriptions against these ailments, whereupon she had a "copious opening." She discharged "sedes" in good quantity, whereupon the rash "dried up." From this evacuation she got well.   (6:9, case 2)

The doctor tried to explain to himself the course of the illness: the feces, the feverish rash, and the inflamed breast were external and internal forms of some "humoral matter, which prior to the pregnancy had issued at the thigh." From the multiplicity of complaints he deduced an inner causal principle: it was *one* form of matter which in the body turned both inward, from the outer leg to the breast (breast inflammation), and outward, expressing itself as the rash. Eventually it was expelled as excrement. It was obviously bad and impure matter, which could move about in the body and had to be gotten rid of. The doctor's gaze turned materials that were quite different into one and the same matter, which he interpreted on the basis of a belief in a continuous inner transformation.

The women's complaints also reflect the notion that all matter, though ultimately the same, is involved in constant transformations. The women said that bad breath appeared when their freckles disappeared (2:454); that sweat smelled of urine (3:225); that loose bowels appeared periodically if the menses failed to flow (8:196, case 47); and that the stopped-up monthly blood exited through bloody sputum—as a chambermaid from the country reported (2:329, case 86). The inside was obviously a place of metamorphosis. How else could freckles transform themselves into bad breath? A woman who felt she was too vehemently assaulted by her husband during marital *congressus* complained of "wind" in her womb. The following day she reported that the "wind had entirely gone out through her ears" (8:365, case 87). Another woman, sick in childbed, sent word that she was having "a strange sensation, as if her breathing and speech went out through her ears" (6:549, case 245). The wind in the womb could rise upward, speech could exit through the ears. In this world the fluid inside the body could apparently assume different forms, yet remain always the same substance. The inside was a porous place, a place of metamorphosis: fluids changed in the body, they transformed their materiality, form, color, consistency, and place of exit, and yet apparently they remained essentially alike.

The Meaning of an Inner Process

On May 17, 1722, a young girl, the daughter of an Eisenach burgher, went for an hour-long walk with her sweetheart, danced at a village dance, and drank some perry; later she went home and complained of a headache. Exhausted, she went to bed early. The next morning the doctor had to be summoned very early. He found her "struck by a fit of senselessness." The girl could not swallow drugs, so Storch had a blister-inducing plaster applied to her calf. But all efforts were in vain. Two days later, on the evening of May 19, the girl died.   (2:127, case 21)

The doctor thinks, "searches," tries to explain the case. Not until eight days later did another girl reveal to him "the incident about the perry-drinking and dancing, and that she had been accompanied and entertained by a sweetheart." Now Storch was certain that he should have insisted, against her parents wishes, that a bleeding at the feet be tried. This, however, had not been done. This is how Storch pieced together the case: the menses rose to the girl's head, they had turned upward from down below. In addition, the blood had been agitated by her amorous feelings, and the perry and dancing had done their part to intensify the inner movement, the maelstrom. It also seemed significant that "her menses had previously been only pale in color."

In order to understand the doctor's thinking and to avoid dismissing his interpretation of the causality in this case as "nonsense," it is necessary to unravel and isolate individual linkages connecting explanatory structures. Nothing was certain, nothing was given as pure factuality. But the ambiguity of each "thing" can be inferred only from its specific meaning, from the causal and material ties that link a specific thing to other phenomena.

What kind of linkages were these? Our source makes many connections between bodily phenomena and the outside world, between bodily phenomena and events, between bodily phenomena and occurrences past and present. These connections give meaning to the various experiences. Each bodily phenomena can point in three directions: it "comes from something," it is introduced with a "because," that is, it has a cause; it "leads to something"—in the source described as "wherefore," that is, it has a result; it has an inner meaning, that is, it has a goal, an orientation which in each case was fought out as a change for the "better" or the "worse." A pain, an external flow, was not simply "there," it was a sign *for* something. The body and individual parts of the body "want" something. In the case of the girl, the headache was a sign of a hidden cause: the agitated blood, caused by perry and love. The upsurge had an effect: the turning of the monthly blood to the head. And it had a goal, for nature was misled by love into letting too much blood surge upward. These three orientations are implicit in almost all of Storch's stories: the linkage of each phenomenon to an event that preceded it in time— the external and internal *cause;* the linkage to the present and the future—the *effect;* and the inner, unexpressed *meaning*—what the body wants. They are ordering elements of his language and form the core of his self-conception as a doctor. After all, it was the ability to interpret signs correctly that distinguished him from the pure empiricists, who considered only superficial phenomena and did not know how to get at the hidden causes. The ability to recognize the "characteristics of diseases" was the secret of true medical learnedness, for the "signs of sickness" are "those clues whereby one can unravel and lay bare an obscure matter, or . . . they are the visible manifestations that reveal a hidden and unknown matter."[6] Interpreting the signs of disease was further complicated by the fact that the doctor and the women did not share the same assumptions. Although the women thought in terms of these orientations—cause, effect, meaning—and expressed this in their complaints, they sometimes did so differently from the doctor. They had their personal signs and their own experience for interpreting things, and a different understanding of what the body needed. A phenomenon that the doctor tried to explain in complicated deductions might be a personal peculiarity that the women could interpret from personal experience. A lady had recurring pustules on her cheek, and she knew that they announced the menses; another woman linked a periodic toothache to her monthlies (2:295, case 70). With another woman, her friends and family knew exactly that her cough and "hoarseness" indicated the "occasion to congratulate her on being pregnant" (3:82, case 7).

The women had their own tradition for understanding the signs; a myriad of phenomena could point to pregnancy, imminent death, the onset of the menses, or an impending consumption. It is here, in the prognostic interpretation of personal signs and in understanding what the "signs of the women" mean, that the doctor and the women diverged most strongly. Their categories of meaning could be far apart. The interpretation of the invisible intentionality may be the locus of the cultural discontinuity that separated the women and the doctor. Here, and perhaps only here, the element that separated Storch as an academically trained doctor from his women—his physiological, philosophical frame of interpretation, the remnants of Aristotelian training—created a gap and a conflict between him and the women. For Storch the body had the ability, even in a malady, to aim at something good: healing. A sign that was bad in itself could thus indicate a good as well as a bad prognosis: vomiting, spitting of blood could be seen as nature's remedies for ridding herself of the filth in the upper body parts. The women speak less of the body's healing power. The doctor seeks to fathom the cause, the nature, the orientation of the inner body, in order to support it. Hence he will "lure" the blood, show it the proper paths from the outside. The women, on the other hand, interpreted the same signs as a call to force open the stopped-up body from the inside. They want to "expel" the blood, to thoroughly "cleanse" the inside. A woman who suffered from rheumatism in her arms cooked up some warm wine with saffron in order to drive the matter out of her arms (8:157, case 36).[7] The doctor saw this as something dangerous: it was better to carefully lead "errant nature" to the proper issues. The signs of the body spoke to the women more of an obstinate and stubborn interior threatened by stoppage. To the doctor they revealed an untimely or erroneous effort of the interior to rid itself of a burden.

The Location of Womanhood

In *Diseases of Women* Storch described only the part of his practice involving women, although occasionally he inserted reflections and cases concerning his treatment of men and children. His view of the male body is revealed in his work on soldiers.[8] From its texts we can get an idea about the physiological difference between women and men. The astonishing finding is that the factors shaping the characteristics of the female body were only tenuously related to what we know as "sex characteristics." Today women, men, and children, while all belonging to the human species, are thought of as differently constituted in morphological and functional terms. Women bleed periodically, they produce children, at a certain age they stop bleeding and this signals the end of their "reproductive" phase. Men do not bleed, do not produce children, experience nothing that might be thought of as biologically comparable to menopause, just as their first nocturnal emissions cannot be equated in meaning with the beginning of the menses in a girl. Children are either small girls or boys, but as biologically immature beings they have neither menses nor emission. To us, biological or physiological conditions are unique and specific as to sex and age. Deviations from this body image are seen as deviations from the norm, or even as pathologies. We understand the biological essentially in an anatomical and physiological materiality, linked to specific bodily phe- nomena depending on gender and age.[9] The doctor from Eisenach attests for himself and his female patients the opposite view, which we also know from the scholarly literature of his time. Many of the man- ifestations that we clearly perceive as sex characteristics, were in the seventeenth and eighteenth centuries not unequivocal signs for the difference between man and woman. And Storch's period did not yet perceive our characteristics of aging. The eye of culture sees in the order of nature what it expects to see.

What distinguished women from men in the view of Storch and the authors he cites was not their monthly bleeding as such but solely the periodic nature of the bleeding or discharge of fluids from the body. The rhythm of discharge, not the blood itself, constituted womanhood. We are faced with a strange contradiction: blood in every form was central to all reflections about the diseases of women, but it was not in itself a necessary element of what gave them their special gender-characteristic. While Storch did work from the assumption that the "monthly affair" should be regarded "as the necessary prerequisite" for the "marriageable years" of a woman, he immediately qualified his position:

> "Except that this is attended with many doubts, since, first of all, there exist not a few stories that children also had menses, and second, there are also many who never saw the menses, and yet once they were married

became happy and fertile mothers. The *bene esse* [well-being] of a woman in her marriageable years includes that she be well developed, have swollen breasts, and the menses; but it is not always part of *esse* [being]." (2:25, introduction)

The literature of the period recorded an abundance of stories in which even very young girls bled: a nine-year-old girl from Danzig, "who gets the menses, though irregularly" (2:548, case 176); a Tübingen bookkeeper's daughter, who began with the red flow in her eighth year (2:549). Examples from all ages follow, including the child of a "messenger or postman, who had true menses from her fourth to her eighth year" (2:550).

> "Anno 1692 the wife of a lawyer in Dresden gave birth to a daughter who had the menses immediate after birth and kept them at regular periods until she was a year and a half. Thereafter a fluor albus appeared instead of the menses and continued monthly for over two years, wherefrom the girl was greatly weakened." (2:552)

Storch then adds a case from his own experience: in 1732 he delivered a noblewoman of a "strong girl," "which . . . on the fourth day after the birth discharged several spoonfuls of blood per pudenda" (2:553).

Just as the monthly bleeding was not an exclusive mark of grown women, it was also not a mark of their *esse*, their being-a-woman. Storch tells of Eisenach women who as adults never had the expected "menses," but instead bled from other parts of the body. Occasionally he observed the "white flux," the "womb-cold," which could discharge below even in small girls (2:420, case 113) or could collect as milk in the breast. [10]

Some women never never had their courses while they were married unless they were pregnant, in which case they had their monthlies regularly (2:547, case 176). Other women experienced different habitual excretions. A "delicate and well-shaped" woman, who always observed only a few drops of the monthly blood on herself, reported "a large recurring blotch on the foot . . . , which grew painfully at the usual time of her menses" (8:74, case 15). Then there were women who reported a periodic bloody sputum (2:99, case 11), diarrhea in the rhythm of the monthlies (8:165), a periodic flare-up of consumption, sweating in the monthly rhythm (6:577, case 248), a periodic "sadness and heaviness of the limbs" (8:99, case 22), and piles that kept a four-week rhythm (8:319, case 80).[11] The movement of time inside the body, a periodic internal, spontaneous surging, along with some cyclical excretion, seem more constant than the material consistency of the issued matter.

This experience of temporary but regular cycles was not limited to women in their marriageable years. Women who were still discharging blood in their old age were nothing unusual in Storch's practice. A seventy-year-old widow, already mentioned, complained in 1723 about pain in her hip, which she had contracted because the "terms," which she had had "unwaveringly" until that time, had not appeared for two periods. After a bloodletting the menses returned. She came back only five years later, in 1728, to complain that a nosebleed was troubling her (8:277, case 72). The regular menstrual flow of old women was not common in Eisenach, but neither was it very rare (8:279). To substantiate this view Storch cites pages of cases from the literature, of old women whose menses had never stopped or who began to bleed again at an advanced age. I shall cite only one case from the abundant evidence:

"A noble lady, Bungardina from Desbeck, had known a fine woman one hundred and three years old, who had gotten her monthly terms again from her one hundred and first year on. Her well-being had thereby improved, and she stayed in good health until her one hundred and third year, when she died just at the time of her courses." (8:279)

We see that a periodic, spontaneous excretion was habitual to women. It is all the more remarkable that a spontaneous issue of blood was also observed in men. Evidently the discharged matter itself was not gender-specific.

One thing distinguished men from women: unlike women, men did not have an inward disposition to bleed periodically from one location. Instead they discharged blood flows from various parts, some almost regularly, some sporadically: from the nose, the piles, a wound, as bloody sputum. The "bleeding piles" especially were seen as analogous to women's "monthlies."[12] In young plethoric men and in men with sedentary occupations it served to discharge the superfluous humors. If the piles of a full-blooded man became "obstructed," he instantly had ailments like those of women suffering from a "stoppage of the month-lies" (2:316, case 77). The "flow of the piles" was as sensitive as the "monthlies." It could be stopped up by a fright, by intervention in the wrong place, or by distempers, so that it never returned. When that happened, a man would get ill and possibly even die:

> "a few years ago I heard that a forty-two-year-old corpulent merchant was having *fluxum haemorrhoidum* and let himself be persuaded by a boastful surgeon and medical quack to have a phlebotomy. The hemorrhoidal fluxus was immediately stopped up and the good merchant . . . died suddenly five days later."   (8:34)

The hemorrhoids and the menses were both seen as spontaneous evacuations of the body; they resembled each other and were interchangeable. This similarity was not a marginal phenomenon, but the subject of a great many learned treatises and disputations.[13] In his *Tractatus de Haemorrhoidibus* (1722) Michael Alberti, a follower of Stahl from Halle, discussed the *consensum* of menses and piles, which he saw in their common task of relieving the body by discharging superfluous, trouble-some, and impure matter. Both flows had such an "affinity," he said, "quomodo ratione objecti, subjecti, instrumenti, mediorum, formae, finis, ordinis, temporis, necessitatis, opportunitatis et causarum etc. haec evacutiones inter se conveniant."[14] The hemorrhoids were a heal-ing, if not a constitutive, blood flow in adult men. Thus the learned tracts echo a piece of popular knowledge that has come down to us in proverbial sayings: namely, that in men the piles take the place of "the menses."[15] Another analogy existed between the flow of semen and a "cold in the womb" ("the whites"), since nature "expelled evil matter also through the excretionem seminis," nocturnal emissions.

   This similarity between men and women in the corporeal habit to relieve themselves through excretions also made possible the phenome-non of a "true" periodic *menses* in men. In his great collection of the medical literature at the end of the eighteenth century, Ploucquet cited the wealth of reported cases from the medical *observationes* of the six-teenth and seventeenth centuries.[16] With information on where they occurred and with a detailed description of the circumstances, the cases reported how men could experience regular menstruation. They bled from the fingertips (*per digitos*), from the left thumb at the full moon, through the varicose veins, and especially, in direct sympathy to menstruation, "per penem."[17] Here is one of the numerous examples, recorded by Wenckh in the Miscellanea of the Natural Science Society: a peasant who diligently performed this monthly discharge from the time of his puberty to his seventy-sixth year, lived a healthy and cheerful life in the process.[18]

Not only did men also issue forth blood flows, not only did they have similar corporeal dispositions in terms of periodicity and body regions, they could resemble women even in a characteristic that would seem to be exclusive to women. According to Storch, women and girls collected milk in their breasts, but "documented experience" showed that boys and men could also have milk in their breasts, enough to "dole it out" to the children. It is true that anatomists—for example, Professor Lorenz Heister from Helmstedt, whose *Compendium* of anatomy Storch used as a guide—excluded this possibility on the basis of their studies; yet, as Storch remarked, "the possibility is not to be entirely denied on these grounds" (7:27). The experience of living bodies refuted the anatomists. Storch recounts cases which he knew from the region around Eisenach (7:26, case 2). If "both genders (have) the same repository, even though in men it is rarely as big as in women" (7:29), if the breasts of men and women are therefore alike, then it is not impossible to find that a man "had milked so much milk from himself that he made cheese from it" (7:28, case 2). Storch stood in the center of a living, if vanishing, tradition. This is made clear by the testimonies which he could add to his stories from Eisenach.[19]

There is an extraordinary range of possible ways in which culture can link sexual identity to corporeality, and interpret corporeality as a sign for the difference between man and woman. No morphological element nor any process such as the flow of semen or the monthly bleeding has been seen at all times and everywhere as unique to a specific gender. Only when such elements are seen by the eye whose vision is shaped by its cultural milieu do they become sexual characteristics. Gender is in the eye of the observer. It was only from the end of the seventeenth century that blood and milk were definitively assigned to the functional sphere of physiological motherhood, and Storch was writing before the new science had acquired exclusive control over the understanding of the female body in Eisenach. Menopause had not yet been "invented," as a word and as a concept of physiology.[20] Menstruation and its problems had not yet been taken hold of by the new field of nosology.[21] The relation between the sexes as it was reflected in the body was not yet interpreted as resting (fundamentally) on "factual" grounds. The process of redefinition that MacLean has described had not yet prevailed.[22] Biology was not yet the science of the body polarized by its sexual characteristics. It was, for Storch at least, still the understanding of life and suffering as told by men and women in their own words.

When Storch talks implicitly about gender differences, he does so with the help of relative categories, not definitive and unambiguous attributes. In doing so he placed himself in the tradition of antiquity.[23] Man and woman are related to each other like right and left, outside and inside, constant and periodic, fullness and deficiency of blood; male or female gender is embodied in relations of analogy and difference.[24] Women, with their disposition to spontaneous discharges, were less threatened by *plethora* (overfulness), that is, illness, than men. And yet they were weaker, colder; they collected more filth and humidity and therefore had to bleed regularly. In their (Aristotelian and Galenic) "inferiority" they embodied the self-healing power of the discharge from the inside. Bloodletting, which Storch prescribed, was supposed to be aligned, like proper menses, with the lunar phase, and it was interpreted explicitly in analogy to the menses.[25] It was prescribed for men as much as for women; in fact men needed it more.

When Storch saw a sick soldier, he did not yet perceive his maleness in the exclusion of milk or menstrual blood, and "seed or sperm," as discussed in Chapter 1, was not at all unique to either woman or man.[26] A woman was not a "woman" because she was of that biological sex; it was the other way round: she suffered from a woman's disease because she was a woman.

Stories about the body flourished within this niche of what was not factually determined. There are many strange cases: a maid in Strasbourg "who had a double uterus" (2:4); a "brave and brazen woman who had denied her sex and served many years as a soldier in men's clothes," and carried a plica on her pudenda (2:7); a woman from

Storch's practice, "of whom it was said that she was still smooth," that she had no hair on her pudenda (2:8). Storch adds that in 1745 he had to use instruments to deliver a "whore" of child, "on whom I also noticed a scanty supply of hair." These last two cases were counterexamples against the notion that smooth pudenda were signs of sterility. In this world everything can acquire meaning, can become a telling sign, since nothing was fixed on the anatomical atlas. A woman's pubic hair, whether frizzy, curly, long, bristly, or soft, could be a sign of her chasteness or virginity. Lasciviousness as well as shyness could be embodied in such details, in hairs, in the belly, in the fullness of blood, but at the same time all these signs could be a *signum fallax,* an erroneous sign. Since there was no anatomy which had once and for all investigated what something had to be, it was not possible to constitute a general female body as a norm. Like his contemporaries, Storch was not sure from where the blood discharged from the vagina came from, and whether a hymen, if it was the subject of a court dispute, was necessarily found in all women. When he spoke about things that are to us objective anatomical characteristics of gender, he surveyed his examples, which attested only a probability that something could be found "if not with all, at least with many women" (2:35). In this situation the various concrete bodily traits could acquire enormous, real metaphorical expressiveness, or, to put it differently, the cultural eye could "see" what it wanted to see. The analogous, dissymetrical complementarity of the sexes, in which the difference was established through complex relationships among similar things, arose from a culture in which gender was constructed only through diverse relationships to each other and to the environment, but could never be unambiguously fixed in one place or in one flow.[27]

Orifices as Exits

My own body becomes real to me as a body only when I observe an order in the bodies of others and in this act of observation subject my body to the same order. Just as my right hand can grasp my left once it itself has been grasped (when the object becomes the organ and the organ the object),[28] the body as the organ of all my perceptions constitutes itself at the same time as the object of all my perceptions. The nature of this perception is determined by its epoch and its culture; the history of the body is the history of this perceptual and order-giving form. Ethnologists[29] and intellectual historians[30] have tried to unravel the meaning of social relations by interpreting the pattern of meaningful references between body parts. Unlike Plügge, v. Weizsäcker, or Zaner, I am not concerned with the theory of the body as the place of self-embodiment. Nor am I concerned with the question of where to place Storch's perceived body in a comparative somatic classification. I want to grasp the meaning of the outer boundary of women's bodies as perceived by Storch and implied in his cases.

I begin with the simplest level. Seen from the outside, a body has a surface—the skin—and holes—the orifices. In addition it has swellings and curves. How many orifices are there? In Storch's stories there are many, more than usually catch the eye: eyes, ears, nose, mouth, breasts, navel, anus, urinary passage, vulva. It seems remarkable that the navel represents an opening and that the breasts were seen that way. First hypothesis: the body openings are exit points. We can see this when we examine Storch's cases from the perspective of what happens at these orifices: something comes out of them, but what is voided changes, can also be excreted in some other place. The body openings are not clearly designated for a single substance. The eyes run with tears, but there are girls who cry bloody tears (2:543, case 174, Horstius); the nose runs, but there are girls who bleed from the nose (2:145, case 26). What comes out is the "monthlies," which are evacuated in this way. Spittle gathers in the mouth, but the menses can flow forth from a gap in the teeth (2:256, case 60) or be vomited up in bloody sputum (2:99, case 11). Menstrual blood can also, though rarely, be passed as bloody urine (2:332, case 88), or, more frequently, through the piles, especially in adult, full-blooded women. The wife of a clergyman, who had her courses stopped by a fright, maintained instead bleeding piles (3:439, case 88), and a "tall, choleric female cook, who was in a kitchen were she could eat well and also drink a glass of good wine," disclosed to the doctor that her "menstrual blood came by the stool" (2:154, case 31). The orifices have a different meaning during different phases of life: young girls bleed above all from the upper part of the body, from the nose and the mouth. The bleedings can occur in the rhythm of the monthly period if the latter does not want to appear "below" (2:333, case 89). Among older women, hemorrhoids are more important. Unmarried women have fewer bleeding piles than do married women.

The body has additional means of issue scattered all over its surface. The skin can open or be induced to open anywhere.

> A maidservant, sixteen or seventeen years of age, who had not yet had her menses, tore open her finger on a wood splinter, and the urge of the blood moved painfully toward the wound. (2:180, case 40)

> A "strong and full-blooded twenty-year-old person," was in prison for a theft. She fell seriously ill, the menses "failed to break out . . . while an oozing flux has appeared on her shoulder with much discomfort" (2:182, case 41); this was her own report to the doctor.

> "A maidservant from the country complained that for several years she has had her courses in small quantity, with an occasional stoppage. At the same time a spungy bump has appeared on her head." When her menses eventually stopped completely, she reported that "the bump grew bigger and spread." (2:249, case 58)

> The sixteen-year-old daughter of a chancery clerk had obstructed menses, and instead a tonsillar abscess, through which "nature"—so Storch— "was emptying out the vicious matter." (2:63, case 4)

From the perspective of the doctor, the surgeon, and the women, wounds, lumps, and cuts were openings that could emit substances blocked from passing through their proper passage. A tonsillar abscess was an issue. What came out there could be the menses or some other substance. The skin itself seems made to be permeable from the inside: it has "sweat holes" which heat could open to allow the discharge of humidity, bloody matter, and impurities. A swelling, a boil on the skin, was a sign for some matter that was pushing toward the periphery in search of an outlet.[31] Wet scabs and ulcers evacuated "the reabsorbed foul matter in the skin" (6:756, case 436). The skin does not appear as a material seal shutting the inside off from the outside. Instead it was a collection of real, minute orifices—the pores—and potential larger openings, especially where the skin was delicate, "seeing that a subtle skin can be easily . . . consumed or torn . . . by a caustic substance" (2:19).

Other phenomena on the skin were also considered as exits: varicose veins showed throbbing blood pushing toward the outside; "redness on the skin," facial burns, Saint Anthony's fire, was caused by peccant matter breaking out; a rash was an issue; scabies seemed a salutary discharge; liver spots were impure stuff brought to the outside. All these cutaneous phenomena could have a connection, a link with the inner blood flow, with the menses. They appeared above all when the menses were suppressed.

> A noble girl's birthmarks swelled when her menses were "stopped up" owing to a fire; the spots diminished when the menses appeared in "proper order." (2:452, case 125)

> A "choleric girl, nineteen years old," complained of "an absence of her terms"; and now, "as the time of the flow should be approaching again, she was getting painful red lumps on her shins." (2:492, case 147)

> A "woman well into her thirties" had a "sore thigh" whence issued the "monthlies," which never came in their proper place. Later, as the regular order of the courses had been restored, "the bleeding through the ulcers . . . did not return." (8:533, case 169)

> A "sanguine, choleric, eighteen-year-old woman," who had never had her menses, had a festering thigh for more than a year and felt fine all along. The wound bled in the rhythm of the terms. When Storch compared her condition with that of her sisters, who also had not yet experienced the onset of bleeding, she seemed better off and healthier with her open thigh, since she had no pains and was not green and pale. In fact she was positively radiant with good health! (2:156, case 32)

The fact that natural body openings and skin spots were interchangeable, that scabies and liver spots were alike, was based not so much on their materiality as on their meaning. What happened at these places was similar: some superfluous or impure matter was ejected. In the case of one noble woman, piles alternated with an "oozing spot behind her ears" (6:677, case 336). Another lady was suffering from "womb cold," the white flux, and this alternated with a "purulent toe" (8:91, case 19). A pregnant woman suffering from the "white flux" observed that her varicose veins swelled up on her right leg. After delivery she suffered from a suppression of the lochia, and these veins became "puffed up and swollen" until that flux was straightened out again" (3:101, case 14).[32]

The skin was fragile and it was a boundary, but it was not meant to demarcate the body against the outside world. It was above all a surface on which the inside revealed itself. A mathematician to whom I read some of Storch's cases, summed up his impressions this way: these women experienced themselves as multidimensional vectors, as bundles of constantly shifting but directed forces.

The doctor saw it as his task to manipulate the orientation of these forces, as the case of a cloth and sergeweaver shows:

> The fifty-three-year-old woman, who maintained a booth at the market, complained in the fall of 1720 of a painful hernia in her side and a costive body. Two paths to recovery were available: to lance the lump in her side, or to drain it off downward and out through internal clysters. Two healers treated the woman: the *chirurgus* used mollifying plasters, whereas Storch worked with numerous clysters. While Storch was attempting to use a natural opening of the body as an outlet, the *chirurgus* was endeavoring to stimulate the skin to open up—in vain, as "no opening followed." (8:222, case 56)

This multifunctionality of the orifices reminds us of Bakhtin's interpretation of body images in Rabelais.[33] But in the sixteenth century the holes of the body were places of continuous exchange between the inside and the outside, between the body and the surrounding world. The body's interior conveyed itself through the body openings, which functioned as points of entry and exit. The permeable boundaries between the body and the environment served the fruitful metamorphosis in both directions. In early-eighteenth-century Eisenach, where this multifunctionality of holes seems to have survived as a tradition, we perceive signs of a shift in the balance, as though the give and take between the inside and the outside was disturbed, and the continuous opening of all openings was a compulsion.

The Inner Flow

In February 1731 one of Storch's female patients, a fifty-two-year-old widow, had a "strange imagination": "wishing to know in her sleep how she is constituted inside" (8:471, case 141), she saw her inside in a dream. This woman chose the only clear path to visualizing the inside that was possible in such a flowing and indistinctly structured body. The wide-awake consciousness found very few certain markers in this inner body, nothing solid, no scaffolding, no bones, no clearly demarcated organs. What it did find were metamorphosis, movement, urges, and stagnating resistance. Since the fluids in the body could change into blood, milk, excrement, sweat, humidity, scorbutic and impure matter, and appear in so many places, we must ask how Storch conceived of these fluids. Was the body some kind of hollow space? Were there directions in its paths, was there a material order to the processes? And what actually caused the inner movement?

> A twenty-nine-year-old noblewoman, who complained frequently about a "white flux," rid herself of this ailment in a surprising way: she "noticed that a large number of lice had settled on her head," and she discovered "that during the time when the bugs were on her head she was relieved of the white flux." (8:90, case 19)

To us this is a very strange connection, in which the somatic order of the differences between above and below, inside and outside seems completely mixed up. Storch interpreted the link between head lice and the disappearing white flux as follows: the lice bite, they suck blood and humidity from the head and therefore attract the "humidity from the lower parts of the body toward the upper" (8:91). This causal connection was by no means a local Eisenach oddity; it appears also in Halle Professor Michael Alberti's 1737 treatise "On the Usefulness of Combing for Good Health." Blood circulation, the venous and arterial systems, but also the traditional mix of humors do not seem to come into play here. In fact it would have been difficult to explain with their help this experienced connection between the lice and the white flux. For the first time we see the body as a place where impulses to movement could be caused from afar, but with a material vagueness: irritations, scratching, itches, or small wounds attract the moisture, lure it even from very far, from the uterus into the head. The inner movement responds to stimulations.

> A maidservant, twenty-three years of age, hit her head against the corner of a shop drawer and suffered a "strong and painful contusion." A few days later she swallowed purgantia at the very time when her menses were

flowing. The menses became "obstructed and regurgitated toward the head, which one could see from the swollen veins on her forehead and temples." This threw the girl into "confusion and melancholy thoughts." Years later this melancholic attack recurred once more. (2:220, case 51)

Storch set to thinking: a lump, the bruise attracted the blood upward, especially since the flow from the womb had become unsure and halting due to the senna leaves the woman had ingested as a purgative. Moreover, this inner marking remained virtually imprinted on the body:

> "Congestiones press . . . from the obstructed evacuation of the menses for the most part toward the head, especially if nature has a chance to do so owing to a former injury." (2:222)

A stimulus lured the blood not only once, directly. It remained as an immaterial groove, an impression, an imprinting on the body with the power of attraction. It engraved its disposition on the flesh. Let us look at another case concerning the inner course of movement.

> A noblewoman suffered from many pains, but the only consistent complaint was a constantly reappearing ulcer on her leg. In January 1723 she complained of "a painful rheum in her face, between the nose and the left cheek," observing that the ulcer receded while this flux was present. Storch administered a variety of remedies to combat the pain in the face, especially a blister-inducing plaster below on the right, unaffected leg. Thereupon "she felt . . . much relief, while the flux sought out its old place in the left thigh with the consequent reappearing lump." (6:189, case 48)

Storch explained the case as follows: "nature," in her habitual "defluxion of rheums down below," had been misdirected by the pains in the face and thus had not kept to her accustomed vein. The impure matter had been driven upward. If this excessive conflux of matter into the head had persisted, a serious disease would have been inevitable. Only by means of the plaster, which irritated the skin to raise a blister and caused pain, could nature "be directed toward the ordinary excretion" (6:190). A discussion about "nature" as an active agent (agens) inside the body must be postponed for now, since we are interested here only in the perception of inner motions. In the body of this noblewoman the doctor suspected rheumatic (slimy) matter, which had taken up a "seat" and time and again pressed toward the ulcer in the leg. Through a stimulus, the pains in the face (and a plaster applied incorrectly on the arm), this habit in the direction of the flow was disturbed and oriented upward. A few days later the patient reported a stomachache, and this pain was also interpreted within the same context: once again, the matter was on the wrong track, the result, as it were, of the newly embodied habit of pushing upward instead of down. It was driven upward since "nature . . . retained this latest diversion" (6:191).

In Eisenach the body is one whose inner motions were channeled through the directed orientation of its urges. These orientations were not embedded in a precise anatomical or physiological structure. Rather, they can best be described as "inducing" a flow, engraving a "habit," "luring" a fluid, "retaining" a path. The body is merely an outer shell for this movement. A stimulus could cause an erroneous path even from a distance, from the opposite end of the body: matter let itself be lured away; it left its habitual pathway and moved in excessive quantity toward the stimulus. A false direction was taken whenever some matter was pushing from the periphery to the inside, or when it was moving upward from below, where it had been closer to an exit. We are far from the inner body as described by the anatomists whom Storch cited: an interior where blood circulates, has the same quantity, moves in a circular flow, flows along predetermined pathways, and in which excess, stagnation, accumulation, and false paths are anatomically and physiologically impossible. The material structure of the inside body in the form of blood paths or vessels was negligible for Storch, or at least it was so undetermined and ineffectual that the actual movement could be triggered by some other impulse. Incidental remarks reveal that Storch could not reconcile these two ways of perceiving the inner body, notwithstanding an ambiguity, indeed a discontinuity, in his thinking. In the case of a seriously ill woman, unable to turn in bed without help, he says: "for this reason all her blood sank to one side, and even before her death . . . she became blue and black on that side" (8:454, case 131). In the case of a pregnant woman he remarked in general about the congestions of blood in the lower belly: "the return flow from the legs, which has to occur upward or rising, is burdensome for nature" (3:112). The blood seems to move in a vague space, or at least the paths along which it travels are like hollow vessels or a sponge.

In March 1736 Storch had to treat a maidservant who reported to him, that her monthly period was irregular, that she was "pale and puffed-up in the face" and often "out of breath, tired, and her feet were swollen." "She accidentally had swallowed a pin the previous year and was afraid that her troubles came from that mishap" (2:535, case 172). Storch appended to this case his own reflections about the possible pathways of a pin inside the body. They are very revealing about his conception, mostly implicit, of the inner anatomical structure. A pin, which surely is more solid than the fluid matters I have mentioned, resembled the latter in that it could exit nearly anywhere: from a lump next to the navel (2:537), through the urine, with the excrement (539), per *vulvam* (540), at the inside of the calf through an abscess (542), after eighteen years through the leg (542). Finally he records the case of a tailor's daughter who swallowed a pin, "which had to be pulled out from the pit of her heart, with none of this having an ill effect on her health" (542). "Nature," as Lanzoni, one of Storch's witnesses, remarked, "knows secret ways inside the human body, hidden to us, which she opens at certain times" (541).

Three interrelated concepts, entirely incompatible with the body system of the anatomists, coexisted in Storch's notions of the inner body: the concept of "urge" and "habit"; the notion of the interior as an unstructured osmotic space, which was characteristic of preanatomical thought; and the auxiliary categories of the mechanistic body model as interpreted by the school of Stahl. This last concept, which gave the metaphorical errant wanderings inside the body a kind of vitalistic-physiological underpinning, must be addressed at least briefly.

By his own admission Storch was an ardent follower of Stahl's theories, and many of his publications were focused on making Stahl's lectures accessible in German to young physicians. He saw himself as treating people in accord with Stahl's method. What attracted him to this interpretation of the inner body, which opposed the ideas of "mechanism," may have been the fact that its central concepts added a physiological systematics to his moral-religious views. All categories of "urge," "enticement," "stagnation," "congestion," and "loosening" were mediated in the central concepts of *motus* and *tonus* as physiological, interior phenomena. The *motus tonicus* was a tension force. This tension force, the *tonus* of muscles and fibers, which was set into motion by a *motus* (an impulse toward movement), was nature's inclination to bring about excretions. It was this impulse toward expulsion that moved the body on the inside, kept it together, and established a "kinship," a *consensus* between the body parts:

> "one should look for the fundamental principle in the *motu tonico* or in the *dispositione naturae* of how, where, and in which manner it goes about producing *excretiones*." (3:119, case 15)

Notwithstanding the multitude of directions that impulses could take, there thus existed inside the body a power capable of producing tension, and this power moved the blood in the direction of due secretions and excretions. The body's *motus tonicus* was guided by "nature," an immaterial agent identical with the preservation of well-being through excretion. Let us look at a case:

> The daughter of a merchant, sixteen years of age, was sickly, pale-faced, and felt racking pains in the arms. The girl had never had her menses. The pain in the arms, a kind of rheumatism, Storch explained as a convulsive *motus tonicus*. It appeared in the arms because "nature" was inclined "to promote an excretion through an increase of the *motus tonici,* and it began the impulse from a distance, forcing the *motum tonicum* in such a way that it manifests itself as a painful cramp." (2:246, case 56)

Once again the body seems like a sponge, though here filled by spasmic, struggling fibers, which obviously are having a hard time moving the blood. "Stagnant" blood is "contracted [by] spasmos" and pressed "from the outside inwards" and finally "ad uterum." The greater the excess of blood, the harder the *motus tonicus* must work to move it, and the stronger the cramps. Abundant, thick, heavy, sticky, gross, and sluggish blood overburdened the *motus* and caused it to produce these cramps.

> "These spasms . . . do not always arise in the proximity or in the lower body. Rather, nature also begins this impulse from afar in very distant parts, and directs the *motus tonicus* such that it contracts the muscles of the outermost limbs to press the blood standing or rising therein . . . *ad uterum:* if then the veins and intervening spaces are too full of blood, the *motus tonicus* cannot so easily and without obstruction move the same into circulation, and thus it transforms itself into a *motus spasticus* and

causes such pains. Not infrequently nature even pushes the *motus tonicus* to the point where, for the sake of this excretion, it turns into epilepsy." (2:248, case 56)

The many cramps Storch had to tend to in his female patients were physiological exorcisms, internally driven, painful expulsions. The doctor's treatment supported this expulsion by letting the "superfluous" blood. The surging was also calmed with internal medications and the matter was cast out.

This metaphorical physiology revealed itself with unique clarity at the end of one's life, when movement inside the body ceased. Storch discussed the bleeding of women who had died:

> A twenty-six-year-old, sanguine woman died in January 1730 in extreme poverty from infectious fever. For fear of contagion the relatives had not looked after her, though they had sent wine and beer. After her death the layer-out noticed "that the monthly period had begun while she was dying and had flowed from her fairly strongly for several days even after her death. The other women living in this room recalled that the same incident had been observed with another inhabitant who had died in this house." (8:456, case 131)

How could a dead woman bleed, seeing that "life," the impetus to motion, must have left her? "One can reasonably consider such expulsion of the blood in the act of dying *pro ultimo naturae conatu,* when frightened nature *in extremis* strives to thrust out." Storch asks himself how it was possible that after death the blood in the cold body not only "oozed out" but even broke out anew. "The very subtle, ethereal part in the blood is that from which the powers not only of the soul but also of the *fibrarum motricium* draw their sustenance, and this can remain concealed in the blood even when the person is already dead" (457). The soul, like the motive power of the fibers, drew its strength from a source: the blood. Whatever was said metaphorically and physiologically about the blood's efforts toward expulsion spoke implicitly also of the soul, which was linked to the blood and mediated by it. In this instance we can grasp not only an obvious but unspoken blending of physiological and religious layers of thinking, but an explicit equating of the two. The language of the humors was the language of the soul. And both separated at death in a manner inexplicable to Storch: "who could finally say beyond doubt how, when, and in what manner the soul leaves its body and dwelling, and whether the soul, for some time still united with the body, may not maintain hidden *motus vitales*" (458).

The Inner and Outer Flux as Mirror Images

The complaint about an inner flux was one of the most frequent reasons why the women turned to the doctor. Just as often they were troubled that the flux may have struck in again. The flux is a strange thing.[34] It described a host of things. "Flux" is the name for pains a woman felt inside from matter flowing in her body. The women also spoke of "flux" when something flowed from their bodies. The menses is a "flux," the "whites" is a flux, and they used the word to describe oozing wounds or open sores on the skin: they "have a flux" or a "defluxion" on them. "Flux" is the term for an illness in our source in which a physiological interpretation on the part of the women finds expression. The word "flux" combined a subjective experience with a complex meaning. The women suffered from an inner flux, but at the same time they were fearful that this flux inside them could be "struck in," be driven back, become stuck. They suffered from the flux and from the fear that it might disappear. "Flux" signified a contradictory echo between inside and outside.

The "inner flux" caused pains: headaches, ringing in the ears, hardness of hearing, loss of sight, stone blindness, a "dull or palsying tongue," gout and rheumatism, stomachaches, colics, suffocation of the womb, sharp pain in the legs. These inner fluxes caused aches where they were felt; they were oppressive, constricting, and burdensome, which is why the women could not hear, speak, or see, why the quickness of their external movements was paralyzed. The women explain the inner distress in a paradoxical way. They call it a "flux," but this flux was characterized by the fact that it did *not* move, that it stagnated, or that it abruptly fell upon some inward part. The pain spoke not of an easy flow, but of a laborious and viscous stream, or of a violent assault of the flux.

> In September 1730 a thirty-year-old woman complained "about the sudden attack of a flux, *circa praecordia*, from which she was struck down

speechless, indicating with gestures the strong and violent pains . . . she had." The following day "she related that she had recovered her speech after taking the second powder." (3:571, case 148)

Early in the morning one day in December 1722 a "woman filled with scorbutic blood" urgently sent for Storch "so that he may help her in a sudden attack of an apoplectic fit." This woman was so "struck" that she could not utter a word. After some powders had been administered and the legs warmed, the fit passed within a few hours. (3:117, case 15)

Other women had a flux quite routinely. They might sense the movement of the flowing matter inside themselves for years. In the case of a noble lady this was felt in the following way:

In September 1722 she was assaulted by a "flux causing cramps and spasms," which she had already felt several times before, the last time violently six years earlier. This time it manifested itself in "swooning, numbness of the tongue, and in a tingling and prickling in one arm, which moved from the left to the right arm, and then within a short period into the left leg." In the following weeks she felt the flux first "tearing" in the leg, then as a boil "on the thigh." In January 1723 she sensed a "flux in the face, while the swollen leg subsided," a "true sign that the flux was striking inward and a change in the body was impending." The flux could keep to its "old place" for long stretches of time, a condition that was relatively bearable, until acute crises arose whenever the matter started to migrate: in the years that followed it moved into the head, the belly, and the limbs. (6:184, case 48)

The outer flux was a mirror image of the inner flux. As women's "flux of reds or whites," it ensured cleansing and unburdening. The external fluxes included, in addition to the periodic discharges, the "oozing sores" that the body created for itself in order to discharge matter. In particular the thin segments of the skin, the swollen venous nodes, boils, and abscesses channeled these flows, the evacuation of "humoral matter," white moisture, pus, and bloody matter. Such a flux, which was uncomfortable, itchy, even painful, was rarely a cause to consult the physician. Unless they came as a sudden hemorrhage, these running flows did not constitute an illness, especially if they were periodic:

A female relative of Storch's "had a flux on her from her youth, which in the beginning showed itself only as a small rash under the nose . . . Beginning in her thirtieth year, this rash emerged below the breasts, but especially under the left breast . . . This flux occasionally also alternated with a light oozing of the navel. Whenever she felt it in either of these issues, she was well and healthy. But if it did not show itself on the outside she was usually costive and bound . . . In her fortieth year she came down with fits of the stone, and by her fiftieth year she had gathered a considerable accumulation of small and medium stones." (7:18, case 1, no. 14)

Different meaning clusters can be read from this case. From the viewpoint of evacuations, body regions were seen as similar by the women: the navel, the breasts, and a sore under the nose were the skin locations of a flux. The opposite to an external ooze was something hard, an accumulation of hard matter. Here the women spoke of a paradoxical inversion: the inner flow, if not drained off, engendered a hardening, a petrification; it was actually viscous and clogging. The flux discharged on the outside was a healthy one.[35] The women were alarmed if an accustomed flow was "striking inward," disappeared from the surface. The "dried-up" flux caused anxiety. The term "dry flux" expressed the darker side of the subterranean flux that seeped into the depths of the body and collected there. The experienced link between an externally invisible phenomenon and the real pains felt somewhere else attests a perception that was plagued not so much by what could be seen, touched, and felt as repulsive, as by its disappearance, a harbinger of an inner stagnation. What fueled the fear was not the discomfort of an evacuation, but the perception of the inner space as a space of induration and stoppage. The evil was inside, not outside. An absent flux, an obstructed evacuation of the body, were interpreted as the causes of later ailments. The women were afraid of driving a flow back.

The wife of a shoemaker, forty years of age, "has had an oozing and sometimes foul-smelling sore under the breast for many years. Having dried up in February 1721, it moved to an untoward place, namely to the genitals, *ad muliebra.*" The pains, especially when passing urine, were so intense that the woman tried to soothe them with cold washes. This bottled up the flux, upsetting the stomach and the guts, causing great anxiety in the stomach and the lower body. During the next years whenever the flux, having returned to its old place, dried up, she immediately requested help, "for fear of dangerous ill effects." Storch gave her sudorifics and a mustard plaster. She placed the plaster under her breast, it dissolved the skin, and already within an hour "the flux could be lured out again, and the woman soon felt . . . relief." This woman died thirteen years later, and the cause of death was this: after she had fallen down the cellar stairs, the flux under the breast subsided and failed to return, whereupon all the matter got stuck in her head. (7:1, case 1, no. 1)

To the women healing meant getting rid of the viscous and hardening matter inside of them. This attitude complicated a possible healing, since it implied a contradictory, nearly irreconcilable balancing act: getting rid of a pain on the outer surface could mean a "repressing" or "repelling" inside. The women wanted to get rid of pustules, rashes, scabs, sores, or measles.[36] They asked the physician for prescriptions. But at the same time they were worried that these matters may be driven into the wrong direction. Between the felt internal flux and the visible external flux was the threat of the flux that had been pushed back inside.

A woman in childbed consulted Storch about her fear that a "recently experienced pustule had been driven back inside." (6:706, case 373)

Another woman in childbed had much vexation and distemper, since her unexpected early delivery indicated to all relatives that she must have begun "congressus" prematurely. Because of this worry she developed a feverish rash, and not just the rash itself alarmed her, but also "her imagining that the spots were being pushed inside." (6:658, case 326)

A fourteen-year-old girl wanted to work in a noble household as a maidservant. Anxious lest a red rash in the face thwart her plans, she drove it out by inducing salivation with a mercurial salve, "without any preparation and purgation." As a result she was "now complaining of stopping in the breast and heavy limbs." The treatment was aimed at luring the rash out. (2:353, case 98)

In Storch's eyes, and no doubt also in the eyes of the women, the art of healing lay in supporting the external flow of impure, dirty, pustular matter until the body had been sufficiently cleansed.[37] Storch believed that the home remedies used by the women were frequently harmful in this endeavor:

A seventeen-year-old girl had been suffering for some time from wild fits and cramps. And whenever that happened her menses were stopped up. Storch reports: "As I was inquiring about some cause or another, she

> remembered that some time ago she had had a blistery flux on one hand,
> which she had cured with a plaster and in part had driven back with cold
> water while washing lace."   (2:116, case 16)

Here a flux in the hand had been driven back; while the hand had been
healed externally, the waste matter caused cramps inside. The girl and
the physician made a connection between the healed hand and these
cramps.

> A "delicate, choleric woman" came to Eisenach, consulted the physician,
> and complained of "persistent cold feet and legs, shortness of breath, and
> hot flashes." On a later occasion "she disclosed that she had had an oozing
> flux between the toes after confinement. She had cured it by sprinkling it
> with white lead powder, and she suspected that this flux had been driven
> back and was now manifesting itself inside. I agreed with her."   (6:749,
> case 440)

> A woman was suffering from gout. She washed the painful limbs with
> well water and found relief thereby. But then she felt an "oppressed
> breast" and "noticed by herself that she had driven the gout pains back in
> with this washing."   (8:261, case 65)

In his reflections and prescriptions the doctor picked up the women's
concern, their fear of driving a flux back inside. He strove to prevent
what, in medical terms, he called a "repelling" of the flux. His aim was
to support the flows gently, to guide them, and, if necessary, to lure
them to the outside. To that end he used in particular blister plasters,
vesicatoria, and fontanels. A blister-raising plaster—of mustard, Spanish
fly, or some such substance—helped above all to divert the flow, to
redirect it, by attracting and drawing it out from a distance. It was
applied to distant parts of the body and created a stimulus by causing
pain. The fontanel[38] (literally, "small fountain") was an artificial wound
that was kept open by a wick made of hair, a seton, to allow the
continuous drainage of fluids.[39]

> A woman clothseller, who was exposed to cold weather at the market and
> to dampness in a cellar while serving beer, suffered for years from an
> errant flow. Finally, after "she had gotten through another attack," Storch
> advised her to let a fontanel be placed on her leg in order to prevent the
> flux from being driven back so often."   (8:234, case 56)

Fontanels and *vesicatorium* were answers to a flux that was causing torment inside, remedies prescribed by the doctor and administered by the surgeons or barber-surgeons. The surgeon induced on the skin no more than what the body itself should be doing and in many cases was doing. Fontanels and blister-plasters resembled the lichen, the so-called weeping exzema: "Once a flux has taken up its permanent seat [in a *Schwindfleck*], patience is the best remedy, since its presence preserves the body from debilitating attacks and takes the place of a fontanel" (7:24). The poorer women in Storch's practice complained about the natural sore. Aristocratic ladies were concerned with one more issue that could become dry: "on the 21st," Storch noted in the case of one patient, "I had to . . . examine an old fontanel on her arm, which had much scar tissue and slough around it. Despite all precautions it was closing up and causing her a defluxion in the eyes and a stoppage of the nose" (8:582, case 180). The afflicted eyes did not improve until the old fontanel had been replaced by a new one on the foot. The remedy worked so well that the patient urgently requested to have an issue made on her other leg as well. Even an abscess, into which an artificial object was placed after it had been lanced in order to keep it open, became thus a kind of natural fontanel.

> A woman who had long suffered from a breast abscess, and whose wound had finally closed, was given the following advice by Storch: "should she again be troubled by the stirrings of old fluxes, she should have them drawn off through a fontanel placed on one leg. But this abscess alone had cleansed her so thoroughly that she remained healthy for several years thereafter." (3:585, case 156)

Finally, one woman experiences such great floods of blood that she was nearly spent. Still she declined to take the prescribed remedies because "she has come to believe that it is a flux which had been withdrawn into the body" (8:470, case 141).[40]

Stagnation and Decay

When the balance between the outside and the inside threatened to collapse, death began to cast its shadow over the sick person. According to the Hippocratic Prognostikon, when this happened, "the nose gets pointy, the eyes become hollow, the temples collapse, the ears turn cold and shriveled. The earlobes turn back, the skin on the face becomes hard and tense, and the color of the face turns pale or blue-black." In Storch's time a physician's training still included the ability to recognize these *facies hippocratica.* "The following must be observed in acute illnesses," the Prognostikon continues: "first the face of the sick person, whether it is like that of a healthy person, but especially, whether it is still like itself." Here, in the entrance hall to death, the body became unlike the healthy person and unlike itself, for it was in the process of transition to becoming a mere body, a corpse. In the *atrium mortis,* the *facies,* like a mask or a negative, brought the phenomenon of corporeality before the doctor's eyes, as Magnus Schmid has said.[41]

The Hippocratic signs were part of the curriculum of medical education in Europe up to the middle of the nineteenth century, and in the United States even to the end of the century. And when they appeared, Storch no longer stood before a sick person who needed his services, but before a dying person whom, as a physician, he could not treat. Whenever he observed the Hippocratic signs, he left the sickbed. He prepared the relatives for the fact that there was little hope of recovery and declared the case now to be beyond his competence. The remedies he continued to prescribe were not prescriptions for the apothecary but instructions for household use. They were intended to ease the act of dying, not to support the struggle for life. "Thus I did not wish to put the husband to great expense," he writes in 1729 in the case of a countrywoman; "instead I prescribed only a meat broth of fresh herbs, namely daisies, watercress, figwort, and chervil, and advised to use fresh primroses as a tea" (8:439, case 122). Though sick, the dying were not patients. To avoid being blamed for false treatment and accused of enriching himself at the expense of the dying, Storch tried at the earliest necessary and possible moment, once he considered it inevitable, to inform the relatives that his prognosis was for a fatal outcome. What he saw as signs of dying were also signs of decay: the pulse faded, speech grew weak, the hands turned brown and cold (8:241), the flesh was emaciated, "the cheeks turn reddish brown, and blood and matter clot in the womb" (8:175).[42]

Though Storch was strongly influenced by the Hippocratic ethic, he was also a man of his own century. If he was able to overcome the reluctance of the relatives, and if the deceased had not explicitly forbidden that her body be opened, he performed postmortem dissections on some women. By dismembering and dissecting matter he hoped to get some information about the course of the disease. In a way Storch was most scientific in the descriptions of his anatomical findings, for here he was trying to separate the body from the lived life story. In the act of dissection the hitherto conjectured inner space was turned inside out. Storch now found in the opened corpse precisely what he had suspected as the site of the patient's fluxes while she was still alive. For him the dismembering of the corpse confirmed the conjectured causality of his categories of diseases. At the dissection table as well Storch looked for and found the invisible.

> "In the afternoon I had to dissect her," he writes of a woman who died suddenly and inexplicably. "In the navel hernia I found no bowels but only an accumulation of the peritoneum, which was all . . . rotten and gave off a black, foul-smelling water. I also found black matter like excrement." (8:435)

The inside of the dead body showed traces of a process of decay, which Storch expressed in the words of stagnating, foul, moist matter. In his dissection reports the organs interest him solely as the bearers of this decay within a kind of amorphous swamp. The images are very similar: a "peritoneum" is "rotten," a spleen is "large and blackish," a liver is "heavy" and "completely shot through by hard, cancerous excrescences and cavities" (8:556), a kidney is "scirrhous and yellow-white in color" (8:438). Hollow spaces he described as stagnant pockets filled with foul-smelling moisture, as indurated petrifications, or as spaces of putrid growths: the "womb is the size of an average pear . . . but in its cavity I found a hard, gristly ball the size of a nutmeg" (8:107), or he discovered it was "filled with ulcers the size of peas, beans, or nutmeg seeds" (8:556), the "ovaries small, like nuts, and whitish-yellow in color" (8:438). These images speak of a perception in which the eye did not dissect but rather imputed the process of dying. The functional inferences that Storch attempted always linked together these three possible and related processes: something was rotten, black, yellow-white, putrid—images of stagnation and *corruptio;*[43] something was ulcerated, cancerlike, gelatinous—images of bad growths; something was callous, knotted, gristly—images of hardening, petrification. All the metaphors point in the same direction. They speak of an inner decay that had been set in motion by accumulation, stagnation, and hardening. The inside of the corpses confirmed the corruption that Storch suspected in the women during their lifetimes. Even in life there was already the threat of mortification inside the body.

> In February 1735 Storch prescribed remedies for diarrhea to a pregnant woman, the wife of a *chirurgus*. The following day she gave birth to a dead child. Much skinny matter was aborted and the blood had a "vile odor." Within a few days she died hallucinating, convulsing, and with a precipitous decline of strength. To Storch all signs indicated "overabundantly"(!) "that a great mass of morbid moistures had accumulated in her, partly in utero, partly in primis viis." The superabundant fluids, "filled with bad moistures and pungency," destroyed the intestines and the fruit in the body. "Nature" did try "its best . . . to expel the evil," but it merely drove out the fruit and the sore uterus turned into a "fatal gangrene; this is especially the case when the uterus also houses next to the fruit false skinny growths that have a tendency to corrupt."   (4/2:202, case 49)

According to Storch, the moist spaces of the body—the lung, the stomach, the womb, the intestines—were particularly "inclined" to accumulate something bad.

> A noblewoman, with a hardened belly, was suffering from dropsy, "since a lot of water was locked up in the hollow stomach." Eventually she died from the inner stagnation of waste matter, "since the monthly period, in view of her age, was no longer issued and this excretion settled inside and caused fatal corruptions at the intestines." Since everything was "closed up" inside of her, the menses no longer discharged. All the bad matter, in particular the fluids of a copper-red rash that had been "struck in," had thus accumulated, corrupting, putrifying, and dissolving the intestines.   (8:328, case 80)

A stagnating flow inside the body caused decay:

> A nineteen-year-old girl, who had never had her menses and had been suffering from a cough and stabbing pains in the breast since the spring of 1735, asked for a prescription. Storch informed her parents of the danger

of a fatal consumption. Because she earlier "had had an oozing flux on one toe, which had been dry for some time," he suspected a bad accumulation. He advised to have a surgeon inspect whether a gathering of purulent matter might not be hidden in the chest, "which . . . could be drained." The surgeon opened the body after the girl's death and found more than "eight pounds of pus." The dissection confirmed Storch's conjecture that "the flux, which previously had voided at the toe, had withdrawn, gotten stuck in the chest and ulcerated the lung." (2:526, case 166)

A young woman lay in childbed with pains in her "left groin." The lochia were stopped up, the pains in the side grew worse. A month later "black clots of blood" were discharged along with the menses. The woman "feared . . . that an abscess might be behind all this." For almost two months they waited and observed an aposteme forming in her left side, using compresses to promote its "maturing." Finally the surgeon lanced the abscess. More than a pound of matter came out, and hours later "again more than one pound of mature pus without blood was drained." (6:623, case 297)

The procedure itself was called "drawing off," a word that was also used for bleeding a patient. This abscess and the act of lancing it finished the illness; in this case, since the matter collected in the side near the periphery, the healers succeeded in preventing an inner "decay."

An abundance of fluids that could no longer be disposed of could collect inside and breed internal sores. If the regular monthly flow of blood "stopped," fear drove the women to seek prescriptions—"to keep a stubborn growth from forming in or on the womb," as one lady told the doctor in 1738 (8:582, case 180). Excrescences, "cancerlike and wild growths," or hardenings, which spread and "devoured" the healthy tissue inside and grew larger, were caused by the one trouble the women complained about most and which stood in the center of everyone's attention: the "stagnation" of the monthly flow. In the case of a soldier's wife, all of whose blood was flowing inward, "the superfluity sat in the *cavitate uteri* and clotted [*geliefern*] (4/2:32). "Geliefern" was the contemporary German word for stagnating, coagulating, curdling. "Clotted blood"—the "clotted lumps" from the womb that are mentioned so often—was hardened, sick blood," it was "burnt," sticky, vitious, "stagnant," "set," or "thickened" blood.[44] The metaphorical term "stagnation" expressed as clotting what people imagined as a very real act of blood stagnation. The womb, from which blood flowed after collecting there for over a month, embodied this constant danger of stagnation by virtue of its shape as a collecting basin for blood. In the women's inside we see the flipside of their periodic flows. In the monthly discharge of their menses women embodied the essence of medical treatment and the prototype of a healthful evacuation. But in their womb they embodied the other side, that of stagnation and hardening. In the middle of the body was the womb, a place of the ever-present threat of stagnation. And stagnation eventually brought on *corruptio,* decay, which is how Storch saw death, in both men and women.

External Dangers to the Body

If we ask what, according to Storch, caused women's diseases, we come first of all to the idea of "mishap." A sudden shower could chill the blood, drive it inside, cause it to stagnate. Peasant girls corrupted themselves in the autumn season, "while combining flax in cold water, or in the winter when exposed to cold and damp" (2:79). Cold wind on bare skin, an uncovered head in the rain, in fact merely a cool breeze blowing against the chest of a heated woman on her way home closed the pores and drove the blood inward, thus explaining violent cramps and epileptic seizures (for example, 2:486, case 142). Washing the feet with cold water during the period of the menses could cause a stubborn constipation of the monthly flow (2:152, case 29). "Mishaps" were incidents that affected the body from the outside, that happened to the body and made an impression upon it. The toils of daily work were very seldom experienced as causes of illness. However, everything out of the ordinary could work as an evil coincidence: anything entering through the mouth (be it a sausage or an overripe cherry), tripping over something, a bolt of lightning, cold air blowing on the face, a damp cloth around the chest.

A fifty-year-old woman caught a "wet cold" in the form of a "rash of St. Anthony's fire" in the face while she was selling her wares at outdoor markets (8:517, case 164); a widow reported that "during the time when her monthly blood was flowing, she had tired herself out with washing and had thereby caused her flow to become stagnant" (8:421, case 113); fatiguing oneself by gathering wood, spinning, carrying loads, digging beets, turning the soil in the garden—off and on women listed such causes.

> With her lord's permission, a maidservant wanted to attend a wedding in the country. "Since she attended to her domestic duties beforehand, she made up lost time by running. Immediately upon her arrival she sat down. After the meal she expended not a little energy dancing," and the next menses came only in a trickle. She complained of weakness in all her limbs and fetched a prescription for a purgative powder. (2:199, case 45)

Such seemingly trivial causes as nighttime dancing, wading through a stream, and a fall in an alley were given as much weight as triggering ailments as were wearing oneself out in the damp environment of a soap factory or at a loom. The spectrum of causes that really mattered had very little to do with injuries caused by toil, hardship, poverty, excessive work, with "class injustices." Even with women in their childbearing years, the wear and tear on their bodies caused by the rapid succession of pregnancies, abortions, and hemorrhages was not mentioned as a factor affecting their physical condition. The things that affected the body by threatening it, making it sick, disturbing it, and causing death were not located within the framework of a somatic materiality. Exhaustion from work was considered significant only if it was unusual. For example, a noblewoman complained of "shivering over the entire body and pains in the legs," because she had done something unusual by sitting down behind the spinning wheel one evening and driving it with her feet (8:58, case 10). This shows that the hierarchy of illness-causing phenomena was conceived as part of the logic of a life story, not as part of the logic of the body as such. The body was not the victim of the circumstances of life, especially not of daily, accustomed toil. Instead, it was a body that attracted and absorbed effects from outside. The soul, one's mood, and specific perceptions triggered an ailment.

> In November 1735 Storch reported "ex officio" as town *physicus* about the case of an "unmarried, pregnant person who had been injured by a beating." He recounts how he found the girl, "who one hour before had been so maltreated by a journeyman-bricklayer with blows from a stick

that she had to be carried home. When I arrived, she still lay speechless and had *convulsiones epilepticas.*" Storch noted the bruises on the skin; the girl, who "recovered her speech" during the visit, indicated where she had been kicked on the front part of the belly. Storch concluded: "Since no *haemorrhagia uteri* showed up, and the two blows I noticed did not seem of great importance, I maintain that the *insultus epilepticus* arose more from fright and anger than from the blows." After the fit of cramps the girl was constipated for three days and was given, in addition to antispasmodic powder, musk pellets to "loosen the belly."   (3:662, case 221)

One could argue that Storch was trying to deflect guilt from the journeyman, that he looked upon an unmarried, pregnant "person" as guilty to begin with, that he was trying, from a male-moralistic stand-point, to downplay the severity of the real blows as the cause for the threat of abortion and the girl's fainting. Even if this were true, in this extreme case his interpretation shows a pattern that overlies a great number of the cases: anger and fright, impressions, delusions, and imagined things were the prime causes of illness. With all these phe-nomena there occurred an exchange between outside and inside, and the inner body mediated what happened to it in the outside world. We have seen already that the skin as a sheath of the inside was also everywhere open to the outside. Here we are talking about the fact that this boundary was also a very thin-skinned mediator of external occurrences.

The bodies of these women seemed closed off against the outside in a fragile way.

In January 1723 a fifty-year-old woman got "into a quarrel with a respect-able tenant, who took her by the arm and showed her the door. She was so vexed by this that her arms and legs trembled, and she got a twinging cramp in her hands and legs accompanied by a *cardialgie.*"   (8:270, case 67)

Storch commented that this woman was usually "so hardened by anger and quarrelsomeness that she did not easily notice any harmful effects from such things." This time, however, since she had been treated with ridicule and the man had refused to quarrel with her, she had this attack of *cardialgie*—a term Storch used interchangeably with "pain in the area of the heart." Thus, "she had to keep inside her the poison she had intended to pour out." Anger as an inner poison drove the women, caused a quick, hot surge, an inner cramp, a choking, a congestion in the womb. If anger swelled too much, it could stagnate the inside, the womb. Anger was the heated, internal upwelling that caused a multitude of pains.[45]

In June 1719 a thirty-year-old woman was seized by a violent anger at the time of her menses, "whereupon she got crampy pain in her hands and feet and became confused." A powder for her head, one to calm the upwelling, and rhubarb as a purgative restored her enough so that on the following day she "had her wits about her once again" and requested a strengthening balsam only for weakness. Two days later the treatment was concluded with a powder for "purging the gall bladder." (8:513, case 162)

The young wife of an artisan, in the third month of a suspected pregnancy, complained in December 1736 "of a headache and swooning after much distress." Storch prescribed rhubarb in the morning along with a sudorific remedy. (3:687, case 245)

The wife of a junior officer, between thirty-six and thirty-eight years of age and of "robust bodily constitution," was quartered with her husband in Eisenach. "Quite often after fits of uncontrolled anger she had to submit to the so-called *cardialgiae hystericae* or suffocation of the womb," and she relieved these fits with rhubarb and a remedy to move the bowels. (8:387, case 98)

A elderly noblewoman, around fifty years old, whom Storch had been attending for over three years and who "in various years had much disturbance of temperament due to worry, anger, and jealousy" (p. 565), was staying in Eisenach. She reported to the doctor "that for some time now she has been more strongly inclined to anger than ever before, wherefore she requested a portion of powders she could take as a preventative after a fit of anger." What tormented this sick woman, who was expected to die very shortly, was the fact that her husband was already sleeping with another woman, "who was to succeed her . . . in order to help revive an extinct line and make it flourish again." But the requested preventives could do no more than help her survive a few more months. She died in November 1739. (8:571, case 117)

A woman who was around thirty years old and "lived with her husband in continual anger, quarrel, and dislike," was pregnant. In June 1731, "when she went into a hop-hill with a feeling of vexation and annoyance, and fatigued herself there by turning over the soil," she felt a bursting, a sudden hemorrhage in her lower abdomen. Even calming remedies could not prevent an abortion.   (4/2:154, case 35)

"A peasant's daughter, between nineteen and twenty years old, was married in 1737 to a young peasant who lived two miles from her parents. After she had been pregnant for four and a half months, she had a fierce quarrel with her husband and his parents and ran to her parents in an irate mood and with trembling limbs"; the next day she suffered an abortion. (4/2:227, case 65)

In these stories we can catch only fleeting glimpses of the women's day-to-day existence. Yet these fragments of their lives form a pattern of the conflicts that provoked the women's anger. And they knew that they had to get rid of this anger, that the anger had to be discharged to prevent its getting stuck inside them. Thus they consulted the doctor for prescriptions.

The doctor's prescriptions were supposed to accomplish the same things the women sought to do with household remedies: bloodletting to draw off the impetuous blood; purgatives to discharge gall and excrement; a drawing plaster of sourdough and herbs applied externally to the chest to entice outward the movements pressing on the breast; hot wine or elderberry juice to drive out the stagnating monthly blood; wine and beer to soothe the "irate womb" (6:367); theriac to sweat out anger (6:340); purgatives to purify the poisoned milk of a nursing mother (7:174). Storch's remedies were no more than an extension of these home remedies, though he believed more firmly in calming remedies (*antispasmodica*) than in expulsive ones. Rhubarb, sudorific remedies, *alexipharmaca* (poison-expelling remedies), rhubarb mixed with *tartarus* to "cleanse" the gall bladder—these were a standard part of his defense.[46]

The frequency with which remedies were requested because a woman was angry reveals a perception of emotions actually inside the body, where they could be and had to be worked on. Emotions affected the body in very immediate and direct ways. Something bad had to be expelled from the inside to keep it from getting stuck and poisoning the inside. The remedies were "preventive," part of preventive care and actual treatment. Phenomena we would consider psychic and part of the noncorporeal realm, were treated in Eisenach in the same way as other ailments.[47] The recourse to remedies points to a paradox. The body very vigorously mediated internal agitation, transforming conflicts into movements of the blood. But at the same time it permitted the idea that anger could be ameliorated with prescriptions.

Anger was real and metaphoric: a poisoned and tense relationship with the husband caused heartaches, trembling, and searing pain. The expulsive remedy prescribed by the doctor acted both physically and metaphorically. This external influence, by which the inside was transformed and which was discharged through the body openings, reveals a context of the person in which there was neither a demarcated, self-contained body nor a social environment that stopped abruptly at the skin. On the level of the body, the Eisenach stories about anger point to a society in which the concept of a body that could be isolated did not yet exist because an isolated individual did not exist. What did exist were people who were bound into social relations down to their innermost flesh.

A second element is also important. Anger as a quickly rising fit of temper was an emotion that had gotten out of control: the body's movements mirrored this uncontrolled reaction.[48]

> "A twenty-two-year-old girl who had been brought up by a rude mother and lived in a tavern became a godmother on June 17, 1727. She drank heavily at the baptismal feast. Upon arriving home, she got into a violent quarrel and anger, and on June 18, toward morning, she fell . . . into an epileptic fit, during which she was bled at the arm. When I came to visit her at noon, she was still lying there without sense and speech, but she could still swallow if given something to drink. I prescribed . . . , whereupon she soon recovered." (2:325, case 84)

Our source is a collection of patient histories. It allows a look at mentality and behavior only in the mirror of those phenomena which the *medicus* recorded as relevant reactions of the body. The description of these phenomena is always filtered through the doctor. Of course Storch noted that individual women and girls were deeply "vexed" after a fit of anger, a rage. In January 1730 a woman sent word that she had suddenly been attacked by a swoon in the evening, "whereupon such a constriction of the throat occurred that she could neither swallow nor breathe" (8:464, case 135). The first prescription against this fit and the swooning did not help; "after an hour the swooning returned, since word was then sent that she had become very angry today and thus made the monthly flow stagnant, but the flow returned after the second swoon-ing." The unmarried, pregnant daughter of an artisan was so vexed by the fact that her fiancé broke his promise of marriage "that she . . . fell into a *cardialgiam hystericam.* Her hands and feet turned deathly cold, and a cold sweat broke out over her entire body" (3:740, case 297). A *specificum* for the head and an *antispasmodicum* relieved the fit. The violent anger of a "healthy and fiery" thirty-year-old woman caused her monthly flow to stagnate. She complained about heart pain and bled herself. The following day, after a fright, she got a "cramp in the hands and *convul-siones* in the arms," and a week later "cramps and *convulsiones,* which almost resembled the evil thing" (8:304, case 75). A youngish widow worked as a maid in a household where she had to suppress a lot of anger. As a result of this she came down with a womb ailment that "trans-formed [itself] into a truly evil thing" (8:418, case 110).

The "evil thing" (*bös Wesen*) was a cramp in which a woman lost her senses and her reason, in which speech and articulation were paralyzed in a convulsive contraction. The "evil thing," a type of suffocation of the womb, was a not untypical, if extreme, reaction within the spectrum of what anger could cause. It is an almost symbolic depiction of the refusal to open oneself. The inside was blocked by a cramp. Storch, who treated many of these fits with loosening, calming, and blood-luring prescrip-tions, also saw in this ailment the movement of the inner blood as the real cause: an excess of blood had flowed into the head or the womb, where, owing to the surge, it caused stagnation, paralysis, and cramp-ing. The cramp was an external manifestation of the inner doings of the blood.[49] At the same time it was a mirror-reversed manifestation of the social conflicts with a lordship, husband, or neighbor.[50]

A twenty-nine-year-old noblewoman had the following "mishap" in Sep-tember 1740: "After a violent fit of anger she had herself bled at the arm. On the 22nd she got an unexpected fright. A few hours later she suddenly fell to the ground and had to be carried to bed, senseless and with stiff limbs; the feet were cold, the face red, the teeth tightly clenched, the breath had stopped. A sudden, violent movement of the breast occurred, after which the breathing consisted of strong snoring and wheezing. I had the feet warmed with bricks and let her body lie quiet and covered. After an hour her face turned pale, and the cramp, both in the limbs as well as in the jaw, subsided, so that I was able to administer an antispasmodic power. This was followed by vomiting and then a quiet sleep, after which she awoke again with her senses." (8:625, case 207)

In the case of this young woman, two causes reinforced each other. A fit of anger was followed by a "fright." Fright was nearly as frequent a "mishap" as anger; young girls experienced it more often than older women, pregnant women and women in childbed in particular were threatened by it. Fright seems to have had an even more intimate relation to the women's two fluxes than anger. Fright "instantly" caused the monthly bleeding to stagnate, reason enough to request a prescription before a tangible reaction set in. Unlike anger, an attack of fright "struck the limbs" and drove the blood to the heart.[51] Heart constriction, anxiousness, fearfulness—these are the afflictions for which the women requested a prescription against fright.[52] The "wife of a grenadier" asked on behalf of her husband's cousin for a bloodletting, because "at the time when she was just having her menses she had suffered fright and fear, whereupon the menses had stagnated and were now driving toward the heart" (2:505). A distinguished burgher lady fell at the time of her flow and broke her hand. Even though the break seemed to be healing well, "she nevertheless noticed that the discharge had stagnated owing to the fright she had suffered. Since evil consequences were feared, I prescribed something to reestablish the menses" (8:66, case 14). "At the time when her menses were flowing for the first time," a girl "was scared by intruding thieves, whereupon the menses stayed away from that very hour" (2:177, case 38). A twenty-year-old woman was caught stealing at the time of her menses, "which immediately ceased, owing to the scare, and failed to reappear for two periods." Because of this Storch treated her in jail for chills, heat, and stabbing pains (2:182, case 41). A forty-two-year-old woman complained that her blood came only irregularly. "But now, when it had just been flowing, she had been greatly frightened and was afraid that henceforth it would stay away while bringing sickly mishaps. I prescribed" (8:619, case 203). The wife of a merchant, far advanced in her pregnancy, was caught in the rain outside the town and fell flat on her face while running; "upon her arrival she therefore requested such remedies as were meant for frights" (3:484).

A major characteristic of fright was that it drove the blood inward and caused it to stagnate. The women spoke anxiously of their concern that their monthlies might therefore stagnate. The fear of amenorrhea in Eisenach resounded with connotations different from the corresponding illness in the nineteenth century. There anemia was a constitutional sign of young bourgeois girls;[53] in Eisenach it was anxiety about undischarged blood, about the blood that failed to come.

Fright was caused by something sudden, something unexpected. The triggering incidents varied: a mouse that jumped at a pregnant woman; a quarrel between neighbors; a fight between drunks; a husband who got into a fight; a thunderstorm; fireworks; two sons who started quarreling upon arriving at home and stabbed each other in the arm (8:376); a thunderbolt; a fire in the neighborhood; being barked at by a dog; finally, great alarms in a family—a husband was brought home seriously injured, a child suddenly had trouble breathing, a sister died unexpectedly.[54]

Thoroughly unusual incidents and extreme occurrences caused fright. A "spectacular fright from a villainous thief and beggar" struck a freshly married young noblewoman early in her first pregnancy, "when he . . . fell down and feigned an epileptic fit." After this encounter she had "imprinted on her mind his fall and contortions such that she soon thereafter complained of headaches that were similar to a congested head cold, and the nose . . . began to bleed." Subsequently she had seventeen epileptic fits and gave birth to a dead child, which bore in its body the marks of the mother's terrible contortions (3:703, case 263). One night, the "sturdy" wet nurse of a noble family in Eisenach was "unexpectedly assaulted on her left arm by a fiery ghost appearing in human form." Storch, summoned at seven o'clock the next morning, found the following: "a large, burning blister on the arm, which gave off at least two spoonfuls of yellowish water, like a blister raised by a *vesicatorium*" (7:123, case 20). Under persisting "anxiety of the heart" this blister drew "ripened matter" in the next days. The woman was not allowed to nurse the baby during these days, since the milk had to be drawn off owing to the pungency that might have gone into her. This story, in June 1725, continued the fright which the mother of the child had suffered in 1718. At that time she had "urgently summoned the doctor at dusk, because she had seen that same ghost standing at the window, a man "of gaunt stature in his nightgown and with a black cap." Storch prescribed the "necessary remedies against the fright."

Fright and anger almost seem to have complemented each other like mirror images.[55] Both affected the body, though in opposite ways: fright penetrated, drove the blood from the limbs to the heart, caused the heart to tighten, to suffocate under the abundance of blood. Anger caused the blood to surge to the periphery, toward the head, into the limbs, into the womb, where it caused cramps by its surging. In extreme cases the women had convulsions and cramps after fright as well as anger. The body mediated external incidents as well as fits of anger that arose inside and in which the self sought to defend itself.[56] In both cases similar remedies were taken to reestablish the balance: remedies to reopen the body.

The Body's Past

Although Storch believed that women's diseases were caused by mishaps, they always had a history in the lives of the patients, their neighborhood, or their ancestors, about whom the doctor "inquired." Storch could understand the ailing body only as a sum of past complaints. It was only in the nineteenth century that the concept of anamnesis constructed a case history as a series of imprints on the body, imprints the doctor had to decipher. For Storch, suffering adhered to the body, was constitutive of the body. Sufferings had a history, which ended only with death. The temporal horizon of the women and the doctor was larger than a single individual's life story. It stretched back in time—to the body history of the parents and grandparents—and forward into the future—the shadow falls on the children.

There was, to begin with, the individual life story. An earlier injury remained engrained in the body:

> In the case of a young woman who was suffering attacks of swooning, speech loss, and much more, the doctor investigated and was told that she had suffered "bad head injuries" in her youth. From these injuries "nature could still now take guidance in directing the surges (*congestiones*) toward the formerly injured head." (8:141, case 28)

An earlier story lurked in the background:

> A twenty-two-year-old noblewoman kept getting fatter. Storch was called in 1720 "to advise her on her violent headaches." "But when I discovered that she had had sickly attacks on numerous earlier occasions, I made it

my concern to investigate further the circumstances, and was informed of the following: several years before, during spring in another village, she had tired herself out very much by dancing. Not only had she cooled herself off at an open window, but at night she also went along on the hunt for mountain cocks. From that time on she had been burdened with intensely painful fluxes and occasionally with womb anxiousness; in fact, she also had an oozing flux in her side (inguine) between her fat belly and thick legs." (8:146, case 29)

An error once made remained imprinted on the body and could not be remedied thereafter:

In 1718 a young woman had herself bled at the arm at the time of her menses—an "improper time" in Storch's view—and she "noticed right away that the monthly flow stagnated." Subsequently she had headaches and "infertility stemming from the improper bleeding." The incorrect bleeding was still remembered in 1737. With this same woman, "one should not forget, after all, that she has been strongly inclined to anger since her youth, on account of which she has during recent years repeatedly caused pains and induced the blood flow to surge." (8:81, case 17)

Nor did the stomach forget:

In 1726 a merchant's wife, "otherwise of a healthy and robust constitution," had "contracted a stomachache by eating stewed pork. This ache stuck with her for over ten years and was rekindled by the least bit of indigestible food." Even when she was a widow, "nature retained the memory of the stomachache, and on November 2, 1738, when she had felt considerable anger for some time, it aroused a vomitum cruentum [bloody sputum]." (8:20, case 2)

The thread that tied together such stories into a particular woman's body could be an incident in the distant past. This way of thinking is strange to us, especially since these causes—an improper bleeding, a fall down the stairs, a fit of anger, a wound, a fright—later could manifest themselves in places far removed from the original locations.

Sufferings remained stuck in the body. Even after they had disappeared, they still were present:

In 1734 a girl cured red spots in her face. When Storch happened to meet her again in 1746, he asked whether these spots had returned. After twelve years he still recalled the trivial incident when the girl had removed a facial blemish. He expected that the vanished mark was still inside the body and could reappear at any time. (2:521, case 160)

Such trivial incidents, which cast lifelong shadows, appear frequently in Storch's cases.

"Heredity," understood as an inclination of the body, linked parents and children, sisters and brothers. This heredity could adhere to all parts of the body, but it sat above all in the chest. Discharges of blood were hereditary, for example, as was the golden vein:

> A thirty-eight-year-old lady complained as a widow of the flow of the golden vein and said that her sister also had this kind of bleeding: "consequently the golden vein should in her be regarded as something hereditary or as a family illness." (8:319, case 80)

A nosebleed was hereditary:

> A twenty-two-year-old noble girl had a nosebleed during the time of her menses. "Her mother reported that it had to be something hereditary, since she herself had been so inclined when she was that age." Storch: "I also knew that two sisters of this young woman had been inconvenienced by it several years before the onset of their menses." (2:225, case 54)

The *pravi humores,* the evil humors, could be hereditary (cf. 4/2:203). Heredity was likely to persist within the same gender, that is, it passed from fathers to sons, from mothers to daughters, but it also could cross over the gender line. "In moralibus as well as vitalibus" children could "take after" their parents (3:442, case 88). "In fact, evil tendencies are more inclined to be passed on than good ones."

This last sentence can serve as a key to understanding Storch's "genetics," for it clearly indicates what he thought was passed on. It was a "habit," a "propensity," or an *inclinatio* in the Aristotelian scholastic sense: "the facility of choosing a certain path which has been acquired by repetition and practice," reads the standard scholastic definition of "habit," *consuetudo* (and thus also of *virtus* and *vitium*). But in Storch's conception it was not the moral personality which acquired these hereditary *consuetudines,* propensities, or habits, but the person's nature, the orientation or tendency of her blood.

There is the case of a woman whose tongue the surgeon depressed with a spatula in order to examine her mouth. She suffered a cramp in "maxillas" and bit her tongue: "she remembered that this had also happened to her father once, and she considered it pro vitio haereditario." (7:3, case 1)

It was incumbent upon the doctor to take preventive measures against the *vitium*.

The sanguine wife of a lawyer had been nursing for a year and a half and observed that her menses did not as usual resume a half-year after she had given birth. She suffered a sudden cramp, a "paroxysmus." Two days later she informed the doctor that she had bitten her tongue during this fit. As a result the monthly blood did resume unexpectedly, but she was concerned about this tongue-biting: "since she had had this attack once before in her sleep, she feared that it might turn into a habit." She consulted Storch not because of the cramp, but with great concern that this tongue-biting, which now had been observed for the second time, might creep in as a regular thing. Storch prescribed a counterremedy. (7:255, case 123)

Evil tendencies of the blood, such as the tendency toward stagnation in the breast, toward consumption, transmitted themselves particularly well.

A merchant's wife came down with a cough during many of her pregnancies, a "wild cough," which always threatened to induce an abortion in the sixth or seventh month. During pregnancies in the summer and fall she did not notice this cough, a fact that was noted as "unusual." The pregnant woman and her sister recalled "that their mother also once aborted during such a cough . . . wherefore it should be considered something hereditary." (3:76, case 5)

A woman in childbed had been "born of a mother who had died of consumption after having given birth to five children." The daughter had several bloody discharges, and when she was in childbed she was worried because of this hereditary burden: "owing to these circumstances she thus wanted to be treated all the more gently." (6:1, case 1)

Storch recorded the following about a lady. As a young woman, she "had expelled stones from the lung by coughing, around the years when the menses appeared." Since her sister had had the same experience, and the brother also had not been spared, Storch noted that "her father had died of a breast dropsy with corruption of the lung, in which various stones had been found." It was clear "that the affectus pulmonum was haereditarius within this family." (6:210, case 53)

Storch listened to the women's complaints in the shadow cast by the past: self-inflicted ailments, things that had happened or were inherited determined the habits of the blood, the orientation of nature. This orientation was unique to each patient, and equally unique therefore was the story each woman told Storch in her own way.

The Migration of Pain

The thread of inherited or ingrained habits of the blood combined the pains into a single story connecting a life and its ancestry. Similarly the women also frequently consolidated the chaotic multitude of painful sensations into one ailment, one "thing." As I have indicated, in many cases the women approached Storch only once or twice. Their stories remain obscure for me, since I hear of them for only a brief moment of their lives. In other cases—in acute crises, during a lingering illness, or in the dense, day-to-day exchange of messages between a patient and Storch—we can trace how the women perceived their illness over the long term. Stringing together a persistent stream of complaints allows an insight into the manner in which the women linked up the individual moments of their illness into a single story. These stories speak of the multitude of tormenting experiences that were conceived of as one and the same thing. The course of an ailment showed itself in the increasing frequency of vague, unexpected pains that left their impression on the inner landscape, now here, now there. In the language of the patients' complaints, pain was "something" that wandered about the body, changed location and form, but was thought of as *one* thing.

In Storch's text every longer story has at least three actors: the woman, the doctor, and the illness. These three subjects are linked with characteristic verbs. A comparison of these verbs shows a social relationship that appears as a triangle:

the women: they say, complain, admit, confess, reveal, entrust something, send word, or report something they experience—the pains at whose command they are, which they must bear and endure, which they feel, which oppress, torment, and overwhelm them.

the doctor: he inquires, investigates, reflects, searches out, believes, prescribes, advises, sends word.

the pains: they present themselves, they happen and manifest themselves, they assail the patient, make an attack, settle here or there, return anew, gain a foothold, take up their seat, attack, change their seat, take their leave, and depart for good.

The women thus reported what was happening to them. The doctor followed the course of events, enquired, and responded with prescriptions. The pains were the active agent, the story revolved around them and they drove the story forward.

Let us follow the case of a "choleric-gaunt" clothseller from Eisenach. She was recorded as a patient for the first time in July 1720 at age fifty-three, and for the last time in June 1741, as she was lying mortally ill (8:222, case 56). I will single out three temporal levels: a few months in 1720; a series of several years; and a few days in April 1732.

date	the woman	the doctor	the complaint
1720	complained		of womb anxiety
		prescribed	
	felt better		
Aug. 15	complained		of an excruciating flux in her right shoulder
		prescribed	
	and relief soon followed		
Nov. 12			chills, heat, and acute pains in the breast
		prescribed	
	good recovery		
			a terrible night

prescribed a
repeat of the
remedy

1721   vomiting, womb
                                               anxiety, and cold
                                               limbs

                          prescribed
                          prescribed

        is well again.

In the years immediately following, the following pains and "symptoms" appeared:

- 1723   tumor on the leg
- 1724   flux in the head, which rendered her hard of hearing
- 1725   attack of fever with a rash on the leg
- 1726   pains in the leg
- 1727   varicose veins in the leg
          hemorrhaging of the monthly period
          bloody urine
- 1729   fatigue in the limbs, attack of chills.

In the spring of 1732:

"on April 12 she sent word that lately the leg had been completely healed and was free of all swelling, but she now felt aches and pains in the breast and also in the abdomen. When I visited her in the afternoon, I found that pleuritic fever was very clearly present . . . except that it had been located initially in the right side with a bloody discharge. When it had run its course there, it moved on the 17th to the left side, whereupon another bloody discharge followed, which . . . persisted until . . . After the pleuritic fever had run its course, she developed in the night of . . . a mild chill, whereupon . . . once again a rash was present on the leg. I gave a prescription . . . , but at the same time, anxious lest the flux continue to be driven back so often, I advised . . . After the rash had been alleviated, colic pains . . . appeared." (8:233, case 56)

Many of the stories resemble the case of this clothseller if they comprise more than a single treatment. We can derive related interpretations from the three temporal levels.

In every case that has a rapid succession of reports, the story unfolds in a "zipper" pattern that interlinks a woman's complaint and the doctor's response. The woman complained and asked *for* something very concrete. The doctor prescribed *against* something, he prescribed very specifically against a reported pain. The chaos of pains and the succession of ever new aches drove the "zipper" interaction forward. These sequences of complaints and responses form nodes of such density that we can read them like dialogues stretched out over many years, despite the fact that the messages were passed through intermediaries. Compared to some other cases, the back-and-forth in the case of the clothseller was actually slow: in times of fear a woman might continue the dialogue with ever new reports of pain several times a day and for weeks on end (e.g.: 8:605, case 198; 8, case 1). If she wanted to continue the "zipper," the woman sent word how she felt after the last prescription, and the doctor sent a new response tailored to the last report. The "zipper" ended when the woman felt "improvement," when she was entirely satisfied with the result or so dissatisfied that she preferred to end the relationship. After every remedy Storch noted the report that came back: the patient had "found it to be good," she "had gained confidence in it," it had "brought relief," she "felt well and healthy," she "had peace after taking it," "the pain had abated" or "had become less," the "fit had died down," she "was livelier," she "was better," she "claimed lasting improvement." The words of "healing" imply only a lessening of pains; they never say that an "objectively" different, "healthy" condition had been reached. The women always had the last word. They judged the merits of the prescription and did so solely in accord with their own experiences. In many cases in which I had assumed, from a modern perspective, that the illness had gotten worse, I was astonished to read that "improvement" had been reported.

For years women reported successions of pains which they identified as various manifestations of the same thing, or as the internal struggle between two things. In the years after 1723, and conspicuously so in April 1732, the clothseller was the "seat" of two alternating illnesses: a flux now in the thigh, now in the breast, now in the ear, was replaced by a rash that "occupied" one leg, struggled with the fever, and kept the "upper hand" (8:235). The internal struggle visible on the body's surface was reported to the doctor, who tried to bring about an issue and relief, whereupon a reaction appeared in another part of the body. The doctor always prescribed after the pain; he followed it on the landscape of the body. Each pain was embodied in a grammatically different agent, which inflicted something on the body, which moved, which was doing something. A woman complained of a thick belly and pains in the body, but at a late date Storch noted that "the pains showed up in a different guise" (8:289, case 73). The experience expressed here is one of a personal ordering: no matter how differently the pains were felt— whether they pinched, hurt, tore, or pricked, and whether all parts of the body were at the mercy of this torment, "had to be at its beck and call"—the experience of the sufferer shaped the temporally disparate and physically scattered sensations into a personal story of suffering. Thus the abundance of expressions for pain lead into the account of an individual story. The contrast in Eisenach between the wealth of words and the way in which these sensations were combined to create meaning in each individual bio-logy of a woman, is very different from today. In in a medicalized culture such as ours, it is not people who are ill with something, but their bodies and organs that are diseased. The impoverishment of the vocabulary goes hand in hand with the inability to impart a personal meaning to pain through the use of language. The reduction of accepted ways of speaking reflects the cultural reduction of the whole spectrum of meaning to a defined body separated from the self. "There is no historical precedent for the contemporary situation in which the experience of personal bodily pain is shaped by the therapeutic program designed to destroy it."[57]

The Precariousness of Pregnancy

"A twenty-year-old woman of small stature was married to a large, thirty-six-year-old man, and during the first two years she had not gotten pregnant; she therefore doubted whether she would ever become pregnant. (3:152, case 20)

With marriage women entered a new phase, the fertile years, which had a beginning but only a very vague ending. What lay in between was not seen as a series of discrete pregnancies, but as a period in which the lifelong flowing and stagnating could take on the meaning of pregnancy or infertility. A woman lived through this period perched on the edge between good growth and evil stagnation, between healthful evacuation and miscarriage. The women lived in a state of ambiguity, caught between the desire to conceive and give birth to a child, and a conception of the body in which inner growth moved perilously close to the threat of stagnation. Women became mothers within the context of this ambiguous corporeality. The physiology of woman was not yet subsumed under the primacy of motherhood, as would be the case from the end of the eighteenth century on.

To help us understand the background of these ambivalencies and the experiences of women, I will sketch the body history of two women. Case one:

"A small woman, twenty-five years old, had "a tendency to get angry." As an unmarried woman she "had been plagued by mensibus dolorificis." Now she had been married for over a year. In the subsequent years the following things happened to her:

1725 Very soon after the wedding the menses failed to come for more than eight weeks, "but then they reappeared with a hemorrhage. Nobody at that time paid any attention whether mola or merely pieces of blood were discharged in the process" (p. 93);

1723 In November she had sixteen weeks of "constipation of the monthly period," which is why she "was quite sure she was pregnant." She did get a bleeding, however, and Storch was asked for a prescription. He gave the remedies which he normally used to expel something from the womb and thus stop a bleeding: "coral, Venitian borax" and his "specif. cephal," the head-powder: "thereupon . . . a mola, along with something skinny, was discharged" (p. 94);

1725 abortion in the fourth month;

1726 in the spring she once again discharged a "molam";

1728 in April she was eight months pregnant. After a fit of anger she was afraid she might abort. She asked for a prescription and gave birth to a living child, "but since she was of an angry nature, the child did not survive for more than two months" (p. 95);

1728 in December she "expelled" a "molam" after an eight-week-long "obstructionem mensium";

1729 At the beginning of January the menses "reappeared"; "her husband was just imagining she was pregnant";

1729   bleeding in February;
1729   suppressed monthly period in March;
1730   abortion after suffering a broken leg.

(4/1:93, case 16, and 3:481, case 102)

For this young woman, blood-stagnation, bloody discharges, abortions, and the birth of one child followed each other in rapid succession. At one point her husband suspected a pregnancy just as the menses started to flow again after the "discharge of a mola." Compared to the many discharges, the one birth stands out as something special.

In the second case, that of a noblewoman (3:120, case 16), the experience was the reverse: six pregnancies in eight years, among them one "untimely child," but the woman often felt compelled to consult the doctor after a fit of anger made her fearful of aborting. In March 1723 she got a fright during the time of her menses; the flow stagnated "instantly," and she reckoned that she was pregnant. In July, however, she had "strong hemorrhaging" from the womb and feared "either that she had an evil accumulation in her or that she was miscarrying." She had such fears repeatedly in the course of the year. In February she gave birth to a child. Looking back, we see that she had felt pregnant long before she could have been: this pregnancy had run its course between fear and hope for eleven months.

Historical demography records the succession of births and the intervals between them. What cannot be read from the statistics is the suffering, the fear, the hemorrhaging between the acts of giving birth, that is, the death that occurred inside the body. Church registers recorded only live births or stillbirths. The doctor's report allows us to construct and bring to light the experiences that formed the basis of an ambiguous perception of pregnancy. Bodily phenomena and the explanations to which they gave rise presupposed each other, and in both the hope for a "true" pregnancy was intimately linked with concern about a putrid inner stagnation.

The retention of the menses could be interpreted as a sign of pregnancy, but could also be a sign of an impending illness, of a "swelling," "dropsy," or the like. The "message of stagnation" was contradictory for a variety of reasons: today we regard the absence of the menses as a likely indication of pregnancy, but in 1720 it was an unclear sign; today

pregnancy and regular bleeding usually exclude each other physiologically, but in 1720 periodic bleeding could be part of a pregnancy
that was progressing *well;* today there is operational verification, while
back then many other signs of a subjective nature were interpreted as
clues since the absence of bleeding gave no certainty—what a woman
felt determined whether she was in the state of being pregnant, the
doctor merely followed the individual system of signs; today what is in
the body should by all means remain inside. In Eisenach pregnancy was
a precarious business, like walking a tightrope. It included the fear of a
miscarriage, a hemorrhaging, as well as the necessity to "expel false
conceptions," and the desire to take "expulsive remedies" in order to
remove "useless stuff" from the body.

The moment the menses stagnated, an ambiguous situation developed.[58] The true pregnancy still had to show itself, it still had to emerge
from the possible negative prognoses. Greater certainty came after the
fourth month, when the fruit quickened in the womb. To outsiders—
the doctor, the family, the neighbors, the priest—the true thing hidden
behind a big belly came to light only with the birth. Prior to that there
were no certain prognoses. On various occasions unmarried women and
widows asked Storch to certify that they were not pregnant, despite
their big bellies. He turned down these requests with reference to a later
time, "when the whole thing would come to light . . . all by itself"
(3:510, case 117). We find cases in which women were certain that they
had a "growth" in the body and therefore requested a prescription, and
time revealed that they were pregnant. Other women stubbornly believed that they were pregnant, and there was nothing to it. Still others,
unmarried, spoke of having a "tumor," and in time a pregnancy revealed
itself:

> A thirty-year-old "artisan's wife" complained "that she believed she was
> carrying a growth in her, which was now seeking to get out with bleeding
> and back pains. For since she had not had a child for several years, and
> could not feel any movement of the fruit in view of the size of her belly,
> she was sure that her feeling could not be deceiving her." Storch asked a
> midwife to inspect her, and she found "a live child." With the help
> of some expulsive remedies she soon gave birth to a healthy child."
> (3:446, case 89)

A "tall, gaunt woman," well into her thirties, who already had three children, complained on February 27, 1724, "that she had felt pregnant for one year for her belly had gotten big while her monthly period had stagnated. But now, since the time for giving birth had passed, and since she had not felt any movement of the fruit, she had to let go of this idea." Instead she had a bloody discharge with "clotted pieces." Storch prescribed expulsive remedies.   (8:341, case 82)

A forty-year-old woman, who had given birth to two children in her marriage and "after the last child had not given birth in eight years," thought she was pregnant, even though her menses came regularly. She very much wanted a child. Storch: "During the visit I soon noticed in her account her passionate feelings, and thus had misgivings about deflating them right away." He prescribed coral, which he considered harmless. Only the passage of time showed that her imagination had nourished false hopes.   (3:289, case 42)

A forty-seven-year-old noblewoman had given birth to but one child in twenty years. "At the time of the cessatio mensium, she started to think that she was pregnant, and was convinced she felt the movement of the fruit. I deferred to her opinion until the calculated date of the birth had passed, even though I never entirely concealed from her my reservations about the matter."   (3:290, case 42)

A young girl, who was usually "eager to get my remedies at the slightest attack" and for the "stagnation of the monthly period," complained to Storch about a "hard and big belly." She said that along with stagnation of the period it was "as though a cramp now and then moved back and forth in the belly and twitched"; she asked for a prescription. Storch suspected a pregnancy and tried to delay prescribing the requested expulsive remedies. In doing so he nearly fell out of favor with the girl. A different doctor was consulted and she took other remedies. This continued until she had a "strong swelling at the legs . . . and the relatives thought that the big belly also originated from this swelling, that both conditions were caused by the stoppage of the monthly period, and that a growth was undoubtedly hidden inside." Eventually came the "birth of a living growth," Storch noted ironically.   (5:298, case 59)

This ambiguous prognosis on the part of the women as well as the doctor about the growing belly was nourished by an imagination in which the stagnating inside could herald something evil; in which the drawing off and expulsion of matter were important aims of remedies; in which anger and fright could "stagnate" the inside; in which a stagnated inside could turn into "corruptio and decay." Added to this concept of corporeal ambiguity, which was inherent in every person, were the elements of a specific ambiguity about the female body. The conception of human beings occurred in that dark and impenetrable space where an excess of blood and phlegm threatened life; in which evil from the outside could imprint on the weak seed. Generation was threatened, above all, by the mood of the pregnant woman herself: woman were physiologically murderous to the fruit, owing to their constitution, their *inner* blood. Hidden in women were death *and* life. The incarnated deadliness was expressed in images of secret, deceitful killing: women could smother and poison the fruit in the womb, even if they did not intend to do so.

I want to explain in somewhat more detail the various aspects of this complex of ideas, which taken together suggest an analogy between pregnancy and excrement, growths, impurity, and evil. This will also make clear why a "real" pregnancy and birth stand out as all the more desirable against the background of anxiety, but also why a calm certainty could be so easily disturbed.

If the monthly blood stayed away, this was easily interpreted as a bad sign: the hope of being pregnant could be overshadowed by the concern that one was "breeding" something "evil" in the body, was initiating a "corruptio." In cases of stagnant monthlies, the doctor was asked for a prescription of opening remedies, to lure or expel the blood; at the same time, however, he had to be careful not to abort a fruit, and he would hold back with the *pellentes* (expulsives), especially with unmarried women. Interventions that seem from our perspective like early abortions can be interpreted as interventions to prevent a threatening mishap inside the body. Such an intervention seems particularly reasonable when external causes could be held responsible for the stagnation: "when the fluxus mensium stayed away owing to an external and patent cause [for example, fright], women rarely want to hear anything about being pregnant until halfway through the term they are convinced by quickening in the womb" (3:440, case 88).

Recourse to the *pellentes* in order to expel the monthlies could always be supported by the notion that impending misfortune was thus averted, evil driven out.[59] What today we consider a "miscarriage" (a construct of reproductive physiology), for the women of Eisenach was a dangerous though necessary discharge, which the doctor should support with expulsive remedies. In all this the doctor's thinking, like that of the women, was apparently oriented along the line that separate good and evil inside the body:

> "A burgher's wife, forty-six years old . . . complained in July 1713 of twelve weeks stagnation of the monthly period attended by nausea, an aversion to food, vomiting, and a growing belly. A neighbor, a medicus who treated in the customary way, considered her to be pregnant. But since she had given birth to only three children during twenty years of marriage, and since she had not been pregnant for seven years, this seemed doubtful to her. Therefore she was now seeking my advice. She admitted in response to my questioning that the stagnation had been caused by fright. I therefore believed she would soon cease to have her monthlies altogether, and that this was a sickly stagnation." A few days later "the stagnation loosened with a strong hemorrhage, and several clotted pieces of blood were discharged." Storch gave a prescription to promote the expulsion of "remnants." (8:43, case 7)

> A noblewoman, who had been pregnant several times, was "frightened" in March 1723, "tempore mensium, wherefrom the menses instantly stopped." Storch gave a prescription and the menses "reappeared." On July 6 she figured she was fourteen weeks pregnant and had a strong hemorrhage from the womb, preceded by winds. "This made her afraid that she had an evil accumulation in her or was aborting. Since . . . I could not reach a definite decision either to expel or to retain, I advised her to hold off to see what would happen next." A few days later she bled once again from the womb. "Since the belly now did not seem big, pregnancy was increasingly doubtful, and I prescribed *Pulv. polychr. Borrac. Ven. Specif. Cephal* . . . But since the menses still did not appear after these remedies, and there was some relief, I was now more mindful of a pregnancy." To support the pregnancy, Storch then prescribed a bleeding. (3:133, case 16)

Whenever Storch concluded that a stagnation was not a pregnancy, he prescribed those medications that he believed would expel the menses: especially the panacea of polychrest pills, Venetian borax, and coral. He said that borax was good for the "quick promotion" of a discharge

(4/2:189, case 43) and prescribed it often. He also gave frequent prescriptions for borax and polychrest taken together (4/2:135, case 30, for example) to evacuate the inner body. These remedies were indicated if one could be certain that something bad was inside the body, which was mostly revealed by a hemorrhage.[60]

The terminology for cases that were ambiguous and dangerous for women is revealing. The concept of "miscarriage" did not apply during the first months of pregnancy. Only in the later phases of a "true" pregnancy did Storch speak of "abortions" and "miscarriage." During the first months of hope and uncertainty, on the other hand, the words deny the meaning of miscarriage. Instead they indicate something deadly: "false conception," something "useless," a "growth," as well as the entire casuistry—derived from learned circles—about "mola," "blood curds," "moon-calves," and "remnants." All these things had to be driven out by labor pains and with the help of "expulsive remedies." They could differ in form and substance: "fleshy, glandulous, bloody, watery, windy, skinny, bubbly, stony, bony."[61]

Notions about the boundary between life, nothing, and evil are amply documented in the medical literature of the period. They testify to the collective imagination—also among the women—about the possibilities of how evil growths can develop: "remnants" are left behind in the body from an earlier birth; "leftover stuff" breeds bad matter; when a "mola was conceived" in a fit of anger (whereby the same word "conceive" was used for the accumulation of matter or fluids as for "conception"); when a mola was generated by the white flux. The terminology about the formation of matter in the body is thus not fertility-specific. In fact it is not even gender-specific. It speaks of the notion that "bad can engender bad."

A newly married woman, eighteen years of age, "sent word on May 29, 1732, that she had had her menses regularly on the fourteenth day after the wedding. Thereafter they had stopped for six weeks and had reappeared in excess after heart-palpitations." The bleedings stopped once more, resumed three weeks later, "taking away black, coagulated pieces." After this she had persistent irregular bleeding "with chills." Storch: "since the flux had stopped for six weeks after the first period, it was to be suspected that something which was to form a foetum had nested in utero. But then, because it was nothing sound, this thing had been driven away by the affluxum sanguinis; since that time . . . some clots remained behind, or something new was formed ex repetitis congressibus, and thus nature was directed to expel again this thing unfit for conception." (4/1:203, case 62)

In December 1718 a forty-two-year-old woman complained that she had "eight weeks stagnation of the monthly cleansing" in the summer, and that "her belly had gotten big." Later the monthly bleeding returned, "but irregularly, and the belly did not grow any more. All the while she had such a painful hipache that she could not walk down the alleys without limping." Storch suspected and reflected "whether a collection of a mola might not be behind it all." (8:80, case 16)

"The menses of the wife of an out-of-town chirurgus, forty years of age, stopped after she had a fright, and did not show up again for twenty-six weeks. In the meantime she felt a lump in the belly, which gradually grew to the size of three fists, and when she lay down it sagged from one side to another. This lump the husband for good reason took to be a mola." She took *Sal. amar. Cruciburgensis,* "whereupon the fluxus mensium appeared, and toward the ninth day a mola of such size came out that it corresponded to the described knot. The bitter salt in this region had many times before given proof of its effectiveness in women suffering obstructio mensium; which is why this woman took it with full confidence, and felt the desired effect." Storch pondered whether the mola "had appeared from the blood that had coagulated in utero owing to the fact that the menses had stagnated because of fright, or whether it had arisen ex congressu." In an unmarried woman Storch would have assumed the former; in this woman, because her husband was frequently drunk, the mola came from his bad semen and from the confusion of the fright, so that "conception took place in *utero male constituto.* Meanwhile it was rare that it had remained in utero until the twenty-sixth week, and undoubtedly would have stayed there even longer, indeed probably ad dies vitae, had it not been driven out by the *sal amarum* that was taken continuously for three days." (4/1:202, case 61)

In this last reflection by Storch there emerges another level of meaning that colored the thinking about growth inside the body: the womb of the women was likened to other organs of the body, to the stomach and the lungs. As a vessel the womb was described in the same words as the stomach. From the stomach too came forth "hard," black, thick "clumps"; it too could clot inside. Both had a retentive capacity, and the fear of closing up and hardening prompted a treatment to make them open up. The stomach retained food; the womb retained remnants, it "buried" a dead embryo. On various occasions Storch compared the womb to a "pickling vat," a barrel in which something can be preserved for a long time and "is safe from decay, especially since it is generally believed that the waters [the amniotic fluid] . . . are like muriae, or pickling juice, in which the children are preserved" (4/2:172, case 39).[62]

From his practice Storch reported similar happenings in the stomach. Take the case of a twenty-year-old pregnant woman who was vomiting. When Storch came to visit, her husband showed him "a piece of white stuff, nearly two ounces heavy, which she . . . had expelled." They were "clumps" of cooked carp milt, which the woman had eaten the year before at a funeral feast, and which had preserved themselves in the body for over five months (3:237, case 36). The words used to describe formations in the stomach and womb, as well as in the lungs, are similar or identical: something "collected," "clotted blood" was vomited up or discharged below, "remnants deposited" themselves (8:74, case 15). Bubbly, watery formations collected in the lungs, of the kind which the womb could also hold in herself; the matter that remained in the stomach was darker, harder stuff.

Another level of meaning is the similarity of the closing of stomach and womb. Certain procedures performed by the midwife, especially the great haste with which the placenta, the afterbirth, was pulled out after a birth, are explained by the fear that the mouth of the womb could close and fail to expel the remnants, and that it might not be possible to open it (for example, 4/2:208, case 51). The mouth of the womb and the mouth resembled each other as voracious openings. Both drew fluids toward themselves, as expressed in the image of the "covetous mother." At conception, the mouth of the womb sucked in the semen, so that the light-colored mucous expelled at birth was seen as male sperm which had been retained inside: "experienced midwives know about this and scold women for their lustiness" (3:301, case 43).[63]

The formation of a "true fruit" was an arduous tightrope walk into life. Often the father's semen was "weak," the fruit was plagued by the overabundance of the woman's body or was in danger of being "marked" by the woman's mood swings. What was imagined as active destruction in this *corruptio* happened through the woman, while passive debilities, a "weakness," a kind of stupidity, came from the semen. Already at conception the fruit could end up as a "futile and spoiled *conceptio*" (3:602, case 168) if the semen was "badly" constituted, if the uterus was not well "cleansed and swept," if it had too much moisture in it by which the seed would be swamped and washed away, if the blood had an excessive "drive ad uterum . . . , so that the weak fruit suffocates, as it were, and is destroyed by the overabundant blood" (3:712, case 263). Judging from the images, the good nesting of a fruit belonged into a field of meaning that was the opposite of everything impure, surging, superfluous, moist, the opposite of the menses. The blood *inside* threatened, above all, to "suffocate" the seed.[64]

Herein lies a contradiction, one we must grasp more clearly in order to understand the ambiguity of the woman's blood. The substance that was to nourish the child, the mother's positive contribution, could also kill through its excess:

"And so it remains certain that the *menses* can be the primary *causa molarum*, which is proved by an anciently observed experience . . . Irregular menses, however, either prevent *conceptionem* or, per nimium affluxum, wash out prematurely what was conceived, or they provide, ex vitio, an opportunity ad conceptum falsum. The natural destiny of sanguis menstruus is that the nourishing fluid formed from it nourishes a fetus conceptus and brings it to growth. If this blood is in excess, the nourishing fluid is also in excess, and this overabundance, especially if it is accompanied by a stronger drive, has the ability to tear the delicate stamina and vessels of a conceived fruit, even to suffocate the fruit, while instead nourishing the secundinam more than the fruit. Thus the causa molarum is manifestly clear, consisting for the most part of an unsuitable and deformed secundina." The uterus is a "locus affectus," whither the blood flows and whither "the congestiones move most commonly, frequently and almost without cease; hence it is easy to understand how quickly it can happen that a delicate and newly conceived fruit can suffer damage in such congestionibus, can suffocate and be corrupted; hereto the animi pathemata, consisting especially of anger and fright, can make the largest contribution." (4/1:185, case 49)

The menses as the expulsion of "filth," of impure matter, are a salutary evacuation. They are salutary because they carry away useless stuff; they threaten suffocation inside because of overabundance. As far as blood was concerned, pregnancy was a precarious business, situated between the need to let off blood and the fear of hemorrhages that could lead to abortion.

> A noblewoman had a stillbirth, and Storch pondered the causes. He noted that she had "taken child-balsam, cinnamon water, and Spanish wine." She had also generally eaten well, and had "thereby increased the blood excessively while at the same time arousing it. As a result, this excess, which in time thickened, became oppressive to the fruit, and its tough-ness eventually prevented the circulation and made it stagnant, where-upon the fruit had to end its life through a kind of suffocation." (3:141, case 17)

On the other hand, there are cases in which the women incarnated an abortive urge, their bodies aiming at "false expulsion":

> "because of this [the woman had been frightened and had suffered an abortion], nature had taken on a habit of calling forth hemorrhagias prematurely and with them drive out the children." (3:305, case 44)

Still other dangers threatened the fruit in the womb from the company it kept. The afterbirth had all the characteristics of a greedy, miserly, or evil thing:

> A soldier's wife, "of a quarrelsome and angry temperament," had an abortion. Judging from the calculated duration of the pregnancy, the fetus was too small. "It was therefore to be suspected that nature had been disturbed by anger or fright in the second month while forming it, and had diverted more nourishment to the secundinae maliformi than to the fruit." (4/2:125, case 26)

> A "deformed secundina, in which the fruit in the first or second month after conception lost its life, and in the juices of which it was preserved without decay as a small figure until its expulsion or birth, because the nourishing fluids had been withdrawn from the fruit and devoted to the secundina." (4/1:152, case 33)

Likewise a mola, a different kind of growth in the womb, could deprive the real fruit of its nourishment, virtually "eating it up":

A woman "aborted . . . a baby girl . . . and this was followed by a blistery mola of considerable size. In all probability, the mola had deprived the child of the nourishing juice and consequently, through the internal heat and the aroused decay, had caused its death."   (4/2:130, case 27)

In another case a mola which had grown beside a fetus deprived it of "strength and growth," so that the fetus "lost its life" (4/1:197, case 56). Still another fruit was "robbed of its proper nourishment" by two molae (4/1:143, case 33).

The images we encounter contradict one another. On the one hand, excessive nourishment threatened the "true fetus" with "suffocation," especially at the beginning of pregnancy. On the other hand, a battle for nourishment could take place inside, in which a kind of evil being, a greedy, blood-sucking thing, stole the food from the fruit. If a woman carried within herself the physiological contradiction between something motherly and something murderous, she could, in the course of the pregnancy, be personally guilty of causing an abortion, a death within the body, through her own anger. Women's anger smothered or poisoned the fruit:

A choleric-phlegmatic woman, nineteen years old, was six months pregnant, "when she was suddenly overcome by a violent anger; whereupon on the next day . . . a strong haemorrhagia uteri followed." After a few days of bleeding and stagnation of the blood, she had an "abortus generis masculini." How was this discharge to be explained? In Storch's view, the bleeding as such was not a sign of anything serious since it merely reduced the amount of blood." "However, at the same time the fruit had been so affected by the anger that it became deathly ill in utero, and died toward the seventh or eighth day. Afterward nature, in order to expel the fruit, produced the regular menses, namely the labor pains attendant on a birth."   (4/2:159, case 37)

Anger of any kind could have a deadly affect on the fruit. Pregnant women feared it; they asked for a prescription if they were angry. The feared physiological effect alternated between the "surge," which was aroused by the anger and drove the blood downward, toward the exit, and poisoning by the gall bladder, which was aroused by fits of anger. It would seem, however, that the ambiguity within the body was almost entirely dissolved from the doctor's perspective in the evacuations themselves and in the interpretation of the abortion, the discharge. Abortions, no matter how unfortunate they might be in individual cases and for the women who were "hopeful," in the end were salutary cleansings. The prescriptions followed this logic: the point was to induce evacuations, cleansing of the womb, and purging of filth. This was to be supported and promoted with remedies, because "if they are not cleansed, it can later happen that nature develops a habit and afterward repeatedly generates forms and expels them" (4/1:169, case 40).

Women came to the doctor driven by fear: before quickening, they were afraid of being stagnated; after the first movements in their body, they were anxious to preserve the fruit. They did not see the doctor to prepare for the birth; that was something that was done among women.[65] The doctor was summoned to lecture about birth only after something had already gone wrong. And the doctor was hardly concerned with preparing the women for birth. Time and again he spoke about the habits which the woman's nature could develop from the processes in her "mother," or womb. "Nature" history was his field.

Nature

Storch could not listen to a complaint, could not imagine a body, without at the same time starting his "research." The object of his investigation was nature. In this he was part of a long tradition of medical understanding; yet he was also very much the town *physicus* from Eisenach, a unique man, a provincial doctor from central Germany with barely four semesters of studies in Jena. In order to prescribe he sought to fathom the nature of each woman—its intentions, directions, and efforts. For he could heal only with nature. The medical-Hippocratic concept of nature which the doctor observed, which he served and supported because it was in the final analysis the root of all healing power, underwent a far-reaching and broad renaissance in the sixteenth and seventeenth centuries.[66] Sydenham had said that "disease is nothing other than an effort of nature, who with all her power is producing the extermination of sickening matter for the patient's welfare."[67] Under his influence "nature" became the basic foundation of medical efforts, regardless of whether it was spiritualized by Helmont following in the footsteps of Paracelsus: "I believe that nature is a command of God, by virtue of which a thing is what it is, and does what it is bidden to do,"[68] or whether it became, with Boyle, a name for a blind mechanism which tended "to secure the preservation of the individual": "the happy things, referred to nature's prudent care of the recovery and welfare of sick persons, are usually genuine consequences of the mechanism of the world and the patient's body."[69] Neuburger has pointed out that the term "nature" was a very unstable concept in medical thinking at the beginning of the eighteenth century: nature was used for "the sum of living manifestations, or the propelling forces, or both."[70]

During Storch's time, the question what nature truly, finally, and essentially was waned in importance. But neither romantic medicine, nor the reduction of nature to a succession of phenomena that could be experimentally ascertained and measured, had yet begun. For Storch, nature was unproblematic; in his countless references to it I could find no trace of the contemporary discussion about its essence.[71] This vagueness of his concept of nature allowed him to let body concept and nature blend into each other. From the bio-logy, the life story, and a woman's complaints he derived his idea of the nature of this woman, and with his prescription he talked to nature, even if in chemical symbols, in order to guide it onto the right paths or reinforce it.

I lost a good deal of time trying to gain an insight into Storch's body conceptions through his prescriptions. To do so I first had to decipher the chemical symbols and contemporary pharmacological nomenclature. Then I had to familiarize myself with the apothecaries of the time. Finally I had to consult the literature of medical history, not so much on the effectiveness as the meaning and significance of prescriptions in the eighteenth century.[72] I tried to wrest from Storch's prescriptions a meaning that might be of importance to me. A few things were obvious: to a large extent Storch prescribed to the women their own home remedies; in specific categories, as we have seen on numerous occasions, his prescriptions ran counter to the women's traditional remedies (always borax instead of saffron as an expulsive); he prescribed the new medicines that were produced in elaborate chemical processes with much greater frequency to the rich than the poor. Despite considerable effort, however, I could cull little else from these remedies. One thing is

clear, though: Storch believed that medicines were effective in helping
him channel the fluids, through the workings of nature, in the directions that seemed right to him. It seems pointless to me to analyze the
remedies for their effectiveness by modern standards, or for the economic interests behind them, or for the traditional meaning of the
ingredients. The remedies make sense within Storch's practice only if I
examine them for their supposed effects on nature and fluids.

The prescription was the doctor's last word. It was the final seal on his
acknowledgment of the complaint, his interpretive reflections, and his
advice. Remedies included procedures we have already encountered:
bleeding, compresses, plasters, and cuppings. But in nearly every case
there were also medicines, the introduction of substances into the body,
the one element that distinguished the doctor from other healers (at least
symbolically) or by which he sought to set himself apart from them. The
remedy was the material part of the doctor's response to the patient,
and, according to the medical ordinances, it was his prerogative. The
prescription was the certificate which the doctor wrote for himself and
the patients as evidence that he understood the patient's nature on the
basis of the complaints brought to him and through his own inquiry
into incidents and shadows of the past.

Time and again Storch came around to speaking of nature. Nature
was "careful," precautionary; he ascribed to her "a wise preparation of
the conditions for self-healing": "inasmuch as nature *provida mater,* as a
prudent and precautionary mother, . . . has made good provisions . . .
through the expulsion of excessive blood. But who properly understands
and appreciates her faithful solicitude (*sollicitudinem*) in such occurrences
of nature?" (3:522). Nature acted in the body; she was located in the
body but could not be found nor was it permanently settled in any one
place, in any organ or body part. Occasionally nature did have a seat,
but she occupied it only for a time, was never always there; it was only
the current locus of its intention. What did nature do? She had a drive
by virtue of which she expelled from the inside of the body to the
outside, moving matter from the inside out. Nature embodied herself in
the excretory urges of the body, so that she took up her seat at the site of
the discharge. Excretion, the expulsion of matter, reflected nature's
highest intention: to protect the body from harm. Looked at in this way,

discharge was the instrument for removing possible harm. The course of illnesses could be deciphered by the doctor as efforts on the part of nature to expel matter in order to restore the body to good health.

> A well-built, forty-seven-year-old woman, who wasted away and died within three months, showed the following "signs": a rash, sores which broke open and contained "hard lumps," bowel movements with lumpy pieces of excrement, phlegm, vomiting. All these manifestations on the skin, the discharges, were interpreted by Storch as healing efforts on the part of nature, which was working against the "corruption" of the liver: "And I really believe of this fatal disease that the liver had a strong corruption and decay, of which a good deal went into the blood, which nature expelled partly through the rash, partly through the many sores, though in the end it was unable to repair the fatal damage of the liver." (8:615, case 199)

In all this "nature" behaved *actively*, that is, the expulsions and secretions were not simply exits, streams of blood and moisture flowing from the body, but active discharges:

> A thirty-five-year-old woman, "who with an idle life-style had grown accustomed to a good appetite and strong beer," was pregnant. She complained during this time of an "urging in utero," then of "violent pains in the joints, tiredness, and occasionally spitting of blood," later still of *mictus cruentus*, blood in the urine. (3:600, case 168)

Storch interpreted the bloody urine as "excretio vicaria haemorrhoidum," as a discharge in place of the blood. Nature "used this discharge for a good purpose in this corpore plethorico. The spitting of blood had been caused in the same way and therefore also did not point to anything dangerous." Nature was thus on her guard in multiple ways. Along different paths she removed from the body vile and superfluous matter which could cause harm. She could alternate between the various paths: a gaunt, fifty-three-year-old woman vomited blood for several years. Storch prescribed rhubarb, whereupon she had "sedes," that is, a passing of "a large amount of black excrement down below." Here the doctor succeeded in supporting nature, so that she "was able to remove the matter down below with guidance from the rhubarb" (8:97, case 21).

A discharge by nature had a number of possible meanings: it could be a cleansing, the expulsion of vile matter, a habit of expulsion, a healing effort. Nature habitually made mistakes; she could err in her urge for expulsion and do too much of a good thing.

> A shoemaker's wife who was in her second childbed, suffered a stagnation of the flux of the womb in childbed, and afterward experienced "a swelling of the body," headaches, loose bowels, and a tumor. Storch: "thus I inquired after various factors in order to get behind the cause of this rapid, dangerous illness, and was told the following: from her youth she had had a propensity to a flux, which at times had caused a swelling of the hands, headaches, and other ailments. Seven years before she had had *anasarcam,* and after that she had developed an abscess under the arm, by which means the swelling had found its exit. In her previous childbed she had had a bad breast with an abscess, and in her current childbed she had been frightened twice around the third and fourth days . . . from which the lochia immediately became irregular and diarrhea set in. After the diarrhea, however, this swelling had for the most part taken over the head." The woman died. Storch: the cause was the "double fright, through which the humores had been lured a peripheria ad centrum, the necessary excretio lochialis had become stagnant, and the congestiones had been driven ad cerebrum. Since nature had once been accustomed to make an excretionem materiae serosae, partly through abscessus, partly through tumors . . . in variis corporis partibus & quidem in locis ad Excretionem minus congruis, it now ex Errore tried such a thing in cerebro, thereby destroying the same as a partem nobiliorem." (6:87, case 17)

Nature's mistakes remained engraved on the body:

> A woman had four stillbirths, each time for understandable reasons (for example, while pregnant, the woman had been chased by a "bold or angry cow"). Storch: "The first four births did have their reasons; however, because of them nature was led to a bad habit, afterward producing the same destruction without cause. In this way I know of a woman in a village, who twice in a row gave birth to children with crushed skulls, the first time perhaps *ex imaginatione,* but the second time only *ex consuetudine naturae.*" (4/2:39)

> A forty-five-year-old woman died from an "apoplexy in the head." Storch pondered the causes, recalled that he had treated the woman fifteen years earlier for "disturbances" owing to stagnant menses, and made a connec-

tion between the sudden death and the ailment fifteen years earlier and the failure of the menses to appear. "The congestio toward the head had its origin in the retention of the monthly blood. The same congestiones had already been the cause of ailments twenty-five years before [it undoubtedly should read "fifteen years"]. Whether nature had still preserved a memory from that time I do not wish to claim with complete certainty. Nevertheless, it can well be considered an error of nature that she prematurely slackened the expulsion of the monthlies, and therefore went wrong with these congestiones in the head." (8:515, case 162)

Nature was impetuous and rash:

A fifty-year-old woman, who had had a bad thigh for many years and whose monthlies failed to appear, complained of various ailments and died. Storch reflected: "if a long absent monthly period returns in women who have already passed their fiftieth year, this should be seen as a sign of a nature behaving errantly . . . For where nature behaves irregularly and impetuously in an excretion, it will also fail to keep proper caution." (8:445, case 126)

Nature was "inventive"; it opened new paths; it created for itself exits where previously there had been none—for example, varicose veins. Storch gives a "notable" example from the literature:

"There was a woman, thirty-six years old, who always was used to having the menses excessively strong . . . when she was pregnant once again, I opened a vein on her right ankle five or six times from the fifth until the eighth month, and each time I drew off up to 12 ounces of blood." (3:602, case 168)

Nature could tire, become powerless; its inherent power to direct the bad could fail:

A sixteen- or seventeen-year-old girl, whose menses had stagnated on account of cold water and had then been brought back by cold water, had a complete "paralysis" of the right side. "Nature" had tried to evacuate through the menses, but it had "not been continuous in expelling the blood, most of which had instead been regurgitated, wherefrom a *stasis emortualis*" had arisen "in one place," "which nature had tried to break up with a *spasmum continuum,* but . . . it could no longer direct the evil." (2:60, case 2)

Elsewhere Storch spoke of the "weakness" of nature—an inability to attain its goal—as a "defectum virium vitalium," a weakness of the vital force. And nature could also be "obstinate," recalcitrant toward the doctor and deaf to his lures. The doctor struggled with nature and was thoroughly absorbed in this struggle.

The women were at the mercy of their ailments. They came to the doctor when fear drove them, when they were afraid that they could no longer on their own get rid of the evil inside them. They complained to the doctor in person, or in their messages to him, and in these complaints they gave their suffering a body. The doctor answered their complaints by something only he could do: perceiving the nature in this body incarnated by their complaints. With his prescription, legible only to the apothecary, he drew up a certificate which was to assure him and his patient that he had discovered her nature, had investigated it, and was trying to guide it. This seems to have been the meaning of Storch's prescriptions, which in their baroque multifariousness were all meant to achieve the same thing: an opening. His entire practice was like a ritual intended to dissolve the death that was trying to gain control of the woman's inside under the sign of hardening. As for their effectiveness, his remedies could never fail, for, no matter what they did, in the end nature was always right:

> "nature, which is called an *amanuensis Dei,* is cautious to observe in her movements certain periods and specific times, and in the human body it is wiser and more knowledgeable than the *medicus.* She is better at observing harmfulness and benefit than all ingenia scholarum: she is the best mistress in healing and is wont frequently to point out to the doctors the paths by which she wants the remaining . . . moistures to be removed most conveniently." (3:324)

The women speak of pains which appear, which attack them, which come and do not wish to let go, which developed and frighten them because they were harbingers of final stagnation. In his concrete body conceptions the doctor was close enough to the women to fashion each woman's complaints into a unique bio-logical (that is, life-story-relating) body history. But he did not see in this his task as a doctor. Everything the women told him he tried to reduce to a common denominator: nature. According to Stahl, nature was "the first . . . real . . . fundamental . . . causative . . . acting force."

Storch penetrated deeply into nature to investigate her and to grasp her innermost essence. Thus, he was perceiving in the blood of each woman the inventive and yet obstinate, the fickle and always active nature, in order to guide her into the proper paths. In this way our doctor faced each woman not only as a physician, but also, in a sensual way, as a man.

Nature was like a rococo costume with which Storch identified the body he *conceived* in his mind. As a doctor, he separated the body of the patients, which he conceived of as nature, from that body experience to which he, as a child of his province, remained sensually attached in images, emotions, and sentiments, and which he could not have encompassed in a self-contained system of concepts and terms. I have tried as much as possible to detach this concretely, traditionally experienced body from the learned Stahlian construct. I have sought to describe this imagined and experienced body according to a dozen subregions and to reconstruct in this way how doctor and patients, from different observation points, oriented themselves in this body landscape.

It would be wrong to try and place Storch as a doctor into a post-medieval, neo-Hippocratic medical tradition simply because he thought of himself as a nature investigator. What he called "nature" existed only in the early eighteenth century, and in this simplistic way surely only in the mind of a small-town would-be scholar. For Mondeville, medical practice was still guided by deciphering the body in the book of nature, in which the order of creation was reflected.[73] In his brief studies Storch adopted a concept of nature which reversed the old one. Nature was no longer the object of tranquil contemplation, but the basic material for describing everything, like plaster in rococo architecture.

Nature withdrew into the body of women. The external correspondences, which Pouchelle was able to uncover in Mondeville, have faded, if not entirely disappeared. It was only in the women's inner body that the doctor could listen to nature, which, in Mondeville's words, "like a fiddler . . . beckoned doctor and surgeon to a dance, a dance to its rhythm."[74] In Storch's conception, nature has turned into a compulsive cleaning woman who "grabs all matter that is foul and improper in the human body, pricks and pinches it, and rolls it around until it is out."[75] His nature no longer knows anything about an order in the microcosm that corresponds to an order in the macrocosm.

In Storch's women little is left of the body which, according to Rabelais, people in the late Middle Ages experienced and perceived: a body that exuded exuberantly, broke all bounds, overflowed, and swept others along in its celebration of life. How different were the women of Eisenach: wretched, stagnating, miserly (the richer ones), and cramped up—this is how they experience themselves, helpless in their suffering bodies, which were supposed to flow but did not. The agony of experiencing an objectified body had begun.

Conclusion

My attempt to make the invisible corporeality of the women of Eisenach the theme of an historical study evoked in me the experience of being an outsider. As I perceived ever more clearly in the women's complaints how different their corporeality was, I realized with growing dismay that my own sense of womanhood is conditioned by history and cannot be compared across time. In order to understand a small-town practice I had to cross into new territory not only as a historian. As a woman too I found myself in a no-man's-land. It became increasingly difficult to gain a footing in the slippery terrain, to create terms that would be understandable to the reader, and at the same time to grasp the object of my investigation and orient my approach at the intersections of various disciplines.

Again and again I ventured into this no-man's-land. Each time I took different authors as my guides, in order to listen to the complaints of girls and burgher women, court ladies and pastors' widows from a different perspective. In so doing, two things astonished me. Historians of art, religion, and science, literary critics, linguists, and anthropologists set me onto tracks that led surprisingly deep into the new territory. Yet these paths beneath the skin also showed me the reasons why the epoch-specific gestalt of the sensory perception of womanhood has so far not become a theme of scholarly investigation.

During these explorations I grew increasingly critical of the approaches I had followed in earlier efforts in which I had tried to reduce the story of the social perception of the female body to the story of how its authentic essence had not been understood. What became more and more important to me were the methods that allow us to reconstruct the historical gestalt of the sensory perception of the body and thus understand the ideas of the macrocosm that corresponded to it. A series of questions arose with increasing urgency. These questions go far beyond understanding a medical practice in the early eighteenth century; they affect the boundaries of historical studies and may well open a new horizon in women's studies.

As from a bridgehead I can now see in this new territory a few mountain ranges that afford perspectives from which the inner body may be integrated into history. My studies up to now have not allowed me systematically to explore and test even a single one of these observation points. But they have made it possible to formulate some hypotheses about how, from these perspectives, we might go about understanding the historically determined perception of the body. I will present them briefly in the form of theses. Each will be formulated with keywords and will indicate a shift in perspective, a change in accent, and the emergence of a new research interest. This approach allows me to avoid placing the new body history in opposition to existing special fields and to present it in such a way that it can be understood as an interdisciplinary suggestion.

Paradigm versus theme. Contrasting paradigm and theme allows me to distinguish between the explanatory and the motivational schemes in Storch's practice: between his learned doctrine derived from Halle and Stahl and his underlying notions of a patient's body. Such a discrepancy has also been noticed recently by historians of science.

Copernicus was reaching for a heliocentric world view in order to guarantee that the curvature of the shell-shaped planetary spheres was perfect. Kepler was guided in his calculations by a belief in the music of the spheres; when he found himself forced to assume eliptical planetary orbits, he saw them explicitly as imperfect circles—as attempts by creation to approach perfection. When Harvey, using a new methodology and new quantitative criteria, demonstrated the circulation of blood, he was, according to his own letters later in life, looking for the circulation in the human microcosm which corresponded to that in the macrocosm. The new paradigms thus often seem to have been independent from the theme that motivated the investigations of the so-called discoverer or creator of the paradigm.

I cannot but assume that a similar dissonance of paradigmatic and thematic elements also explains the practice of a doctor like Storch. For example, he occasionally performed an autopsy on a deceased patient, yet, with few exceptions, this was no reason for him ever to wish to see and examine with his hands more of a patient's body than the face. For him, the paradigm of three-dimensional exterior space carried over only into the dead inner body. The living flesh, its blood, its stagnations, and its fluxes took place in an "inside" that was only analogous but not identical to the external space. I think it is important to place the study of practice-orienting, epoch-specific themes into the service of body history. Only such an approach will make it possible to distinguish the corporeal experience of an epoch and realize how different it was from the contemporary, learned body image. Only in this way might we bring forth from out of the shadow of the history of science the perception and interpretation of the body that was most concretely lived.

From Discovery to invention. This thesis contrasts, in an ideal way, two attitudes a historian can assume in trying to deal with the appearance of a new theme, such as the theme of the heart as a pump, the circulation of matter, or the theme of homogenous, three-dimensional space. The monopoly of Cartesian three-dimensionality over space, time, and experience is too readily seen as the "discovery" of a topology that was "always" imminent in every reality. But the new concept of space can also be understood as the invention or creation of a new theme. Time and again this second perspective, in which the emphasis is on historical discontinuity, proved useful for my investigation.

First, this way of looking at the past sharpened my alertness for vanished perceptual and conceptual forms, even if I adopted it only as a heuristic attitude. With the rise of the Cartesian sense of space, other dimensions faded out, for example, the importance of the olfactory and tonal spaces. The Cartesian space obliterates the complementary-disymmetrical relation between inside and outside.

Second, this perspective focused on invention contributes to the study of the sociogenesis of my own self-evident corporeality. In other words, it contributes precisely to understanding what it is in myself that I must not transfer to Storch's patients. Before we begin to form an idea of vanished body perceptions, we must shed some light on the sociogenesis of our "corporeality," on what today is taken for granted and hardly seen as in need of a history.

From written to oral transmission. Every one of Storch's cases contains the protocol of a woman's statement followed by the doctor's description of her ailments. At the center of my analysis when I first began this work was the difference between these two types of texts in terms of gender and social class. Later, another difference assumed vital importance. The women speak, complain, disclose, reveal, suspect. Their bodies emerge as the *expression* of a suffering that is related only in oral form; it is an undescribed, undefined, undefinable body of which they speak. By contrast, Dr. Storch *describes*. He investigates to discover what a woman actually suffers from. The body he presents is created by his written record. In my source the woman's body appears as a fragile synthesis, combining elements of the mentality of oral culture such as cheese and rennet with concepts from the written medical tradition—embryology, for example. But elements from various currents of tradition flow together both in the life stories of the women and in the objectification of their ailments by the describing doctor (the pathography). What the women said was also shaped by what they had adopted from medicine, and the learned expositions of the doctor also drew upon popular ideas, which he had probably absorbed with his mother's milk.

To avoid misunderstanding the relation between these elements, it would be necessary to clarify much more fully than I was able to do the differences between the reception of oral themes and the tradition of ideas transmitted in writing.

From theory to practice. Medical practice is usually studied from the perspective of cultural and social history. As a result, research is focused on the shaping of this practice by the medical theories of the doctor, on the unscientific customs of the patients, and sometimes also on the enforcement of class-specific interests by way of this practice.

Beneath the questions that arise from this approach lie in most cases a biased view of history as the story of progress ("What did people back then know, what did they not yet know?") and the special concerns of the historian ("How did this practice implement social prejudices or support them ritually?").

I could not venture to interpret Storch without asking myself these questions in relation to him, and without making it clear to myself how many of them remain unanswered. My topic, however, was not the doctor's practice, but the body image and body experience expressed in it. It was my intention to describe not the place of the female body within the learned system of Halle, but the gestalt of a body conception that shaped the women's complaints and the doctor's response. In order to accomplish this, I created the device of the "orientational patterns of perception of the body." They allowed me to probe the differences of perception between the women and the doctor. I was conscious of using a fragile auxiliary device, but one I could not do without as long as I was concerned about the concrete reality of the body as reflected in the dialogue of this practice. For my theme was not the ideology of the doctor or his class-interest, which distorted his perception of the objective entity "woman." Nor was I interested in dealing with my source in a purely literary-historical way. I wanted to understand the body as the experienced object of women's complaints, anxieties, fears, and self-perception—the body as a conception shaping these sufferings. To that end I also had to investigate the conceptions that shaped the doctor's behavior over twenty years.

From medical to social history. As long as I saw Storch as a mere epigon of Hippocrates and Galen, or as a predecessor of the modern family doctor or gynecologist, I had already attributed my own body percept to the women patients of Eisenach. After all, one goes to the doctor if one is sick, thinks one is sick, or is afraid one might get sick.

My studies on the history of midwifery had made clear the way the doctor's technical claim to competence had changed in the eighteenth century. But in the literature this standardization of the medical profession is described as a development in the specialized treatment of a body that is essentially nonhistorical, a body whose well-being earlier had been the concern of herbwomen and doctors, pilgrimage sites and barbers, witches and faith healers.

My reflections on the symbolic components in Storch's practice showed the extent to which the modern body has been created through the symbolic effectiveness of nineteenth- and twentieth-century medical and hygienic practices. The synthesis of the bourgeois body was accomplished only after its care was monopolized by medicine. Without the process of ascribing to "the" medical profession the responsibility for health, the modern Western body could not have emerged.

It would be misleading to try and understand Storch the doctor by comparing him to doctors of a later age. In many cases I had to ask myself: Was this woman coming to Storch because she wanted advice or because she wanted a remedy she could no get in any other way? Did she come to disclose her ailment? To find comfort in telling her suffering? In any case Storch's most important function is symbolic. He is a mediator between the age's self-evident certainties and the age's flesh. Just as modern medicine mediates my age's certainty and the body I ascribe to myself, Storch's practice has led me to look with entirely new eyes at the sociogenesis of modern sexuality, reproduction, hygiene, and health, no trace of which can I find in the writings of this eighteenth-century doctor.

WORKS BY JOHANN STORCH
NOTES
INDEX

Works by Johann Storch

Diseases of Women

1. *Unterricht vor Heb-Ammen* . . . welcher als das erste volumen zu einem bald folgenden Opere casuali practico de morbis mulierum betrachtet werden kann (Instruction for midwives . . . which can be seen as the first volume in a soon-to-follow work of practical cases on diseases of women). Gotha, 1747.

2. *Von Kranckheiten der Weiber, zweyter Band,* darinnen vornehmlich solche Casus, welche den Jungfernstand betreffen, auf theoretische und practische Art abgehandelt . . . (Diseases of Women, volume two, wherein primarily such cases as concern maiden women are discussed theoretically and practically . . .). Gotha, 1747.

3. *Von Kranckheiten der Weiber, dritter Band,* darinnen vornehmlich solche Casus, welche die Schwangeren betreffen . . . (Diseases of Women, volume three, wherein primarily such cases as concern pregnant women are discussed theoretically and practically . . .). Gotha, 1748.

4.1 *Von Weiberkranckheiten, vierten Bandes 1ster Theil,* darinnen vornehmlich solche Zufälle, welche Molas oder Muttergewächse und falsche Früchte betreffen, auf theoretische und practische Art abgehandelt . . . (Diseases of Women, volume four, part one, wherein primarily such mishaps as concern lumps or womb growths and false fruits are discussed theoretically and practically . . .). Gotha, 1749.

4.2 *Von Weiberkranckheiten, vierten Bandes 2ter Theil,* vom Abortu oder Mißfall. (Diseases of Women, volume four, part two, of abortions or miscarriages). Gotha, 1749.

5. *Von Weiberkranckheiten, fünfter Band,* darinnen solcherlei Zufälle, welche ordentliche und schwere Geburten betreffen, auf theoretische und practische Art abgehandelt . . . (Diseases of Women, wherein such mishaps as concern normal and difficult births are discussed theoretically and practically . . .). Gotha, 1750.

6. *Von Weiberkranckheiten, sechster Band,* in welchem vornehmlich solche Zufälle, so die Wöchnerin und Kindbetterin betreffen . . . (Diseases of Women, volume six, wherein primarily such mishaps as befall women in childbed are discussed theoretically and practically . . .). Gotha, 1751.

7. *Von Weiberkranckheiten, siebenter Band,* in welchem solche Zufälle, so die stillenden Weiber und Säugammen betreffen, auf theoretische und practische Art abgehandelt . . . (Diseases of Women, volume seven, wherein such mishaps as concern nursing mothers or wet nurses are discussed theoretically and practically . . .). Gotha, 1751.

8. *Von Weiberkranckheiten, achter und letzter Band,* worinnen vornehmlich solche Zufälle, Kranckheiten und Gebrechen, so man der weiblichen Mutter zuschreibt, und den Weibern außer dem Schwangergehen begegnen, abehandelt werden (Diseases of Women, volume eight and final volume, wherein are discussed primarily the mishaps, illnesses, and infirmities attributed to the female womb and found among women outside the state of pregnancy). Gotha, 1752.

Other Works

Medicinischer Jahrgang oder Observationes clinicae, darinnen er zeigt, wie die ihm anvertrauete Patienten im Jahr . . . curiret worden (Medical Yearbook or observationes clinicae, wherein he shows how the patients entrusted to him in the year . . . were cured), volumes 1–8. Leipzig, 1724–1735.

Quinque partitum practicum, oder eine in fünf Classen eingetheilte *Praxis casualis medica,* welche er als eine Continuation seiner bisher edirten Jahrgänge von 1731 zusammengetragen (Quinque partitum practicum, or a practical work of medical cases, divided into five sections, which he has compiled as a continuation of his edited Yearbooks since 1731). Leipzig and Eisenach, 1738.

Quinque partiti practici, oder der in fünf Classen eingetheilten *Praxeos casualis medicae,* Tomus II, vom Jahr 1732 (Quinque partiti practici, or practical medical cases, divided into five sections, volume II, from the year 1732). Leipzig and Eisenach, 1740.

Wohlmeynender *Unterricht,* auf was Art ein Mensch, bei anfallenden Kranckheiten seiner wahrzunehmen habe . . . (Beneficial instruction on how a person should look after himself in case of illness . . .). Leipzig, 1730.

Theoretisch-und practische Abhandlung von *Kranckheiten, denen vornehmlich Soldaten unterworfen seyn* . . . (Theoretical and practical treatise of diseases which affect primarily soldiers). Eisenach and Naumburg, 1735.

Leitung und Vorsorge des Höchsten Gottes, Das ist: Dessen Lebenslauf, Schicksale, fatale Kranckheit und seeliger Abschied, nebst dem Sections-Schein; theils aus dessen Autographo aufgezeichnet . . . von Jacob Storchen (Guidance and providence of the Lord God, that is, his life, fate, fatal illness, and blessed parting, along with the dissection report; based in part on his own autobiography . . . by Jacob Storch. Eisenach, 1752. (An appendix, pp. 40–48, contains the complete list of the publications of Johann Storch, alias Huldericus Pelargus.)

Notes

1. Toward a History of the Body

1. Marcel Mauss, "Die Techniken des Körpers," in *Soziologie und Anthropologie,* ed. Wolf Lepenies and Henning Ritter (Frankfurt, Berlin, 1978), 2: 197–220. This essay set off the contemporary discussion on the epistemology of body perception. For Mauss, "the unknown is found at the boundaries between scholarly fields, the place where the professors 'devour each other,' as Gothe put it." As an ethnologist he looks for "facts which have not yet been embraced by concepts . . . have not even been organically grouped . . . which are given the label 'unknown' . . . and are classified under the heading 'miscellaneous.' " "This is where scholarship has to take off. Here one can be certain of finding truths" (p. 199). Mary Douglas, *Natural Symbols* (New York, 1982), said: "Mauss's denial that there is any such thing as natural behavior is confusing. It falsely poses the relation between nature and culture" (p. 69). "The social body constrains the way the physical body is perceived. The physical experience of the body . . . sustains a particular view of society" (p. 65). (Mary Douglas, *Ritual, Tabu und Körpersymbolik: Sozialanthropologische Studien in Industriegesellschaft und Stammeskultur* [Frankfurt, 1981], p. 123). "The human body expresses universal meanings only insofar as it reacts as a system to the social system . . . what it can express symbolically in a natural way are the relationships of the parts of the organism to the whole . . . The 'two bodies' are the self and society". In the discussion among anthropologists the historian cannot help but be conscious of the question whether, on account of this intertwining, the entity that is "culturally" determined is a "natural body." Important research approaches to this question are being explored in Germany, for example, through the long-time efforts of A. E. Imhof, an introduction to which can be found in his *Leib und Leben in der Geschichte der Neuzeit* (Berlin, 1983). There are also inventories of body perceptions from foreign cultures dealing with the connection between cosmos and body. A monumental example is Alfredo Lopez Austin, *Cuerpo Humano e Ideología: Las Concepciones de los Antiguos Nahuas,* 2 vols. (Mexico, 1980).

2. The genesis of the modern body probably could also be read as a commentary on the formation of the "possessive individual," which C. B. MacPherson, *The Political Theory of Possessive Individualism: Hobbes to Locke* (Oxford: 1962), has described as follows: "The individual was seen neither as a moral whole, nor as part of a larger social whole, but as an owner of himself. The relations of ownership, having become for more and more men the critically important relations determining their actual freedom and actual prospect of realizing their full potentialities was read back into the nature of the individual. The individual, as it was thought, is free inasmuch as he is the proprietor of his person" (p. 3). Spicker, as a phenomenologist working in a hospital, has this emphasis on having at the expense of being: "The patient's lived body is reduced to the weakened image of a physical body, not only by the physician, but, paradoxically, by the patient as well. For the patient responds to the request of the physician to live in his or her body during the physical examination, as a body that he or she *has,* not as the body that they *are* . . . the patient is asked to live in his or her body as a thing, in order to attain medicine's end—health. This thing-body . . . is something merely possessed, an object, a thing with physical, anatomical and physiological property." Stuart F. Spicker, "Terra Firma and Infirma Species: From Medical Philosophical Anthropology to Philosophy of Medicine," *The Journal of Medicine and Philosophy* 1, 2 (1976): 119.

3. To social historians of my generation historical demography has become a primary source of statements about body-mediated phenomena. Demography became a modern science only with the use of statistical methods. Statistics constructs "population" as some kind of entity. A population has a number of arbitrary features, and these are studied to determine the probability that they constitute a specific characteristic. The characteristics of the body within a statistical population are thus perceived as probable attributes of an object: as rates of birth, morbidity, reproduction, and mortality. The body appears, for example, in the context of the production of children, or accidents and diseases, or in relation to the growth or decline of population units. Jean-Pierre Peter and Jacques Revel, "Le Corps: L'Homme malade et son histoire," in *Faire de l'histoire,* ed. J. le Goff and P. Nora (Paris, 1974), 3: 169–191, have described the encirclement of the body by demography and speak in this context of a silencing of the body.

4. David Armstrong, *Political Anatomy of the Body: Medical Knowledge in Britain in the Twentieth Century* (Cambridge, 1983), p. xi. This book was important to me for two reasons. Armstrong deals with a profound transformation of the subject of medical activity, one that coincides with my own lifetime. He examines the transformation of the "patient" in medical practice: around 1950 the patient had been fully constituted as an object of medical intervention; but in the mid-1980s he was being reconstituted as the subject of medical communication. Armstrong reveals this transformation of the perception and self-perception of the patient from the perspective of Foucault. Medical sociologists William Ray Arney and Bernard J. Bergen, in

Medicine and the Management of Living: Taming the Last Great Beast (Chicago, 1984), come to the same conclusion as Armstrong, the philosophically trained doctor. So far, scholars have hardly examined the relation between medical ritual and discourse and the process whereby the patient constitutes himself, in an epoch-specific way, both as an object of treatment and a subject participating in the treatment.

5. Michel Foucault, *The Birth of the Clinic. An Archaeology of Medical Perception,* trans. A. M. Sheridan Smith (New York, 1973).

6. Karl Figlio, "The Historiography of Scientific Medicine: an Invitation to the Human Sciences," *Comparative Studies in Society and History* 19 (1977): 277. In the light of the scientific discourse in the late eighteenth century, Figlio examines historiographically the appearance of this epistemologically new understanding of the human person, which was based on axioms that were radically new compared to previous models. One consequence of the linguistic-conceptual dissociation of a body defined as sick from the body lived every day, was the separation, the isolation, "le renfermement" of this body in a "realm of disease"; this was a process which had already begun in the late sixteenth century. It was only in the course of the nineteenth century that the healthy body as well was seen that way.

7. "The perception of ego as a *human,* and the demand that social institutions fit the ego's egalitarian human needs, represent a break with all pre-modern forms of consciousness—including body perception. On the discussion of what constitutes the precise characteristics of this radical change in thinking and experiencing, see Ivan Illich, *Genus: Zu einer historischen Kritik der Gleichheit* (Reinbeck, 1983), pp. 136 ff.; translated as *Gender* (New York, 1982).

8. That science does not create facts, even if it produces them socially as facts, is a central argument of a group of English historians of science, who also deal with the sociology of the science of the body. My own analysis depends in part on the attempt of these authors to understand descriptive concepts as expressions of social relations; see R. M. Young, "Science is social relations," *Radical Science Journal* 5 (1977): 65–129; Steven Shapin, "Social Uses of Science," in *The Ferment of Knowledge: Studies in the Historiography of Eighteenth-Century Science,* ed. G. Rousseau and Roy Porter (Cambridge, 1980), pp. 93–143; Figlio, "Historiography," esp. p. 265 on the modern state of knowledge.

9. Robert A. Scott, *The Making of Blind Men: A Study of Adult Socialization* (New York, 1969), showed that in the United States today, 50 percent of the people defined as blind read the newspaper every day, and that the same number of people who cannot see are not diagnosed as being blind and in most cases do not even consider themselves blind. Blindness in the United States is fundamentally dependent on the creation of a client-relationship. Irving Zola, *Missing Pieces: a Chronicle of living with Disability* (Philadelphia, 1982), himself a seriously disabled sociologist, has been studying for years the creation of the "cripple" by social service systems.

10. Gaston Bachelard is an epistemologist who taught the history of philosophy

and science at the Sorbonne. Neither in France nor in Germany can his teaching be classified into existing disciplines. The materiality of elements reveals itself to him as the source of imagination. See, for example, his commentary on Novalis, for whom the essence of water conjured up in the imagination the image of "delightful young girls": *Water and Dreams: An Essay on the Imagination of Matter* (Dallas, 1983; Paris, 1942), p. 126.

11. Utz Jeggle, "Im Schatten des Körpers: Vorüberlegungen zu einer Volkskunde der Körperlichkeit." *Zeitschrift für Volkskunde* 76, 2 (1980): 172: "Corporeality would thus be the experiential form of the body that is created by a historical society." Imhof, *Leib,* p. 5: "the satisfying of basic bodily needs, such as eating, drinking, sleeping, dressing, moving, procreating, already has as a further dimension a strong cultural imprinting with a temporal, spatial, and social differentiation, structuring, and standardizing."

12. Ivan Illich, *H₂O and the Waters of Forgetfulness: Reflections on the Historicity of "Stuff"* (Dallas, 1985). This book is the product of the author's reflections on an interdisciplinary seminar of phenomenologists, psychologists, and historians, which he and I conducted at the Dallas Institute of the Humanities and Culture. The theme was Historical Heuristics of Body Images.

13. André Malraux, *La Tentation de l'Occident* (Paris, 1926), p. 158; trans. R. Hollander, *The Temptation of the West* (New York, 1961).

14. A wealth of examples can be found in Fridolf Kudlien, "The Seven Cells of the Uterus: The Doctrine and its roots," *Bulletin of the History of Medicine* 39 (1965): 415–423; and in Thomas G. Benedek, "Beliefs about Human Sexual Function in the Middle Ages and Renaissance," in *Human Sexuality in the Middle Ages and Renaissance,* ed. Douglas Radcliff-Umstead (Pittsburgh, 1978), pp. 97–119.

15. In my selection of the sociohistorical literature I list primarily works dealing with the eighteenth and early nineteenth centuries, both because they are chronologically closest to my period and because this period is relatively unexplored. I do not consider works dealing with the second great wave of medicalization in the late nineteenth century.

16. Louisa Accati, "Lo spirito della Fornicazione: virtù dell'Anima e virtù del corpo in Frìuli, Fra '600 e '700," *Quaderni Storici* 41 (1979): 650. In the later sixteenth century the Church began to discipline strictly the clergy by means of inquisitorial procedures in order to sever their ties to the late medieval world of popular magic; see Mary R. O'Neill, "Sacerdote ovvero strione: Ecclesiastical and Superstitious Remedies in 16th Century Italy," in *Understanding Popular Culture,* ed. Steven Kaplan (Paris, 1984), pp. 53–83.

17. Robert Muchembled, "Le Corps, la culture populaire et la culture des Elites en France (XVe–XVIIe siècle)," in *Leib und Leben in der Geschichte der Neuzeit,* ed. A. E. Imhof (Berlin, 1983), p. 151; see also his "La femme au village dans la région du Nord (XVIIe–XVIIIe siècles)," *Revue du Nord* 63, 250 (1981): 585–593.

18. Jean Delumeau, *La Peur en Occident, XVIe—XVIIIe siècles* (Paris, 1978), p. 306. Delumeau marshals a wealth of evidence that fear of women grew from the sixteenth century on, and that the female body took on an increasingly threatening form in the imagination; cf. pp. 305—325.

19. Muchembled, "Le Corps," p. 146.

20. Ibid., p. 145. Martine Segalen, "Quelques réflexions pour l'étude de la condition féminine," *Annales de Démographie historique* (1981): 16: "The image of woman . . . is made of a permanent ambiguity . . . Every female gesture seems to possess an obverse and a reverse side." On woman as the bearer of traditional powers, see also Françoise Loux and Jean-Pierre Peter, introduction to the issue focusing on Langages et images du corps, *Ethnologie Française* (1976): 215—218.

21. Accati, "Spirito," p. 649.

22. Muchembled, "Le corps," p. 141.

23. Piero Camporesi, *Il sugo della vita: Simbolismo e magia del sangue* (Milan, 1984), pp. 16—18. Michel Foucault, *Discipline and Punish: The Birth of the Prison* (New York, 1979), chap. 2: "The Spectacle of the Scaffold," is rich in details for the period 1650—1720. Foucault also describes the public butchering and disemboweling of the "patient" immediately after his execution. Robert Muchembled, *Culture populaire et culture des élites dans la France moderne (XVe—XVIIIe siècle)* (Paris, 1978), p. 248: "The executed body allows the act of justice to become visible to all. For the people crowd to the executions as onlookers." Trans. Lydia Cochrane, *Popular Culture and Elite Culture in France, 1400—1750* (Baton Rouge, La., 1985).

24. Owsei Temkin, "The Scientific Approach to Disease: Specific Entity and Individual Sickness," *The Double Face of Janus and Other Essays in the History of Medicine* (Baltimore, London, 1977), describes, pp. 451 ff., the contrast between the "anatomia publica" as a public investigation of man as such and the later prevailing individual autopsy. Ernst Ackerknecht, "Primitive Autopsies and the History of Anatomy," *Medicine and Ethnology* (Stuttgart, Vienna, 1971), pp. 91 ff., emphasizes that it would be wrong to draw premature conclusions about any kind of "anatomical knowledge" of the inner body from a society's skill in cutting up the body and penetrating into it; see also Gunter Mann, "Exekution und Experiment: Medizinische Versuche bei der Hinrichtung des Schinderhannes," *Lebendiges Rheinland-Pfalz* 21, 2 (1984): 11—16.

25. Heinrich Haeser, *Lehrbuch der Geschichte der Medizin und der epidemischen Kranckheiten* (repr. Hildesheim, New York, 1971), 2: 280.

26. On this, see also Peter Linebaugh, "The Tyburn Riots against the Surgeons," in *Albion's Fatal Tree: Crime and Society in 18th Century England*, ed. D. Hay et al. (New York, 1976), pp. 65—111. The battle for the integrity of one's own corpse lasted into the early twentieth-century. According to David C. Humphrey, "Dissection and Discrimination: The social origins of Cadavers in America, 1760—1915," *Bulletin of the New York Academy of Medicine* 49 (1973): 819—827, more than half the

dissected corpses in America were still supplied by body snatchers; "the Blacks lacked the power to protect their dead" (p. 820), and: the "prudent line of stealing only the bodies of the poor" remained the rule until around 1915. On the conflict between the city and the university of Halle over the supplying of corpses, see W. Piechoki, "Zur Leichenversorgung der Halleschen Anatomie im 18. und 19. Jahrhundert," *Acta Historica Leopoldina* 2 (1965): 67–105.

27. Marie Christine Pouchelle, "La prise en charge de la mort: médecine, médecins et chirurgiens devant les problèmes liés à la mort à la fin du Moyen Age (XIIIe–XVe siècles)," *Archives Européenes de Sociologie* 17, 2 (1976): 274.

28. Foucault, *Discipline,* pp. 54 ff.

29. Giulia Calvi, *Storie di un Anno di peste: Comportamenti sociali e immaginario nella Firenze barocca* (Milan, 1984), trans. Dario Bocca and Bryant T. Rogan, Jr., as *Histories of a Plague Year* (Berkeley, 1989).

30. "The blood in the town of the 18th century . . . this natural element, as much present as waste, filth, excrement, dirt, water, and mingling with them. Nevertheless it avoids being defined as unclean," writes Arlette Farge in "Signe de vie, risque de mort: Essai sur le sang et la ville au XVIIIe siècle," *Urbi* 2 (1979).

31. Michael MacDonald, *Mystical Bedlam: Madness, Anxiety and Healing in Seventeenth-Century England* (Cambridge, 1981). This was an important book in connection with my work. It is the only attempt known to me to give a monographic description of a doctor's practice from the seventeenth century. As a student of Keith Thomas, MacDonald examined about 2000 case descriptions of an "astrological physician." These cases concern people from all social classes in a rural area who came to him for help. If this book had been available to me earlier, I would have dealt in my own work with the perspective that distinguishes MacDonald's understanding from my own. For MacDonald, many of the patients' complaints can be grasped objectively only as psychopathologies; I was very careful to avoid this sort of reductionism and classifying.

32. Robert Burton, *The Anatomy of Melancholy* (London, 1968), 1: 408. Cited here after MacDonald, *Mystical Bedlam,* p. 112.

33. MacDonald, *Mystical Bedlam,* pp. 170 ff.

34. Ludmilla Jordanova, "Guarding the Body Politic: Volney's Catechism of 1793," in *1789: Reading, Writing Revolution, Proceedings of the Essex Conference on the Sociology of Literature,* ed. Francis Barker et al. (Essex, 1982), pp. 12–21, describes one tool of health education, the health catechisms; C. F. Volney is the example cited here, p. 18.

35. Shapin, "Social Uses," p. 129. C. Lawrence, "The Nervous System and Society in the Scottish Enlightenment," in *Natural Order,* ed. S. Shapin and B. Barnes (London, 1979), pp. 19–40, examines the adoption of Albrecht von Haller's model in Scotland at the end of the eighteenth century and finds "that the model of the body was developed, evaluated and deployed in the context of

legitimation" (p. 35), and, "Sympathy is a transmission of sentiment (Hume) . . . with this theory Hume moved away from the 18th-century fascination with the individual's invariable characteristics . . . The principle of sympathy was taken over from Hume by Adam Smith . . . as the basis for his social theory . . . It is transmitted by the nervous system and depends on the latter's conditions . . . it is the great cement of human society" (pp. 31–32). "in France the major thinkers developed a vitalism stressing the *independent sensibility* of each organ; in Göttingen Albrecht von Haller (1752) elaborated his theory of *irritability* as an autonomous property of muscle. In each *'foreign'* case the model of the body was more decentralized than that developed in Edinburgh" (pp. 34 f.). On this, see Edwin Clarke, "The Neural Circulation: The Use of Analogy in Medicine," *Medical History* 22 (1978): 291–307; Karl Figlio, "Theories of perception and the physiology of mind in the late 18th century," *History of Science* 13 (1975): 177–212: from the end of the eighteenth century, the nervous system expressed an individual's overall constitution.

36. Norbert Elias, *Über den Prozeß der Zivilisation: Soziogenetische und psychogenetische Untersuchungen,* 2 vols. (Basel, 1939); trans. Edmund Jephcott, *The Civilizing Process,* 2 vols. (Oxford, 1978–82).

37. Ute Frevert, *Krankheit als politisches Problem 1770–1880: Soziale Unterschichten in Preußen zwischen medizinischer Polizei und staatlicher Sozialversicherung* (Göttingen, 1984), describes the contradictory, parallel, and countervailing factors of the "medicalizing process" in Germany: doctors fighting for more influence; a state that took a cautious wait-and-see attitude; a health-conscious bourgeoisie; reluctant urban "under classes" clinging to their accustomed behavior. With the exception of Lesky's study for Austria, the few essays dealing with Johan Peter Franck, and Stürzbecher's essays on medical institutional history, the German region has been hardly worked on; only Frevert offers in this work a first panoramic view of the medicalizing process in Germany.

38. Ludmilla Jordanova, "Earth Science and Environmental Medicine: The Synthesis of the Late Enlightenment," in *Images of the Earth: Essays in the History of the Environmental Sciences,* ed. J. Jordanova and R. Porter (Chalfont, 1979), p. 121.

39. On the "non-naturals" see L. J. Rather, "The Six Things Non-Natural: A Note on the Origins and Fate of a Doctrine and a Phrase," *Clio Medica* 3 (1968): 33–347, and P. H. Niebyl, "The Non-Naturals," *Bulletin of the History of Medicine* 45 (1971): 486–492.

40. W. Coleman, "Health and Hygiene in the Encyclopédie: A Medical Doctrine for the Bourgeoisie," *Journal of the History of Medicine and Allied Sciences* 29 (1974): 419. Roy Porter, "Lay Medical Knowledge in the Eighteenth Century: The Evidence of the Gentleman's Magazine," *Medical History* 29 (1985): 138–168, examines the literary expression of the new glorification of health in the *Gentleman's Magazine,* esp. pp. 145 ff.

41. On the medicalization of the concept of the family and familial discipline, which began at the end of the eighteenth century, see Jacques Donzelot, *Die Ordnung der Familie* (Frankfurt, 1980). On the importance of the doctor as an adviser drawn into the family in this process, see Angus McLaren, "Doctor in the House: Medicine and Private Morality in France, 1800—1850," *Feminist Studies* 2, 2/3 (1975): 39—54. Varying degrees of cleanliness became acknowledged demarcations in a new social stratification. For Victorian England, see Leonore Davidoff, "The Rationalization of Housework," in *Dependence and Exploitation in Work and Marriage* (London, 1976), ed. D. L. Barker and S. Allen, pp. 121—151. The cognitive order, which was projected onto the woman responsible for it through the obligation of maintaining cleanliness, became more important for social demarcation than the visible cleanliness; see Leonore Davidoff, "Class and Gender in Victorian England: The Diaries of Arthur J. Munby and Hannah Cullwick," *Feminist Studies* 5, 1 (1979): 87—141. The class-specific delay in the adoption of medical instructions concerning the feeding of infants by two successive generations is discussed by Luc Boltanski, *Prime education et morale de classe* (Paris, 1969). The lower-class baby was thus created several decades after its bourgeois counterpart.

42. Michel Foucault, *The History of Sexuality,* Vol. I, *An Introduction* (New York, 1980), p. 148: "The new procedures of power that were devised during the classical age and employed in the 19th century were what caused our societies to go from a symbolics of blood to an analytics of sexuality. Clearly, nothing was more on the side of the law, death, transgression, the symbolic, and sovereignty than blood; just as sexuality was on the side of the norm, knowledge, life, meaning, the disciplines, and regulation."

43. Mikhail Bakhtin, *Rabelais and his World* (Cambridge, Mass.: Harvard University Press, 1975), pp. 320 ff. Richard Sennett, *The Fall of Public Man* (New York, 1977), chap. 5, esp. pp. 164 ff., describes for the early nineteenth century the continuation of this retreat in the tight, gray costume of the man and the corseted silhouette of the woman. Philippe Perrot, *Les dessus et les dessous de la bourgeoisie* (Paris, 1981), allows us to follow the creation of underwear as a deeper level of this retreat (and thus also as a representational possibility).

44. Marc Bloch, *The Royal Touch: Sacred Monarchy and Scrofula in England and France* (London, 1973).

45. Robert Mandrou, *Introduction à la France moderne 1500—1640: Essai de psychologie historique,* 2nd ed. (Paris, 1974), pp. 76—81.

46. Alain Corbin, *Le miasme et la jonquille: l'odorat et l'imaginaire sociale: 18e et 19e siècle* (Paris, 1982); trans. *The Foul and the Fragrant: Odor and the French Social Imagination* (Cambridge, Mass.: Harvard University Press, 1986). On how body odor became offensive and thus a means of social exclusion, see pp. 167—188.

47. J. P. Goubert, "Die Medikalisierung der französischen Gesellschaft am Ende des Ancient Régime: die Bretagne als Beispiel," *Medizinhistorisches Journal* 17, 1/2

(1982): 108 ff., on the outbreak of a cultural conflict in northern France caused by the Enlightenment propaganda for a new body. Even today, in the midst of industrial society, this conflict occupies debates between public-health planners and practicing doctors. See Cecil Helman, " 'Feed a Cold, Starve a Fever'—Folk Models of Infection in an English suburban Community, and their relation to Medical treatment," *Culture, Medicine and Psychiatry* 2 (1978): 107–137. Paradoxically enough the latest biomedical systems planning allows taking the "popular belief" into service as a positive factor; see, for example, Arthur Kleinman, "The Meaning Context of Illness and Care: Reflections on a Central Theme in the Anthropology of Medicine," in *Sciences and Cultures,* ed. E. Mendelsohn and Y. Elkana (Dordrecht, 1981), pp. 161–176.

48. Loux and Peter, "Présentation." On similarities between the marginalization of peasants and women, see also Jean-Pierre Peter, "Les mots et les objects de la maladie: Remarques sur les épidémies et la médicine dans la société française de la fin du XVIIIe siècle," *Revue historique* 499 (1971): 34: "In these end products of a thousand-year slavery, the physiology itself, the humors, the deep texture of the body . . . have lost their specificity of being human." For parallel statements from the contemporary literature, see Jean-Pierre Peter, "Entre femmes et médecins: violence et singularités dans les discours du corps et sur le corps d'après les manuscrits médicaux de la fin du XVIIIe siècle," *Ethnologie française* 6, 3/4 (1976): 341–348.

49. Quoted from H. Mitchell, "Rationality and Control in French Eighteenth-Century Medical Views of the Peasantry," *Comparative Studies in Society and History* 21 (1979): 98.

50. For an overview of the polemic on the therapeutic value of bloodletting around 1800, the indispensible work is still Josef Bauer, *Geschichte der Aderlässe* (Munich, 1870; repr. Munich, 1966), esp. pp. 197 ff.

51. Urs Boschung, "Geburtshilfliche Lehrmodelle: Notizen zur Geschichte des Phantoms und der Hysteroplasmata," *Gesnerus* 38, 1/2 (1981): 59–68. Concerning the reform of midwifery in France, Jacques Gélis, "L'Enquête de 1786 sur les 'Sages-femmes du Royaume,' " *Annales de démographie historique* (1980): 299–314 and appendix, has worked up the results of the survey of the Societé Royale de Médecin from 1786 and made it quantitatively accessible for 26 departments. One consequence of the so-called reform of midwifery was the official devaluation of the old woman: the new "midwife . . . is the reflection of a totally different notion of midwifery . . . [but] it is highly unusual for women to place their trust in a young person" (p. 306). See also Jacques Gélis, "Sages-femmes et accoucheurs au XVIIe et XVIII siècles," *Annales E.S.C.* 32, 5 (1977): 927–957. In a very detailed regional study, Brigitte Menssen and Anna-Margareta Taube, "Hebammen und Hebammenwesen in Oldenburg in der zweiten Hälfte des 18. und zu Beginn des 19. Jahrhunderts," in *Regionalgeschichte: Probleme und Beispiele,* ed. E. Hinrichs and W. Norden (Hildesheim, 1980), pp. 165–224, come up with a similar result for

the Oldenburg region: according to a survey conducted in 1793 in the parishes, only 12 of the 143 women surveyed said they would be willing to be trained to continue their work (p. 200).

52. Mireille Laget, *Naissances: L'accouchement avant l'âge de la clinique* (Paris, 1982). With a deep understanding of the symbolism of the event, the author gives a lively and detailed description of the talking, interpreting, drinking, and goings-on in the birth room, which she calls a "chamber of initiation." In the distribution of tasks she sees a ritual, the embodiment of an imagination (pp. 134–137), in which the various birth attendants ("la femme, la bonne femme, la sage-femme, la bonne mère, la leveuse, la levandière, la ramasseuse, la reveleuse, la matrone") exercise their office as a charitable task. No similarly realistic study of the process, which the nineteenth century transformed in accordance with its own wishes, exists for other parts of Europe. Gernot Böhme, "Wissenschaftliches und lebensweltliches Wissen am Beispiel der Verwissenschaftlichung der Geburtshilfe," in *Wissenssoziologie,* ed. N. Stehr and V. Meja (Opladen, 1980) (Kölner Zeitschrift für Soziologie und Sozialpsychologie Heft 22), pp. 445–463, tries to construct sociological categories with which we can examine the medicalization of the birth process by contrasting "forms of knowledge." Claudia Pancino, "La comare levatrice: Crisi di un mestiere nel XVIII secolo," *Società e storia* 13 (1981): 593–638, compares the changes in the language of the Italian midwifery ordinances between 1596 and 1819 in regard to which personal qualities were expected of a midwife and what names were given to the objects used in confinement.

53. On this, see Ute Frevert, "Frauen und Ärzte im späten 18. und frühen 19. Jahrhundert: Zur Sozialgeschichte eines Gewaltverhältnisses," in *Frauen in der Geschichte II,* ed. A. Kuhn and J. Rüsen (Düsseldorf, 1982), pp. 177–210.

54. Quoted by Frevert, "Krankheit," p. 54.

55. See Kurt Reuber, *Die Ethik des heilenden Standes in Ordnungen des hessischen Medizinalwesens, 1564–1830* (Berlin, 1940), p. 81.

56. Krünitz, *Oeconomische Encyklopädie* (1788), 17:806.

57. Ludmilla Jordanova, "Policing Public Health in France, 1780–1815," in *Public Health: Proceedings of the 5th International Symposium on the Comparative History of Medicine East and West,* ed. T. Ogawa (Tokyo, 1981), pp. 12–32. Erwin H. Ackerknecht, "Hygiene in France 1815–1848," *Bulletin of the History of Medicine* 22, 2 (1948): 117–155, examines the further development of the notion of "santé" year by year from 1815 to 1848.

58. Stephen R. Kellert, "A Sociocultural Concept of Health and Illness," *The Journal of Medicine and Philosophy* 1, 3 (1976): 223, 224. See also Joseph Margolis, "The Concept of Disease," *The Journal of Medicine and Philosophy* 1, 3 (1976): 238–255. Medicine, he says, is "systematically concerned with rendering judgments that are at once informed by selected norms of human functioning and characterizable as findings of fact" (p. 238).

59. Jordanova, "Public Health," pp. 22 f. As religion once did, "so health transcends the immediate needs and interests of the individual in the service of the collectivity and the threatened sanctions are moral and at first glance not repressive" (p. 22).

60. Karl Figlio, "The Metaphor of Organization: An Historical Perspective on the Bio-medical Sciences of the Early Nineteenth Century," *History of Science* 14 (1976): 19, 25–28.

61. Ludmilla Jordanova, "Natural Facts: A Historical Perspective on Science and Sexuality," in *Nature, Culture, Gender,* ed. Carol MacCormack and Marilyn Strathern (Cambridge, 1980), pp. 64. ff.

62. Carolyn Merchant, *The Death of Nature: Women, Ecology and the Scientific Revolution* (New York, 1980).

63. Brian Easlea, *Witch-Hunting, Magic and the New Philosophy: An Introduction to Debates of the Scientific Revolution 1450–1750* (Brighton, 1980), chap. 5: "The Appropriation of Nature," pp. 196–252: "in the 17th century mechanical philosophers not merely all but banished life conceptually from the cosmos but minimized the role of women in procreation, declared nature incapable of giving rise to life, and proclaimed matter . . . inert and passive, possessing . . . the ideal female qualities" (p. 244).

64. The cultural shift of the demarcation between, on the one hand, the natural and the social sphere, and, on the other, man and woman, was the theme of anthropological theorizing in a symposium, introduced by Carol MacCormack, "Nature, culture, and gender: a critique," in *Nature, Culture, Gender,* ed. C. P. MacCormack and M. Strathern (Cambridge, 1980), pp. 1–24. On page 7 the discussion is focused on the question when and how the issue concerning the extent to which gender-difference is "natural" (and inevitably implies a natural hierarchy) became a problem in European history.

65. Jordanova, "Natural Facts," p. 46.

66. Gianna Pomata, "La storia delle donne: Una questione di confine," in B. Bongovanni et al., eds., *Il mondo contemporaneo,* vol. 10, pt. 2, *Gli strumenti della ricerca* (Florence, 1983), pp. 1435–1469, has reviewed and examined in great detail the recent anthropological debate on the naturalization of the concept "woman."

67. For a critique of the naturalized concept of family, see Michelle Z. Rosaldo, "The Use and Abuse of Anthropology: Reflections on Feminism and Cross-Cultural Understanding," *Signs* 5, 3 (1980): 389–417, and Rayna Rapp, Ellen Ross, Renate Bridenthal, "Examining Family History," *Feminist Studies* 5, 1 (1979): 174–200, who begin their critical survey of the concept of the family as used in scholarship by examining its alleged naturalness.

68. Annette B. Weiner, "Trobriand Kinship from Another View: The Reproductive Power of Women and Men," *Man* n.s. 14 (1979): 328–348, exposes the

biologism of Malinowski and demands an examination of the "cultural/symbolic meanings of reproduction, rather than the traditional biological grid" (p. 346). On the conceptualization of the anthropological debate over "reproduction," see F. Edholm, K. Young, and O. Harris, "Conceptualizing Women," *Critique of Anthropology* 3, 9/10 (1977): 103–130, and Olivia Harris and Kate Young, "Engendered structures: Some Problems in the Analysis of Reproduction," in *The Anthropology of Pre-capitalist Societies,* ed. J. Llobera and J. Kahn (London, 1981).

69. The implied presuppositions of the concepts of kinship and household as used in scholarship are analyzed by Olivia Harris, "Households as Natural Units," in *Of Marriage and the Market,* ed. Kate Young, Carol Wolkowitz, and Roslyn McCullagh (London, 1981), pp. 49–68. She shows how a naturalized, that is, biologized, understanding of kinship makes it impossible to understand the complex language of kinship as social relationship. On the anthropological debate, see also E. Leach, "Polyandry, Inheritance and the Definition of Marriage," in *Rethinking Anthropology,* ed. E. Leach (London, 1961), pp. 105–113, and Annette B. Weiner, "Plus précieux que l'or: relations et échanges des hommes et femmes dans les sociétés d'océanie," *Annales E.S.C.* 37, 2 (1982): 222–239.

70. Ellen Ross and Rayna Rapp, "Sex and Society: A Research Note from Social History and Anthropology," *Comparative Studies in Society and History* 32 (1981): 51–72, criticize the notion that there exists within sexuality a biological, universal "kernel": "In sexuality as in culture, as we peel off each layer (economics, politics, families, etc.), we may think that we are approaching the kernel, but we eventually discover that the whole is the only 'essence' there is" (p. 54).

71. Olivia Harris, "Households and Their Boundaries," *History Workshop* 13 (1982): 150.

72. Harris, "Households as Natural Units," p. 49.

73. Edward Shorter, *A History of Women's Bodies* (New York, 1982). See also the critique of Jordanova in *Times Literary Supplement* (April 29, 1983), p. 436.

74. Alexander Berg, *Der Krankheitskomplex der Kolik- und Gebärmutterleiden in der Volksmedizin und Medizingeschichte* (Berlin, 1935), allows us to trace in popular pharmacopoeias, miracle books, and consolation tracts the whole range of meanings ascribed since the Middle Ages to the pains located in a "mother/womb." Rudolf Kriss, *Das Gebärmuttervotiv: Ein Beitrag zur Volkskunde nebst einer Einleitung über Arten und Bedeutung der deutschen Opfergebräuche der Gegenwart* (Augsburg, 1929), examines the sculptural depiction of the "womb" and its use and experience in popular piety.

75. Shorter, *Women's Bodies,* p. 287.

76. Barbara Ehrenreich and Deirdre English, *For Her Own Good: 150 Years of Experts' Advice to Women* (New York, 1978).

77. Ludmilla Jordanova, "Conceptualising Power over Women," *Radical Science Journal* 12 (1982): 124–128 (review of Ehrenreich and English; see note 76).

78. Yvonne Knibiehler and Catherine Fouquet, *La femme et les Médecins* (Paris, 1983), p. 148.

79. Yvonne Knibiehler, "Les médecins et la 'nature féminine' au temps du Code Civil," *Annales E.S.C.* 31, 4 (1976): 824–845, examines the notions of the female body that were explicitly and implicitly formulated in French medical handbooks, encyclopedias, and in the medico-legal literature. See also Yvonne Knibiehler, "Les discours médicals sur la femme: constantes et ruptures," *Romantisme* 13–14 (1976), special vol.: "Mythes et représentations de la Femme au XIXe siècle," pp. 41–55, and Thérèse Moreau, *Le sang de L'Histoire: Michelet—l'histoire et l'idée de la femme au XIXe siècle* (Paris, 1982).

80. Jordanova, "Natural Facts."

81. The expression was used in this context by Claudia Honegger in a lecture she gave in the fall of 1983 at the Technische Universität in Berlin.

82. Jordanova, "Natural facts," p. 57.

83. Emily Martin, "Pregnancy, Labor and Body Image in the United States," *Social Science and Medicine* 19, 11 (1984): 1201–1206, examines the internalization of this body construct in the United States of today. The women interviewed speak of a separation in the body; they feel that their uterus is working independently of them. This perception corresponds to the medical view of the uterus as an "involuntary muscle" and to the birth practices in a modern clinic. See pp. 1204 f. on the women's helpless and failing efforts to speak in "their own voice."

84. Roy Porter, "The Physical environment," in *The Ferment of Knowledge: Studies in the Historiography of Eighteenth-Century Science,* ed. Roy Porter and G. S. Rousseau (Cambridge, 1980).

85. From obscure studies like that of William Denny Baskett, *Parts of the Body in the Later Germanic Dialects* (Chicago, 1920), we can see how many meanings and perceptions that were variously described and evaluated in the dialects and popular belief were lost in the wake of the triumph of a medicalized colloquial language. There are ten different groups for the hand or fist, each with regional variations; the palm, the paw, and the individual fingers are listed in the same way. For the *pudendum femininum,* see ibid., pp. 114–119, with twenty-two meaning classes; penis, pp. 106–111, from group I, "that which dangles," to seventeen additional groups that are clearly different from scrotum and testiculus.

86. Gianna Pomata, *Un tribunale dei malati: Il Protomedicato bolognese 1570–1770* (Bologna, 1983), pp. 71 ff.

87. Gianni Pomata, "Barbieri e comari," in *Medicina herbe e magia* (Bologna, 1982), pp. 162–183.

88. Margaret Pelling and Charles Webster, "Medical Practitioners," in *Health, Medicine and Mortality in the Sixteenth Century,* ed. Charles Webster (Cambridge, 1979), p. 166.

89. Gerald Holton, *Thematic Origins of Scientific Thought: Kepler to Einstein*

(Cambridge, Mass.: Harvard University Press, 1973), speaks of these as "themes."

90. Owsei Temkin, "The Historiography of Ideas in Medicine," *The Double Face of Janus and Other Essays in the History of Medicine* (Baltimore, 1977), p. 116.

91. H. E. Sigerist, "William Harvey's Stellung in der europäischen Geistesgeschichte," *Archiv für Kulturgeschichte* 19 (1929): 158–168.

92. Figlio, "Metaphor," pp. 29 f.

93. N. D. Jewson, "The Disappearance of the Sick-Man from Medical Cosmology," *Sociology* 10 (1976): 225–244.

94. Margaret Lock, "L'homme-machine et l'homme-microcosme: l'approche occidentale et l'approche japonaise des soins médicaux," *Annales E.S.C.* 35 (1980): 1119: "Medicine became . . . one component of a larger system of sociocultural and intellectual organization in the particular society in which it was practiced: it constituted a subsystem."

95. This English school of sociological history of science was very helpful to me in my attempt to create, through a critique of the sociogenesis of contemporary body notions, the intellectual space in which I could interpret the Eisenach body through the context of its own time. For an orientation about specific findings in regard to concepts that are closely related to body history, see the following four collections: G. Rousseau and R. Porter, eds., *The Ferment of Knowledge: Studies in the Historiography of Eighteenth-Century Science* (Cambridge, 1980); B. Barnes and Steven Shapin, eds., *Natural Order: Historical Studies of Scientific Culture* (Beverly Hills, London, 1979); P. Wright and A. Treacher, eds., *The Problem of Medical Knowledge* (Edinburgh, 1982); W. F. Bynum and R. Porter, eds. *William Hunter and the Eighteenth-Century Medical World* (Cambridge, 1985).

96. Shapin, "Social Uses," p. 135.

97. Anne Marcovich has examined this continuity in the writings of a doctor, "Concerning the Continuity between the Image of Society and the Image of the Human Body: An Examination of the Work of the English Physician J. C. Lettsom (1746–1815)," in *The Problem of Medical Knowledge,* ed. P. Wright and A. Treacher (Edinburgh, 1982), pp. 69–87.

98. The expression was coined by Ludwik Fleck, *Genesis and Development of a Scientific Fact,* ed. Th. Trenn and R. K. Merton, with a foreword by Th. Kuhn (Chicago, 1979); a translation of *Entstehung und Entwicklung einer wissenschaftlichen Tatsache: Einführung in die Lehre vom Denkstil und Denkkollektiv* (Basel, 1935). Fleck tries to create a theoretical framework to help us understand how in the thought style of a period the "bad blood" of syphilis is transformed into the scientific fact of syphilis that corresponded to the Wassermann test. Thomas Kuhn realized as early as 1962 "that Fleck anticipated many of my ideas." Thaddeus Trenn, "Ludwik Fleck's 'On the Question of the Foundations of Medical Knowledge,'" *The Journal of Medicine and Philosophy* 6 (1981): 237–256, has pointed out that Kuhn overlooks

the fact that he failed to take into consideration something essential: Fleck's reference to the social matrix, the epoch-specific stylistic elements to which he relates the leitmotifs of scientific thought or from which he deduces them.

99. The history of the word "reproduction" clearly shows the uniqueness of modern concept formation. In French the first use of this word in an economic context is ascribed to Raynal, 1758: "production nouvelle de ce qui a été consommé" (Roberts Dictionary refers to Littré, *Dictionaire de la langue Française*). Voltaire speaks of "les arbres, les plantes, les polypes et l'individu, tout semblable reproduit son semblable." In German the word arises in the late eighteenth century as a substantival prefix formation to the word "Produktion" (cf. H. Schulz and O. Basler, *Deutsches Fremdwörterbuch*, 1977, vol. 3, cols. 335–337), but the first mention of the "Reproduction bei Thieren" is listed for 1810. For English the OED lists the "reproduction" of destroyed limbs in salamanders as early as 1727, "The process of producing new individuals" (1785), and then explicitly in Buffon's Natural History: "without limiting our research to the generation of man . . . let us contemplate the general phenomenon of reproduction" (1791). "Reproductive apparatus" appears in 1836, "reproductive organs" in 1859, the first pairing with "sexus" in 1888: "ordinary nephridia . . . take on a sexual function at the reproductive season." The OED Supplement VIII (O-S) adds a 1782 quotation of John Wesley, founder of Methodism: "He [Buffon] substitutes for the plain word *Generation* a quaint word of his own, *Reproduction,* in order to level man not only with the beasts that perish, but with nettles or onions." In Spanish "reproducción" in connection with fertility is used only in cattle-breeding: a "reproductor" is a prize bull. Compare also "generation-reproduction" in W. F. Bynum, E. G. Browne, and R. Porter, eds., *Dictionary of the History of Science* (Princeton, 1981).

100. The eighteenth century had neither a word nor a concept for what we call "sexuality." "Sexual" is only rarely used. Goethe speaks of the sexuality of plants in 1812. Only around the turn of the century did the word and its compounds become common usage; first came the sexual diseases and selective breeding around 1860, then the sexual division of labor and the secondary sexual characteristics around 1890. From 1900 on, Freudian conceptualization shaped sexual love, the sexual life, the sexual instinct, and sexuality as such. (On this, see *Deutsches Fremdwörterbuch,* ed. H. Schulz and O. Basler, vol. 4, cols. 159–163). The word "Naturtrieb" (natural drive) or "Geschlechtstrieb" (sexual drive) was not used until the late eighteenth century. Prior to that the German word "Trieb" was known only in hunting, cattle-breeding, in plants, and with regard to humans only when a person did something of his own accord ("aus eigenem Trieb") (*Trübners Deutsches Wörterbuch*). Only with Freud did "Trieb" become a "Arbeitsanforderung, die dem Seelischen infolge seines Zusammenhanges mit dem Körperlichen auferlegt ist." The "drive" could thus acquire a "fate" or "destiny." Thus, "Triebschicksale . . . sind von vornherein . . . Beziehungsschicksale. Trieb läßt sich begreifen als Körperlichkeit,

die in Beziehung zu den Triebobjekten gebildet wird." A. Lorenzer in *Wissenschafts-theoretisches Lexikon,* ed. Edmund Braun and Hans Radermacher (Graz, Vienna, 1982), p. 610.

101. The images in which the processes of impregnation were conceived are of fundamental importance for the new understanding. The notion that all living things were created from the influence of sperm on a *primordium* (an egg), has been common knowledge of enlightened thinking since the late seventeenth century; see Elizabeth A. Gasking, *Investigations into Generation, 1651–1828* (Baltimore, 1967). And here Harvey's view came to prevail (*de generatione animalium,* 1651). Harvey made obsolete the doctrine, traced back to Aristotle, according to which the *vivipara* were created from the coagulation of *menstruum* and sperm, *ovipara* from eggs, and other "growths" from *scolex* (often already present in the environment). In the first half of the eighteenth century there was a learned consensus about the universality of sexual reproduction. Linné assigned sexual organs to all plants, and divided plants into those that displayed their reproductive organs and those that concealed them. Until around 1840 everyone, with the exception of a few *animalculists,* ascribed to spermatozoa at best a triggering or chemical function. See Jacques Roger, *Les sciences de la vie dans la pensée française du XVIIIème siècle: la generation des animaux de Descartes à l'Encyclopédie* (Paris, 1963).

102. Michel Foucault, *History of Sexuality,* vol. 3: *Le souci de soi.* (Paris, 1984), points out, esp. pp. 51–85, that at least in classical antiquity the attitude toward excess in regard to *tá aphrodisia* underwent a historical change. In the fourth century B.C. moderation was one precondition for the citizen to claim political influence. By Galen's time it was already seen primarily as an issue of "dietetics," as "culture de soi." Translated by R. Hurley, *The Care of the Self* (New York, 1986).

103. For twenty years Michel Foucault sought new approaches to the history of the reality-creating power of topics of discourse. His last work on the history of sexuality, interrupted after four volumes by his death, had the aim "of seeing how an 'experience' came to be constituted in modern Western societies, an experience that caused individuals to recognize themselves as subjects of a 'sexuality' . . . What I planned, therefore, was a history of the experience of sexuality, where experience is understood as the correlation between fields of knowledge, types of normativity, and forms of subjectivity in a particular culture." *History of Sexuality,* vol. 2 (New York, 1984), p. 4.

104. Uwe Pörksen, "Zur Terminologie der Psychoanalyse," *Deutsche Sprache* 3 (1973): 7–36.

105. See G. J. Barker-Benfield, *The Horrors of the Half-Known Life: Male Attitudes toward Women and Sexuality in Nineteenth-Century America* (New York, 1976).

106. Figlio, "Historiography," pp. 278, 279.

107. Jewson, "The Disappearance."

108. In 1943 Canguilhem wrote a doctoral dissertation on the history of the idea

of normality in the nineteenth century and its influence on pathology, in particular in Claude Bernard. It was published in 1966 with a postscript of equal length. Georges Canguilhem, *Das Normale und das Pathologische,* trans. M. Noll and R. Schubert (Munich, 1974), seems fundamental to me for the history of the norm by which an event becomes a "disease," and for the study of the body-possessing individual who evaluates himself against the norms. On the measuring of the French population, which began with large-scale surveys of the weight and height of recruits under Napoleon I, see W. Coleman, *Death Is a Social Disease: Public Health and Political Economy in Early Industrial France* (Madison, Wisc., 1982): "Death played the leading role in their drama, for the most striking feature of these empirical studies is the hygienists' effort to express collective social conditions in terms . . . of the seemingly irrefutable language of number" (pp. xx ff.). Creating the national body requires both measurements and norms.

109. H. Tristram Engelhardt, "The Concepts of Health and Disease," in *Evaluation and Explanation in the Biomedical Sciences,* ed. H. Tristram Engelhardt and S. F. Spicker (Dordrecht, Boston, 1975), p. 139.

110. Erna Lesky, *Die Zeugungs- und Vererbungslehren der Antike und ihr Nachwirken* (Wiesbaden, 1950), p. 3.

111. G. E. R. Lloyd, *Magic, Reason and Experience: Studies in the Origin and Development of Greek Science* (Cambridge, 1979). Lloyd outlines the task as follows: "a contribution to what might be thought . . . a very hoary problem, namely the relationship between what may be called *traditional* and *scientific* patterns of thought . . . between two distinct mentalities, the one *prelogical* or *prescientific,* and the other *logical* and *scientific*" (p. 1); and: "the aim of my inquiry is to analyse within Greek thought both the conditions under which confrontations between contrasting belief-systems were possible and the nature and limits of such confrontations as [they] occurred" (p. 2).

112. Lloyd, *Magic,* esp. pp. 226 ff. G. E. R. Lloyd, *Science, Folklore and Ideology: Studies in the Life Sciences in Ancient Greece* (Cambridge, 1983): "Ancient science is from the beginning strongly marked by the interplay between, on the one hand, the assimilation of popular assumptions, and, on the other, their critical analysis, exposure and rejection, and this continues to be a feature of science to the end of antiquity and beyond" (p. 1). It seems to me that this remained a problem right up to Eisenach in the early eighteenth century, except that in post-Medieval Europe, "popular assumptions" were themselves largely but still only partially shaped by the written tradition.

113. Lloyd, *Science,* chap. 2, pp. 58–111: "The Female Sex: Medical Treatment and Biological Theories in the Fifth and Fourth Centuries B.C."; words quoted, pp. 59, 61.

114. Pedro Lain Entralgo, *The Therapy of the Word in Classical Antiquity,* ed. L. J. Rather and J. N. Sharp, with an introduction by Walter J. Ong (New Haven, 1970).

115. Bruno Snell, *The Discovery of the Mind: The Greek Origins of European Thought,* trans. G. T. Rosenmeyer (Oxford, 1953). Chapter 1, "Homer's View of Man" (pp. 1–22): "The early Greeks did not . . . grasp the body as a unit." Homer referred only to the embodiment of feeling and of extremities, not to the body as a whole. This perception of the body, to which is opposed an I or a soul as a totality, was a later "invention." In the same way ambiguous feelings were not yet possible. It is said of Homer: though his hand was willing, his *thymos* was not. Only with Sappho did eros become bittersweet, the speaker could at the same time both want to and not want to.

116. Lain Entralgo, *Therapy,* p. xii. On the fundamental heterogeneity between an oral and a written way of being, see Walter J. Ong, *Orality and Literacy: The Technologizing of the Word* (London, New York, 1982). This book is also an excellent introduction to the literature and the state of the debate on this topic in Anglo-American scholarship.

117. Eric A. Havelock, *The Literate Revolution in Greece and its Cultural Consequences* (Princeton, 1982). This work compiles in one volume the author's most important essays on this topic. Havelock shows that the first generation of Athenian citizens who had learned writing in school were Plato's contemporaries. Ivan Illich in *Schule ins Museum: Phaidros und die Folgen* (Munich, 1984), discusses (chaps. 2, 3) the contrast between orality-based and literacy-based modes of thinking.

118. Richard B. Onians, *The Origins of European Thought about the Body, the Mind, the Soul, the World, Time and Fate* (Cambridge, 1951), pp. 73–76. The theme of this splendid book is not the origins of the body as described in Greek literature and science, but the fleeting shadows of those body percepts that persisted from early archaic Greece into the surviving sources. This book became important to me for two reasons: it taught me to search in the past of my own traditions for the very different body that so often surprised me in anthropological descriptions of other worlds; and Onians sharpened my awareness to look in the statements of my source for the possibility that the historical stream of unwritten tradition had dragged along remnants of this other body into the eighteenth century.

119. Yvonne Verdier, *Façons de dire, façons de faire: La laveuse, la couturière, la cuisinière* (Paris, 1979).

120. Sandra Ott, "Aristotle among the Basques: The 'Cheese-Analogy' of Conception," *Man* n.s. 14 (1979): 699–711.

121. Emmanuel Le Roy Ladurie, *Montaillou, village occitan de 1294–1324* (Paris, 1975), trans. B. Bray as *Montaillou* (New York, 1978), pp. 172 f.

122. See Michela Pereira, "Maternità e sensualità femminile in Ildegarda di Bingen: Proposte di lettura," *Quaderni storici* 44 (1980): 564–579, who presents a collection of passages from Hildegard's original Latin on feminine sensuality.

123. Hildegard von Bingen, *Heilkunde,* trans. into German with commentary by H. Schipperges (Salzburg, 1957): "When a woman has received the male seed, the

reception of this seed is so strong that it attracts all female monthly blood to itself, just as a cupping glass, which a bloodletter places onto the skin of a person, draws a lot of blood and pus (tabes). At first the semen is within the woman's organism like milk, then as curdled milk, and finally as solid matter; in like manner milk first curdles, whereupon cheese follows." Hildegard von Bingen, *Liber Causae et Curae,* ed. P. Kaiser (Leipzig, 1902), pp. 67 f.: "Unde, cum semen viri in locum suum cadit, tunc sanguis mulieris cum voluntate amoris illud suscepit, et in se introrsum trahit, sicut spiramen in se aliquid tollit. Et sic sanguis mulieris cum semine viri miscetur, et unus sanguis fit, ita quod etiam caro ejusdem mulieris de hoc permixto sanguine fovetur, crescit et augmentatur. Ac ideo sic est mulier una caro cum viro de viro . . . sed vis eternitatis, quae infantem de ventre matris sue educit, virum et feminam sic unam carnem facit."

124. Mikhail Bakhtin, *Rabelais and His World,* trans. H. Iswolsky (Cambridge, Mass.: MIT Press, 1968), pp. 3, 5, 12, 22, 471.

125. M.-Ch. Pouchelle, *Corps et chirurgie à l'Apogée du Moyen-Age* (Paris, 1983), p. 125, trans. R. Morris as *The Body and Surgery in the Middle Ages* (Oxford, 1990).

126. A good deal of material on the permanence of the link between specific peasant tools and the hands of men and women is given by Günter Wiegelmann, "Erste Ergebnisse der ADV-Umfragen zur alten bäuerlichen Arbeit, *Rheinische Vierteljahresblätter* 33 (1969): 208–262.

127. Françoise Loux, *Le Corps dans la société traditionelle (Pratiques et savoirs populaires),* introduction by Jean Cuisinier (Paris, 1979). In the illustrated catalog to this exhibit, the author emphasizes the "timeless" seeming "pratiques du corps" in work, celebration, and suffering.

128. Rudolf Allers, "Microcosmus: from Anaximandros to Paracelsus," *Traditio* 2 (1944): 319–407, attempts an ordering of the macro-microcosm-"types." L. Barkan, *Nature's Work of Art: The Human Body as Image of the World* (New Haven, 1975), examines the ideas about the body as a mirror of the cosmos and the political world, and as a microcosm of architecture and aesthetics, in order "to depict the history of an idea, to suggest poetic techniques which the idea may have produced . . . an attempt to define a habit of thought . . . in the history of ideas, and . . . in poetic imagery and metaphor" (pp. 6 f.).

129. Pouchelle, *Corps,* p. 158; a paraphrase of Mabille.

130. Ian MacLean, *The Renaissance Notion of Women: A Study in the Fortunes of Scholasticism and Medical Science in European Intellectual Life* (Cambridge, 1980).

131. For an introduction to the debate over the language of science, see Brian Vickers, "Analogy versus Identity: the rejection of occult symbolism, 1580–1680," in *Occult and scientific mentalities in the Renaissance,* ed. Brian Vickers (Cambridge, 1980), pp. 95–164. My insights into the sociogenesis of my own body—on which my understanding of the women of Eisenach is based—would not have been possible had I not learned from Professor Pörksen to see what he calls the mathema-

tization of colloquial language as a disguised metaphoric language. For an orientation on this topic, see Uwe Pörksen, "Zur Metaphorik naturwissenschaftlicher Sprache," *Neue Rundschau* 89 (1978): 63–82.

132. Pouchelle, *Corps,* p. 159.

133. Ibid., p. 224.

134. MacLean, *The Renaissance,* pp. 33 ff.

135. Hendrik van den Berg, *Things: Four Metabletic Reflections* (Pittsburgh, 1970). The author is not so much concerned with the history of the body as with the experience of its mutability, not with psychological history but with historical psychology. His work takes off from "discoveries," the historical moments in which the newness of the body was described as such before familiarity with the new had blotted out the experience. On the reception of this work, see Dreyer Kruger, ed., *The Changing Reality of Modern Man. Essays in honor of Jan Hendrik van den Berg* (Juta, Capetown, 1984). The following essays in this volume were of particular importance to me: Bernd Jager, "Body, House, City or the Intertwinings of Embodiment, Inhabitation and Civilization," pp. 51–61, and M. Jacobs, "Geometry, Spirituality and Architecture in their common historical development as related to the Origins of Neuroses," pp. 62–86.

136. C. R. S. Harris, *The Heart and the Vascular System in Ancient Greek Medicine from Alcmaeon to Galen* (Oxford, 1973), a critical source collection by a philologist. Harris argues that the Greeks, against the background of their world view, would not have known what to do with the concept of circulation.

137. Arnold Huttmann, "Eine imaginäre Krankheit: Der Polyp des Herzens." *Medizinhistorisches Journal* 18, 1/2 (1983): 43–51.

138. Patricia Berry, *Echo's Subtle Body: Contributions to an Archetypal Psychology* (Dallas, 1982).

139. Robert S. Sardello, "City as Metaphor: City as a Mystery," *Spring* (1982): 95–111.

140. Robert D. Romanyshyn, *Psychological Life: From Science to Metaphor* (Austin, 1982), esp. pp. 100–142.

141. Richard Zaner, *The Context of Self: A Phenomenological Inquiry Using Medicine as a Clue* (Athens, Ohio, 1981).

142. F. Hartmann and K. Hädke, "Der Bedeutungswandel des Begriffes Anthropologie im ärztlichen Schrifttum der Neuzeit," *Marburger Sitzungsberichte* 85 (1963): 39–99.

143. O. Schwarz, *Medizinische Anthropology* (1929), quoted in Ritter, *Historisches Wörterbuch der Philosophie,* vol. 1, col. 376.

144. Helmuth Plessner, *Philosophische Anthropologie: Lachen und Weinen. Das Lächeln. Anthropologie der Sinne* (Frankfurt, 1970), p. 232.

145. Viktor von Weizsäcker, "Krankengeschichte," in *Arzt und Kranker,* (Stuttgart, 1949), 1:120–148.

146. Herbert Plügge, *Der Mensch und sein Leib* (Tübingen, 1967).

147. Viktor von Weizsäcker, *Der Gestaltkreis: Theorie der Einheit von Wahrnehmen und Bewegen* (Stuttgart, 1940).

148. Armstrong, *Political Anatomy,* and Arney, *Medicine.*

149. Rudolf zur Lippe, *Naturbeherrschung am Menschen,* vol. 1: *Körpererfahrung als Entfaltung von Sinnen und Beziehungen in der Ära des italienischen Kaufmannskapitals;* vol. 2: *Geometrisierung des Menschen und Repräsentation des Privaten im französischen Absolutismus,* 2nd ed. (Frankfurt on the Main, 1981).

150. Ibid., vol. 2, pp. 215, 211.

151. Natalie F. Joffe has shown this with the example of menstrual blood, "The Vernacular of Menstruation," *Word: Journal of the Linguistic Circle of New York* 4, 3 (December 1948): 181–186.

152. Verdier, *Façons,* and Ruth Kriss-Rettenbeck, "Am Leitfaden des weiblichen Leibes," *Bayrische Blätter für Volkskunde* 8, 3 (1981): 163–182, reviewed this book and initiated a discussion of the methodology of body history that was very inspiring to me.

153. Anne Hollander, *Seeing through Clothes* (New York, 1975), pp. 237–311.

154. Ibid., pp. xii, 152–156.

155. Leo Steinberg, *The Sexuality of Christ in Renaissance Art and Modern Oblivion* (New York, 1983).

2. Johann Storch and Women's Complaints

1. Johann Storch (alias Pelargus), *Leitung und Vorsorge des Höchsten Gottes. Das ist: Dessen Lebenslauf, Schicksale, fatale Kranckheit und seeliger Abschied, nebst dem Sections - Schein; theils aus dessen Autographo aufgezeichnet . . . von Jacob Storchen* (Eisenach, 1752). This autobiography, published posthumously by his brother, is the basis for Friedrich Börner, *Nachrichten von den vornehmsten Lebensumständen und Schriften Jetztlebender berühmter Ärzte und Naturforscher in und um Deutschland,* vol. 1 (Wolfenbüttel, 1749); on Storch, see pp. 485–528. See also Johann Georg Meusel, *Lexikon der vom Jahr 1750 bis 1800 verstorbenen Teutschen Schriftsteller* (Leipzig, 1813), 13: 427–433, and A. Hirsch and E. Gurlt, *Biographisches Lexikon der hervorragenden Ärzte aller Zeiten und Völker* (Leipzig, 1887), 5: 553. J. Geyer-Kordesch considers Storch's life typical for a doctor of his time, "Medical Biographies of the 18th Century: Reflections on Medical Practice and Medical Education in Germany," in *Heilberufe und Kranke im 17. und 18. Jahrhundert,* ed. W. Eckart and J. Geyer-Kordesch (Münster, 1982), pp. 124–147.

2. Storch, *Leitung,* p. 7.

3. See Büchner, *Miscellanea Physico-Medico Mathematica* (1729), Mens. Decembr., p. 750, for Storch's discussion of arnica.

4. Börner, *Nachrichten,* p. 489.

5. See Wolfram Kaiser and Karl-H. Krosch, *Zur Geschichte der medizinischen Fakultät der Universität Halle im 18. Jahrhundert,* 2 vols. (Halle, 1964–1967).

6. On the history of the faculty of medicine in Jena in the eighteenth century, see E. Geist and B. von Hagen, *Geschichte der medizinischen Fakultät der Friedrich-Schiller Universität Jena* (Jena, 1958). On Wedel, see Heinrich Haeser, *Lehrbuch der Geschichte der Medizin und der epidemischen Krankheiten,* vol. 2 (repr. of 3rd. ed., 1875–1882; Hildesheim, New York, 1971), p. 380. On the teaching activity of Wedel and Slevogt, see *Proempticon inaugurale de privata dispensatione medicamentorum* (Stahl) (1704): Wedel lectured on *Institutiones medicinae, Materiam medicam, Politiam medicam,* and *Formularia et Semeiotica;* Slevogt lectured on *Botanica et anatomica.*

7. Lester S. King, "Some Basic Explanations of Disease: An Historian's Viewpoint," in *Evaluation and Explanation in the Biomedical Sciences,* ed. H. T. Engelhardt and S. F. Spicker (Dordrecht, 1975), pp. 11–27, examines the materialistic explanation of diabolical influences on the body in Friedrich Hoffmann, *Fundamenta Medicinae* (1695), pp. 17–20.

8. On Storch's studies in Jena, see Wolfram Kaiser, "Beiträge zur Geschichte des Thüringischen Gesundheitswesens im 17. und 18. Jahrhundert, VII. Der Schwarzburg-Rudolstädter Arzt Johannes Storch (1681–1751) und sein Beitrag zur Kinderheilkunde," *Rudolstädtische Heimath* 21, 3/4 (1975): 64 ff., and Börner, *Nachrichten,* p. 492. References to cases in Storch's *Diseases of Women* are given by volume, number of first page, and case number where applicable. See preceding section, Works by Johann Storch, for titles and descriptions of these volumes.

9. Storch, *Leitung,* p. 13.

10. Unlike Halle, Jena had anatomical training built into its curriculum. As the century progressed, knowledge of anatomy increasingly became the central credential of the ability of the *medicus;* for Prussia, see W. Artelt, *Medizinische Wissenschaft und ärztliche Praxis im alten Berlin* (Berlin, 1948), pp. 54 ff.; see also Puschmann, *Geschichte des medizinischen Unterrichtes* (Leipzig, 1889); for Halle, see Wolfram Kaiser, "Medizinisches Grundlagenstudium im frühen 18. Jahrhundert," *Zeitschrift für die gesamte innere Medizin und ihre Grenzgebiete* (East Germany) 34 (1979): 419–428.

11. Storch spent the money to get his doctorate in 1718.

12. On the *collegia medica,* see, for Prussia, Manfred Stürzbecher, "Zur Geschichte der brandenburgischen Medizinalgesetzgebung im 17. Jahrhundert," *Beiträge zur Berliner Medizingeschichte* (Berlin, 1966), pp. 1–66; for the Saxony region, see Wolfram Kaiser and Arina Völker, *Universität und Physikat in der Frühgeschichte des Amtsarztwesens* (Wissenschaftliche Beiträge der Martin Luther Universität Halle-Wittenberg 53) (1980), p. 6 f.

13. R. Jauernig, "Die Gestaltung des Gesundheitswesens durch Herzog Ernst den Frommen von Sachsen-Gotha vor 300 Jahren," *Wissenschaftliche Zeitschrift der Friedrich-Schiller-Universität Jena, Mathematisch-naturwissenschaftliche Reihe* 3 (1953–54): 213, 211.

14. See ibid., p. 218, on the licensing requirements in neighboring Gotha.

15. Storch, *Leitung,* pp. 17, 14.

16. Schuhmacher, *Merkwürdigkeiten der Stadt Eisenach und ihres Bezirkes* (Eisenach, 1777). Quoted in Karl Schrader, *Die fürstlich-sächsische Residenzstadt Eisenach 1672–1741* (Eisenach, 1929), p. 45.

17. Schrader, *Eisenach,* pp. 53–59.

18. On the population of Eisenach, see ibid., pp. 47–52, and Hermann Helmbold, *Geschichte der Stadt Eisenach mit einem volkskundlichen Anhang* (Eisenach, 1936), p. 81.

19. J. Limberg, *Das im Jahre 1708 lebende und schwebende Eisenach* (Eisenach, 1709). Quoted by Schrader, *Eisenach,* p. 84.

20. Schrader, *Eisenach,* pp. 95 ff. on the *Braugerechtigkeit* (privilege of brewing and selling beer), pp. 104 ff. on sheep-raising, pp. 106 ff. on trade.

21. Ibid., pp. 51 f.

22. On the office of the town *physicus,* see Manfred Stürzbecher, "The physici in German-speaking countries from the Middle-Ages to the Enlightenment," in *The Town and State Physician,* ed. A. V. Russell (Wolfenbüttel, 1981), pp. 123–129 (a collection of essays on the state of European scholarship). A description of the development and duties of the town *physicus* in Halle in Storch's time is given by W. Piechocki, "Das Hallesche Physikat im 18. Jahrhundert," *Wissenschaftliche Beiträge der Universität Halle* 36/20 (1977), 185–206. See ibid. for the oldest surviving letter of appointment for the town *physicus* from 1720. For a comparison, see W. Bubb, *Das Stadtarztamt zu Basel: Seine Entwicklungsgeschichte vom Jahre 1529 bis zur Gegenwart* (Zürich, 1942).

23. Kaiser and Völker, *Physikat,* p. 46.

24. Jauernig, "Die Gestaltung," p. 219.

25. According to Kaiser and Völker, *Physikat,* p. 59, in small residential towns the personal physician was often at the same time the municipal medical officer.

26. Storch, *Leitung,* p. 29.

27. Jean-Pierre Peter and Jacques Revel, "Le Corps: L'Homme malade et son histoire," in *Faire de l'histoire,* ed. J. Le Goff and P. Nora (Paris, 1974), 3: 177.

28. Roy Porter, "The Patient's View: Doing Medical History from Below," *Theory and Society* 14 (1985): 175–198, examines the mental concepts which have blocked the "view from below" in medical history: the history of medicine is seen as the history of treatment; the doctor is not examined as a social reference point. Porter demands that we "*defamiliarize* ourselves with the assumptions of modern physician focused history" (p. 176). This has been done in concrete studies in *Patients and Practitioners,* ed. Roy Porter (Cambridge, 1986).

29. Porter, "The patient's view," pp. 182 ff. On the problem of sources, see also his "Lay Medical Knowledge in the Eighteenth Century: The Evidence of the Gentleman's Magazine," *Medical History* 29 (1985): 139 ff.

30. Françoise Loux and Philippe Richard, *Sagesses du Corps: La santé et la maladie dans les proverbes regionaux français* (Paris, 1978). The transmission and reception of body-related proverbs often allows insight into an epoch-specific interpretation of popular conceptions.

31. Storch, *Medicinischer Jahrgang I* (Leipzig, 1724), preface.

32. A classic example of such a collection is Th. Bartholin, *Acta Medica et Philosophica Hafniensia* (Hafnia, 1673 ff.), a continuous collection of cases. At first glance they seem similar to the later German-language collections, since the collection also published cases submitted by local doctors. The fantastic is outdone by things even more fantastic. For example, Buxtehude, vol. 4 (1677), "De Mola Virginum," pp. 37 ff.: "novi juvenculam Buxtehudanam foeminam, quae cum partu simul paeperit monstrum capite leonino praeditum, sed demortuum" (I know of a young woman from Buxtehude, who together with her child gave birth to a monster endowed with the head of a lion, though dead). Then we hear more about the penis of the monkey, crickets, remedies, the weather, and the comet of 1671. On this genre, see K. Park and L. J. Daston, "Unnatural Conceptions: The Study of Monsters in Sixteenth- and Seventeenth-Century France and England," *Past and Present* 92 (1981): 20 ff.

33. Paul Slack, "Mirrors of health and treasures of poor men: the uses of the vernacular medical literature of Tudor England," in *Health, Medicine and Mortality in the Sixteenth Century,* ed. Charles Webster (Cambridge, 1979), pp. 237–273, examined the vernacular medical literature in sixteenth-century England. He says: "It is in their reflection of common assumptions and attitudes that the main value of the text-books and collections of remedies . . . lies . . . There were not two distinct medical cultures" (p. 273). On the persistence in popular medicine of traditions that had become scientifically anachronistic, see Janet Blackman, "Popular Theories of Generation: The Evolution of Aristotle's Works: The Study of an Anachronism," in *Health Care and Popular Medicine in Nineteenth Century England,* ed. John Woodward and David Richards (London, 1977), pp. 56–88.

34. Jutta Dornheim and W. Alber, "Ärztliche Fallberichte des 18. Jahrhunderts als volkskundliche Quelle," *Zeitschrift für Volkskunde* 78 (1982): 28–43. This essay is among the few attempts to give a critical account of the patients' understanding of the medical gaze and the medical activities on the basis of German-language descriptions of patients' behavior.

35. An evaluation of these German-language patient histories from the early eighteenth century as a new genre within German literature, or at least within medical literature, can be found in Johanna Geyer-Kordesch, "Fevers and other fundamentals: Dutch and German medical explanations c. 1680–1730," in *Theories of Fever from Antiquity to the Enlightenment,* ed. W. F. Bynum and V. Nutton (Medical History, suppl. 1) (London, 1981), pp. 99–120: "They have been almost completely but unjustly ignored by medical historians" (p. 101); "This turning to the

vernacular was certainly polemical. It meant that medical information—in the view of these physicians—should be discussed and judged by anyone capable of following the argument, and it put knowledge in the hands of patients as well as doctors" (p. 102). This is not true for Storch's writing, at least it was not the primary intention behind his writing and publishing. Storch wrote for younger colleagues. Next to Kaiser, "Beiträge," Geyer-Kordesch, pp. 109–110, is one of the few instances where Storch is mentioned in the modern literature. I should add that there is a monograph on Storch: Alfred Nußbaumer, *Die medizinische Berufsethik bei Johann Storch (1732) und seinen Zeitgenossen* (Zurich, 1965). This work describes Storch's commentary to his edition of the Prooemium (Introduction) of the *Praxis Stahliana* (Leipzig, 1728), and places it in the contemporary context.

36. Storch, *Medicinischer Jahrgang I* (Leipzig, 1724), preface: "I am writing for practitioners who are in training, who are eager for knowledge, and for those who take the welfare of their patients to heart but have a moderate income" (Storch, 3/1: 294).

37. Lentilius, Preface to Storch, *Dritter Medicinischer Jahrgang* (Leipzig, 1726).

38. The debates about the use of the vernacular in science and what contemporaries saw as its impact on scientific thinking itself was the topic of conversations with Professor Uwe Pörksen (Freiburg) during his visit to Pitzer College Claremont in the fall of 1984. See also Pörksen's essay "Der Übergang vom Gelehrtenlatein zur deutschen Wissenschaftssprache," *Zeitschrift für Literaturwissenschaft und Linguistik* 51–52 (1983): 227–258.

39. Gerhard Baader, "Die Entwicklung der medizinischen Fachsprache im hohen und späten Mittelalter," in *Fachprosaforschung,* ed. G. Keil and P. Assion (Berlin, 1974), pp. 88–123, shows that the medical terminology of classical Rome drew on the earthy vernacular and up to the eleventh century continually absorbed neo-Latin words. Only under the influence of Constantinus Africanus in Salerno around 1065 and a little later in Toledo, did a new specialized Latin emerge, to a large extent to translate Arabic texts into a Church-shaped Latin. The gap between the oral expression of a complaint and the medical verdict must have been particularly wide in the late Middle Ages. Audrey Eccles, "The Reading Public, the Medical Profession and the Use of English for Medical Books in the Sixteenth and Seventeenth Centuries," *Neuphilologische Mitteilungen* 75, 1 (1974): 143–156, shows that the attempt to frame medical knowledge in the vernacular began in England quite early and for the benefit of midwives. Eccles describes the controversy surrounding this attempt.

40. Michael Alberti, *Tractatus de Haemorrhoidibus . . . Pathologice et practice* (Halle, 1722), pp. 67, 95.

41. Storch, *Praxeos Casualis Medicae,* Tom. II (Eisenach, Leipzig, 1740), preface. This type of diary as a way of conducting personal research and continuing one's education differs from doctors' diaries that recorded the treatment of the patients so

that the bills could be made out. The greater expressiveness of Storch's cases is revealed if we compare them, for example, to a contemporary diary of an English pastor and doctor, who decided in 1729: "I think it is now proper to keep a more exact account of my patients, their diseases, the Remedies prescribed" (p. xliii). But the entries contain little more than the names of the patients, the dates of their visits, and the prescriptions, but no "complaints." For example, Dec. 18, 1729: "was called to Armin Middleton. Found her distracted, I fear with hott liquors. Ordered her a blister and some Bolus but with little hope of success, she being in a Fever of the spirits and exceedingly puffd up of late." V. S. Doe, *The Diary of James Clegg of Chapel-en-le-Frith 1708–1755* (Matlock: Derbyshire Rec. Soc., 1978), 1: 73.

42. See the complete list of his publications in the appendix in Storch, *Leitung und Vorsorge*, pp. 40–48.

43. Storch, *Weiberkrankheiten* 6, preface. How important his records were for Storch himself can be seen in the following small detail: the year the aged Storch moved to Gotha he finished his *Hebammenkatechismus* (Catechism of Midwifery) and recorded the birth of triplets as three boys. Ten years later, in the volume on nursing women (volume 7), he mentions the triplets once more, noting that the first time he had misidentified girls as boys: "this happened, however, ex lapsu memoriae, since I had forgotten the actual year and season of the year, and thus could not look it up in the diary" (p. 512).

44. Storch, *Leitung*, p. 23.

45. Storch, *Praxeos Casualis Medicae*, Tom. II, preface.

46. In many cases Storch lists under one number, as a single case covering many pages, the history of a woman's illness which dragged on for years. In other cases he refers at the end to entries about the same woman in another volume. Since his reference is the only way for me to discover the identity of a woman who was discussed in two or more cases, I tried in a variety of ways to understand the logic of his referencing. For example: of 307 cases in the volume on pregnancy (volume 3), only 10 give a reference to volume 6, on childbed and confinement; but in only 6 of the cases in volume 6 is there a reference back to the woman in her pregnant state. But of the 462 cases on confinement, 29 give references to the woman's pregnancy in volume 3. The more I tried to derive something important about the history of the body from my register and such calculations, the more I became convinced that I was on the wrong track. A number of considerations led me to assume that there are 60 to 80 women behind the 228 referenced cases, and thus we are talking about a total of about 1650 women.

47. In each volume I counted the cases in which Storch referred to additional entries on the same woman and compared these references with the total number of cases. The following picture emerges: the references are most numerous in volume 4 (on uterine growths and abortions); nearly a third of the "aborting women" were

treated by Storch in a different context. The references are least numerous in volume 2 (maids) and volume 8 (general diseases of the womb). Here we find one reference for every thirty cases; it is interesting to note that reference from other volumes to volume 2 are twice as numerous as references *from* volume 2. Storch sees one out of ten girls again, for example when they get pregnant. In the three other volumes the percentage for references lies between 11 and 17 percent.

48. The women in *Diseases of Women* are nameless. They are and remain for me anonymous. Case 24, vol. 3, is a gaunt, tall, slightly melancholy pregnant woman of choleric temperament, who sought Storch out before her third childbirth in 1722, and whose history is told up to the year 1726. Through a cross-reference we find her again on Nov. 11, 1726, as a thirty-eight-year-old, sanguine-choleric woman, with another reference to the now forty-year-old woman in the same volume 6 as case 176. This reference really gave me pause. I compiled complete registers of the referenced cases for all the volumes of case studies. For about 1816 numbered cases I have a total of 228 referenced cases (about 13 percent) But I did not succeed in determining the exact number of real women behind these 228 cases. If I subtract the referenced cases from the total, I arrive at 1588. Since Storch seems to have been a tenacious referencer, there may well have been that many women. On the other hand, I found a dozen cases which appeared in several volumes as different, cross-referenced entries about the same woman. These were the women I got to know better, and I examine some more closely in the section on pregnancies.

49. In this regard my source differs from doctors' account books or diaries that have been analyzed from a sociohistorical perspective. Jacques Gélis, "La pratique obstétricale dans la France moderne: Les carnets du chirurgien-accoucheur Pierre Robin (1770–1797)," *Annales de Bretagne* 68, 2 (1979): 191–208, uses the diary of the Rheims surgeon Robin to examine his obstetrical practice between 1770 and 1797, with precise statistics on the expansion of the practice, his income, the social position and geographic distribution of his patients, and the frequency with which the forceps was used. E. M. Sigsworth and P. Swan, "An Eighteenth-Century Surgeon and Apothecary: William Elmhirst (1721–23)," *Medical History* 26 (1982): 191–198, were able to derive from a billing and treatment book details such as the radius of the practice and the forms of payment ("imperfect dividing-line between cash-payment and barter," p. 195). Irvine Loudon, "The Nature of Provincial Medical Practice in Eighteenth-Century England," *Medical History* 29, 1 (1985): 1–35, examines the ledger of a young surgeon between 1757 and 1760 and compares his income with the data from other "medical ledgers." He thereby arrives at a new assessment of the relative prosperity of a small-town surgeon in the eighteenth century, and he broadens the meaning of "income" which included agricultural activities and the sale of brandy and medications. See also I. S. L. Loudon, "A Doctor's Cash Book: The Economy of General Practice in the 1830s," *Medical History* 27 (1983): 249–268. E. Hobhouse, ed., *The Diary of a West Country*

Physician (London, 1934), on the other hand, is based on a precise personal diary from 1718–1726, which recorded income, visits to relatives, and impressions about the Sunday sermon, as well as brief notices about patients and remedies. In addition there are details like this from July 16, 1719: "Mr. Bragge, Mr. Arthur Chichester, and I . . . went into the great Fish-Pond, a Swimming" (p. 70). These sources allow insights into doctors' lives and forms of practice of the past, which in Storch's case I could derive only through speculative inference.

50. The stories of the swallowed pins, which found different exits from the body, Storch found attested in authors such as Walter, Bierling, Stalpart, Hildanus, and Ettmüller, among others.

51. Licentiate Jacob Storch, brother of the diseased, in the Preface to Storch, *Leitung.*

3. Medical Practice in Eisenach

1. Jewson, "Medical Knowledge," pp. 375 ff. Ivan Waddington, like Jewson, a sociologist, uses categories that are actually unhistorical—such as "power" and "control"—and thus sees the break between the eighteenth and the nineteenth century as the transition from a "patronage system" to a "colleague control system": "The Development of Medical Ethics: A Sociological Analysis," *Medical History* 19 (1975): 36–51.

2. Frevert, *Krankheit,* pp. 57 f., mentions factors of this kind. Manfred Stürz-becher, "Über die medizinische Versorgung der Berliner Bevölkerung im 18. Jahrhundert," in his *Beiträge,* pp. 97 ff., examines doctors' fees on the basis of the Prussian medical tax of 1725 and emphasizes the inaccessibility of the doctor to the lower classes.

3. Goubert, "Medikalisierung," p. 95: the network of doctors was identical with the network of cities. On this, see also Jean-Pierre Goubert, "Résau médical et médicalisation en France à la fin du XVIII siècle," *Annales de Bretagne* 86, 2 (1979): 221–229. On the classification of healers at the end of the *ancien régime,* see his "L'art de guérir: Médecine savante et médecine populaire dans la France de 1790," *Annales E.S.C.* 32, 5 (1977): 908 ff. Goubert has long emphasized that to speak of the "medical wasteland" of the countryside in the eighteenth century refers only to the absence of academic *medici,* not the absence of all kinds of healers.

4. Pierre Dockès, *L'espace dans la pensée économique du XVIe au XVIIIe siècle* (Paris, 1969).

5. Pelling and Webster, "Practitioners," began their study of the world of healing in Norwich in the sixteenth century with the premise "to accept that the entire body of individuals identified as healers by the community should be regarded as eligible for inclusion in a study" (p. 232). From town charters they gathered every healer identifiable by name: the result was a previously unimaginable variety and multitude of healers, among them a large number of practicing women. For a city like

Norwich, with around 17,000 inhabitants, they came up with at least 73 healers resident in the town, and 170 resident in the surrounding region, which yields a ratio of one healer per 220/250 inhabitants (p. 225). Pomata, *Protomedico,* examined the world of healing in Catholic Bologna between the middle of the sixteenth to the eighteenth century through approximately forty court cases concerning healing, how it was defined and paid for. She explains (pp. 70 ff.) the surprising quantitative distribution of the healers and their stratification: "a medical density much greater than what we have come to expect" (p. 73).

6. We can assume that Storch recorded in his diary about one-third of all the women who in the course of one generation resided in Eisenach or the immediate vicinity. He cultivated a long and close relationship with about four dozen noble women and, I suspect though I cannot prove it, with three dozen bourgeois women from Eisenach and pastors' wives from the countryside. This relationship is reflected in frequent entries that stretch over many years. He records the entire social spectrum of humankind, which he treats in prison and all the way up the social scale to the Duchess (though he withheld the story of her ailments), but a disproportionately large part of the entries refers to a circle of a few dozen regular patients.

7. After an introductory volume, a Handbook for Midwives, Storch distributes his cases among seven volumes. By analyzing the social composition of the women patients in the individual volumes, we can get a rough estimate of the percentages of women in the various social classes who wanted something from the doctor in specific phases of their lives. In two-thirds of the cases we can learn something about the social stratum to which a patient belonged. Sometimes we can do this only on the basis of a conjecture based on the context; far more often through very concrete descriptions. Noblewomen are identified by social class, others by the position of father or husband, dependent working women by the circumstances of their employment, some through their connections with the local garrison, and some by geographic factors—as a woman from the country, a peasant woman, the wife of a schoolmaster in the country, or a "peasant person." Volume 2 (Maids) contains 220 cases: 183 cases are identifiable, 37 are not. The former break down roughly as follows: personally employed by the town or the court, 55; from the nobility and the upper-level administration, 36; from the bourgeoisie, 35; from the artisan class, 20; peasant folk, i.e. maidservants, 5; from the poor, 4; from the school or parish, 12. What is notable is the large number of unmarried women who got to the doctor through their employment. Maidservants, and the daughters of merchants and artisans give this part of the practice a bourgeois-urban-artisanal flavor. Volume 3 (Pregnant women) has 307 cases. Two-fifths cannot be determined (123), but 184 can be identified (about the same number as in volume 2). These include: from the artisan class, 59; soldiers' women, 25; unmarried women, 15; wives of pastors from the countryside, 7. About half of the women come from the urban-artisanal class and the lower class. Country women, 18 (7 of them primiparae); from the nobility,

36. What is notable is that patronage is unimportant and that urban patients are strongly represented. Unlike aristocratic women, who in the course of a pregnancy were treated repeatedly by Storch, a large portion of the urban pregnant women wanted advice or a prescription only once, or at most twice. Volume 6 (women in childbed) has 462 cases: unidentifiable, 124; identifiable, 338. This volume contains by far the largest number of cases. Storch has included here twice as many cases as in the volume on unmarried women. In comparison with the unmarried women, socially referred to in relation to their fathers or their employment, most women in this volume are identified by their husbands' social status. It is notable that the proportion of artisans, peasants, and poor doubles compared to the proportions in volume 3. Maidservants shrink in number (5 unmarried women in childbed; in addition, 22 wives of servants). The nobility is relatively underrepresented (20 women); their confinement appears for the most part in the context of their stories in volume 3. For the wives of peasants, soldiers, day-laborers, and artisans, confinement was the one occasion on which they called on the doctor. Volume 8 (general diseases of the womb) has 211 cases: unidentified, 84. Identifiable, 127, but of these 21 are known only as "widow." This leaves only 106 women with social classifications. The relative percentage of nobility (29 ladies) and of the bourgeois upper class grows (14 described as "burghers" or "respectable women"). Peasants and women from the urban artisan class dwindle in number.

8. The source permits some conjectures about the size and structure of the area from which Storch's patients came. Sigsworth, "Surgeon," pp. 192f., and Loudon, "Medical Practice," pp. 9 f., are able to give precise distances from other medical sources. Gélis, "La practique," pp. 198 ff., sees the connection of the surrounding suburbs and villages to the practice of the surgeon Robin along the roads. Storch, who uses more than four dozen terms for urban professions, distinguished in the countryside the nobility, the parish, the school, the peasant, the maidservant. Frequently he contents himself with the classification "women from the countryside." C. Karnoouh, "L'étranger, ou le faux inconnu: Essai sur la définition spatiale d'autrui dans un village lorrain," *Ethnologie Française* (1972): 107–122, has tried to reconstruct how rural space was experienced. He speaks of "shells." The doctor in Eisenach was probably among those people who were occasionally accessible, even if, geographically, they were part of the first or second "shell" of a peasant.

9. Just as Storch received news and patients in his house, he sometime traveled for days to get to individual patients in the countryside, particularly noble patients. Scattered throughout the cases are hints about night travel on horseback, incidental visits with peasants during a visit to a manor house, a stay of several days on one estate while awaiting a birth. Richard Kay noted in his diary the long distances in his rural practice with all the attendant imponderables; see W. Brockbank and M. L. Kay, "Extracts from the Diary of Richard Kay of Baldingstone, Surgeon (1737– 50)," *Medical History* 3 (1959): 58–68.

10. Günter Risse, "Doctor William Cullen, Physician, Edinburgh: A Consultation Practice in the Eighteenth Century," *Bull. History of Medicine* 48 (1974): 338–351, examines, through a collection of about 3000 letters from the estate of a leading member of the medical establishment in Edinburgh, the central importance of the letter in a medical practice, though in the second half of the eighteenth century.

11. Walter Hoffmann, *Schmerz, Pein und Weh: Studien zur Wortgeographie deutschmundartlicher Krankheitsnamen* (Gießen, 1956), offers insight into the regional differentiations of the terms for pain, see pp. 16– 29.

12. In late medieval iconography, the urine flask is an identifying attribute of the university educated doctor, and the flat basin, mostly of hammered brass, the sign of the barber. In the sixteenth and seventeenth centuries the doctor began to make specific observations about changes in the quality of the blood during the procedure, and the "bleeding cups" became medical attributes in art. See Friedrich Lenhardt, "Zur Ikonographie der Blutschau," *Medizinhistorisches Journal* 17, 1/2 (1982): 63–77.

13. Richard Töllner, "Die Umbewertung des Schmerzes im 17. Jahrhundert in ihren Voraussetzungen und Folgen," *Medizinhistorisches Journal* 6 (1971): 36–44.

14. Dietlinde Goltz, "Krankheit und Sprache," *Sudhoffs Archiv* 53 (1969): 225–269, examines the ways in which patients expressed themselves in the consulting hours of a German doctor after the war. In the words of the male and female workers she finds ways of expression and images that differ from the "findings" of the doctor, but which in many ways seem timeless to her. A similar asynchronicity of the way in which ailments were conceived was found by Helman, "Feed a Cold," in a practice in a suburb of London. The medical profession's inability to listen, which had begun with the health catechisms mentioned in Chapter 1, reached a highpoint in this medical devaluation of the patient's complaint as the latter became a "symptom." During the course of the 1960s the medical profession became convinced that this gap in medical practice was counterproductive. The result has been described by Armstrong, *Political Economy*, as the medical creation of the patient as the subject of clinical interaction. In 1960 the "ideal patient" took his body or his soul to the doctor in expectation of a finding. Today doctor and patient work together in trying to create the case. The patient as object and the patient created as a conscious subject through medical efforts have nothing in common with the people who sought help in the eighteenth century. Both perspectives can lead the historian to alienate the patient of the past, more subtly and thoroughly if the patient is approached from the second perspective.

15. See, for example, B. Hieronymus Braunschweig, *Haußarztney-Büchlein: Gute gebreuchliche und bewerte Arztneyen zu allerhand Gebrechen des gantzen Leibes, außwending und innwendig, von dem Haupt bis auff die Füß* . . . (Leipzig, 1591). The prescriptions follow the pains: from the "aches and pains of the head" to the "flux in the feet."

4. The Perception of the Body

1. Jerome J. Bylebyl, "The Medical Side of Harvey's Discovery: The Normal and the Abnormal," in *William Harvey and His Age: The Professional and Social Context of the Discovery of the Circulation*, ed. J. J. Bylebyl (Baltimore, 1979), pp. 28–102. For me this was central to understanding the break between what is dead and what is alive. Bylebyl shows why Harvey himself could not have been influenced in his practice by the insights he derived from anatomy, and above all why autopsy findings revealed nothing conclusive about the "normal" condition inside the body, why thus also a man like Storch was immune to the concept of circulation. "There would have been no way for him [Harvey] to tell for certain what goes on in the undisturbed depths of the body" (p. 89), for no matter what became visible through anatomy, "a given observation is misleading or inconclusive because it represents a postmortem change in the body, not a true reflection of the normal situation" (p. 32).

2. On the gap between anatomy and pathology, see Temkin, "Scientific Approach," pp. 452 ff.

3. Not until the mid-eighteenth century did Haller think to interpret a postmortem examination from the perspective of an *anatomia animata*, "to determine the relationship between the living body and the findings of the postmortem examination," P. Diepgen, G. G. Gruber, and H. Schadewaldt, "Der Krankheitsbegriff, seine Geschichte und Problematik," in *Altmanns Handbuch der Allgemeinen Pathologie* (Berlin, 1969), 1: 2. Owsei Temkin, "The Role of Surgery in the Rise of Modern Medical Thought," in his *The Double Face of Janus*, pp. 487 ff., points out that anatomy as a science was institutionally separated from the cutting of the surgeons. Scholars very often had no experience with the sick, surgeons did not engage in research.

4. Discussed by Lippe; see Chapter 1, notes 149 f.

5. The "false paths" of the milk, by which it appeared as an excretion in places other than the breasts, were discussed in learned medicine right up to the end of the eighteenth century; see, for example, B. Bose, *Programmata de lacte aberrante* (Leipzig, 1772); Heymanns, *Diss. de aberratione lactis et morbis ex ea pendentibus* (1781).

6. See Zedler, *Universallexicon*, vol. 20 (1739), cols. 902 ff. The entry "Characteristics of diseases" compiled the medical casuistry of the first half of the eighteenth century. What the doctrines of signs have in common is that external signs open a way to an understanding of the inside. On the deduction of causes from external signs according to the Stahlian school, see Johannes Juncker, *Conspectus medicinae theoretico-practicae, Tabulis CXXXVII omnes morbos Methodo Stahliana tractandos* (Halle, 1724), plate I.I: Morbis in genere, p. 2: Signa.

7. "because she had had heard how fluids of this kind were caused if the blood was not copiously evacuated" (8:157, case 36).

8. Storch, *Theoretische und Practische Abhandlung von Kranckheiten, denen vornehmlich Soldaten unterworfen seyn, nach sicherer und vieljähriger Erfahrung bekräftigter Methode entworfen* (Eisenach, Naumburg, 1735).

9. Only if we understand the gender-ambiguity of heart, breast, and milk can we interpret a whole host of topoi in late medieval piety. See Leon Dewez and Albert Iterson, "La lactation de Saint Bernard: Légende et iconographie," *Citeaux in de Nederlanden* (1956), 7: 165–189; Paule-V. Bétérous, "A propos d'une des légendes mariales les plus répandues: Le 'lait de la Vierge,' " *Bulletin de l'association Guillaume Bude* 4 (1975): 403–411, and C. W. Bynum, *Jesus as Mother: Studies in the Spirituality of the High Middle Ages* (Los Angeles, 1982).

10. On the periodicity of the "white flow" of women, cf. Johannes Juncker, *Conspectus Medicinae* (Halle, 1724), pp. 752 ff.

11. See, for example, also Zedler, *Universallexicon,* vol. 15 (1737), col. 1643, "Krätze" (scabies): "Finally, scabies is also orderly, or *periodic* . . . we see this . . . in that the itching rash observes a certain timing . . . the girls . . . are afflicted by scabies . . . at the same time as their cleansing . . . should flow."

12. Max Höfler, *Deutsches Krankheitsnamenbuch* (Munich, 1899), p. 4, derives the German term "golden vein" for the piles from the fact that a person saved the doctor's fees if he bled from them. On the "golden vein," see also Zedler, *Universallexicon,* vol. 11 (1735), and "Haemorrhoides," vol. 12 (1735), col. 123: "this discharge seems to be somewhat equal to the monthly cleansing of women." The flow sometimes kept an orderly rhythm, "like among women."

13. See, for example, Georg Ernst Stahl, *De Motus Haemorrhoidalis et Fluxus Haemorrhoidium Diversitate* . . . (Paris, 1730); Michael Alberti, *Diss. de haemorrhoidibus secundam et praeter naturam* (Erfurt, 1702); Hamberger, *Diss. Doctrina de haemorrhoidibus* (Jena, 1745).

14. Michael Alberti, *Tractatus de Haemorrhoidibus . . . Pathologice et Practice* (Halle, 1722), part 2: De Haemorrhoidum et Mensium Consensus, p. 3.

15. Höfler, *Krankheitsnamen,* p. 4.

16. Wilhelm Gottfried Ploucquet, *Literatura Medica digesta, sive Repertorium Medicinae practicae, chirurgicae atque rei obstetricae* (Tübingen, 1809), 4 bks. in 2 vols. See the literature cited under the entries: *Menstrua Marium* (3: 10), and *Haemorrhagia ex pene* (2: 255).

17. Martin Schurig, *Haematologia Historico medica, hoc est sanguinis consideratio physico-medico-curiosa* . . . (Dresden, 1744), relates, on p. 275, the case of a servant, who since his childhood "experienced regular bleeding in the thumb of his left hand. From the right side near the finger at the time of the full moon (it was rare indeed for this flux to appear the day before or after the full moon) and without any headache . . . the blood suddenly sprang forth from various rivulets"; see also menses in men, ibid., p. 302, Menses in viris, and also Martin Schurig, *Parthenologia Historico-Medica, hoc est virginitatis consideratio, qua ad eam pertinentes pu-*

bertas, menstruatio . . . (Dresden, 1729), Caput IV, De Menstruatione in Maribus et Brutis, pp. 118–127.

18. Schurig, *Haematologia,* p. 303.

19. On the "milk" of men, see also Ploucquet, *Literatura,* article "Lac" (2: 477), and Zedler, *Universallexicon,* vol. 21 (1739), where article "Milch," col. 145: mentions "milk" in men and boys.

20. On the "invention" of menopause by nineteenth-century medicine (for France), see Joel Wilbush, "La Menespausie: the Birth of a Syndrome," *Maturitas* 1 (1979): 145–151.

21. Patricia Crawford, "Attitudes to Menstruation in Seventeenth-Century England," *Past and Present* 91 (1981): esp. 72, documents the change in the conception of menstruation during the seventeenth century. According to Crawford, it was in this period that menstruation as a sign indicating "a less perfect being" began to be reinterpreted as the mark of a being "designed for procreative and domestic activity." She stresses that female inferiority was emphasized in both interpretations. "Menstruation served as a reminder of the axiom that women had inferior bodies" (p. 73). Menstruation appeared with an opposite meaning both in popular therapy and in the context of humoral pathology; here woman became the prototype of the self-healing body. On this, see Gianna Pomata, "Menstruation and Bloodletting in XVII Century Bologna: The Symbolic Link," unpublished manuscript (Bologna, 1984), esp. pp. 17 ff. Only in the nineteenth century did menstruation emerge as a "problem" and as a disposition to pathologies; see Elaine and English Showalter, "Victorian Women and Menstruation," *Victorian Studies* 14, 1 (September 1970): 83–89. How the monthly blood has created a female type in the medical theories since antiquity has been traced by E. Fischer-Homberger, "Krankheit Frau—aus der Geschichte der Menstruation," in E. Fischer-Homberger, *Krankheit Frau* (Bern, 1979), pp. 49– 84.

22. See Chapter 1, note 130.

23. In the interpretation of classical and medieval texts, which still influenced the thought of the Baroque to a large degree, this ambiguous reciprocity has usually been overlooked. The history of the interpretation of the classical trope of the *mas occasionatus,* of woman as a failed man, is one example. A. Mitterer, "Mas occasionatus oder zwei Methoden der Thomas-Deutung," *Zeitschrift für katholische Theologie* 72 (1950): 80–103, discusses the scholastic sources. Madeleine Jeay, "Albert le Grand entre Aristotle et Freud: La femme est-elle un acte manqué?," in *Le Racisme: Mythes et sciences. Pour Leon Poliakov,* ed. Maurice Olender (Paris, 1981), pp. 1–13, tries to indicate this complementary ambiguity through a structuralist textual commentary on Albert's *De animalibus.*

24. On the embodiment of "right" and "left" in and through man and woman, with special consideration of theories of procreation, see Lesky, *"Die Zeugungs- und Vererbungslehren,* pp. 1263–1294. Storch quite often discusses the male and female

connotation of right and left in relation to breast, testicles, and sides of the uterus; see, for example 7:74 or 3:155. The analogy is carried through into details: for example, in Storch (2:316) a man is scared by the first bleeding of the golden vein, whereupon "it immediately became stopped up and regurgitated toward the breast and head."

25. Pomata, "Menstruation," pp. 12 ff., tries to show that bloodletting was an artificial continuation of the body's self-evacuation.

26. On the tradition, see Wolfgang Gerlach, "Das Problem des 'weiblichen Samens' in der antiken und mittelalterlichen Medizin," *Sudhoffs Archiv* 30, 4/5 (1938): 177–193.

27. On the gender-unspecific anatomical nomenclature that still existed in the eighteenth century, see the articles of Zedler, *Universallexicon*, "Gebärmutter," "Gebär-Vater," "Geburtsglieder" (male/female), and the analogies in the articles "Mutter" and "Magen"; see also Höfler, *Krankheitsnamen*, on "Manns-Mutter" and "Bär-Vater." According to G. E. Stahl, *Ausführliche Abhandlung von den Zufällen und Kranckheiten des Frauen-Zimmers*, 2nd ed. (Leipzig, 1735), pp. 110, 132 ff., men also had a kind of "womb disorder," the "Malum Hypochondriaticum," which was located in the stomach region, below the "pit of the heart," and, when a running flow had "become stopped up" (p. 36), it caused the same anxieties. The similarity is attested down to votive offerings: see Erwin Richer, "Einwirkung medico-astrologischen Volksdenkens auf Entstehung und Formung des Bärmutterkröten-opfers der Männer im geistlichen Heilbrauch," in *Volksmedizin*, ed. E. Grabner (Darmstadt, 1967), pp. 372–398.

28. Zaner, *The Context*, pp. 38 ff., tries to give a philosophical-historical introduction to this topic. In a commentary on the texts of Sartre, Zaner also points to a very specific contemporary difficulty in dealing today with the body as the place where being is embodied: *la nausée*, the disgust we feel when we notice that someone else perceives this body, which we think we *have*, as an object. According to Sartre, we are then horrified by the other person, who remains always at our heels. While I was working on this commentary to Storch, I had to wrestle with my own feelings: horror and shame, curiosity and consternation. Only by engaging such feelings was I able to interpret the embarrassed giggling that overcame me when I first read many passages in the text as a sign that I lacked the inner freedom for historical studies of this kind.

29. Roy Ellen, "Anatomical Classification and the Semiotics of the Body," in *The Anthropology of the Body*, ed. John Blacking (New York, 1977), pp. 342–373, attempts a classification of the ethnological studies dealing with body classification, with many examples for the metaphorical usage of the environment, tools, grain, the house, or furnishings in naming the body.

30. Mario Vegetti and Paola Manuli, *Cuore, sangue e cervello: biologia e antropologia nel pensiero antico* (Milan, 1977), have related early Greek body images, the meaning

of heart or brain, to corresponding social images; see also M. Vegetti, "Metafora politica e immagine del corpo nella medicina greca," *Tra Edipo e Euclide: Forme del sapere antico* (Milan, 1983).

31. That the skin was understood as a potential issue can be seen, for example, in the use of the word *transsudare*. In the literature it was used for the sweating out of blood, pus, and other matter; see Schurig, *Haematologia,* pp. 269 ff., and Johannes Juncker, *Conspectus Therapiae generalis cum notis in materiam medicam* (Halle, Magdeburg, 1725), pp. 83 ff. The skin was seen therapeutically as a place where the body could be induced to open: "sweating . . . is an evacuation through the porous periphery of the body, by means of which pungent, superfluous, or even noxious humors are expelled."

32. J. S. L. Loudon, "Leg Ulcers in the Eighteenth and Early Nineteenth Century," *J. R. Coll. Gen. Practitioners,* part 1, 31 (1981): 263, and part 2, 32 (1982): 301–309, points out, first, that ulcerated legs, which often remained that way for years, were very common in the seventeenth and eighteenth centuries, and, second, that their interpretation and treatment changed substantially as humoral pathology faded away. Until the eighteenth century leg ulcers were routinely seen as an outlet for pungent fluids from the body and accordingly were kept open—even those of sailors and soldiers, who had them often. These notions survived the emergence of the "closed" body. We have a testimony from mid-nineteenth-century London, where a smith reported on his wife's salve: "it has been the saving of my wife . . . this salve keeps the wound open and this wound does act as a safety-valve to her heart; were it allowed to close she would die of heart disease . . . it draws off the bad humour." John Thompson, *Street Life in London* (New York, London, 1969), p. 35.

33. Bakhtin; see Chapter 1 in this book.

34. Höfler, *Krankheitsnamen,* pp. 159–164, distinguished ten main groups of the flux: among them catarrh, wound secretion, intestinal or bowel flux, apoplectic fit, rheumatism, fontanel, menses, and lochia. "Flux" included "every ailment whose causes the people cannot fathom," "sudden and swift illnesses in general." The term was used until the end of the eighteenth century, by humoral pathologists as well as in popular medicine.

35. Ernst Bargheer, *Eingeweide: Lebens- und Seelenkräfte des Leibesinneren im deutschen Glauben und Brauch* (Berlin, 1931), p. 377. Drawing on vernacular language, customs, and proverbs, the author compiled examples of ideas about the inside body, such as: "if the rash actually appears, the 'sour blood' has settled" (Styria).

36. Zedler, *Universallexicon,* vol. 15 (1737), "Krätze" (scabies), cols. 1646, 1647: "Scabies is an ailment that has no danger, unless it is driven back and into the body . . . For the fact that the matter when driven back and into a nobler part of the body can give rise to dangerous, serious, and deadly effects, can be seen from the deadly shortness of breath caused by it." With many diseases scabies was actually

hoped for, "since the matter which has caused such very dangerous effects in the nobler parts will settle in the ignoble parts. This is why, when ill, one must not drive away the scabies without cause, but must keep it open for a while."

37. Michael Alberti devoted an entire chapter of his *Therapia* to "de expulsione morborum repulsorum" (quoted from Storch, 2: 455).

38. "Fontanel," derived from the Latin "fons," is the term for the artificial wound as well as for the flux that is kept flowing by a seton or some other obstacle (see Höfler, *Krankheitsnamen,* p. 160); cf. also W. Schönfeld, "Die Haut als Ausgang der Behandlung: Verhütung und Erkennung fernörtlicher Leiden," *Sudhoffs Archiv* 36 (1943): 43–89, and Robin Fåhraeus, "Grundlegende Fakten über die Pathologie der Körpersäfte und ihre Relikte in Sprache und Volksmedizin," in *Volksmedizin,* ed. E. Grabner (Darmstadt, 1967), p. 458, on the fontanel as an issue for the phlegm in the tradition of humoral pathology.

39. Loudon, "Leg Ulcers," pp. 265 ff., examined three eighteenth-century texts in which swellings on the calves were classified, along with instructions on which ones should be kept open. See also Loudon, "The Nature," p. 13.

40. We find the same image in a common pharmacopoeia from the end of the seventeenth century: "The synovial fluid should not be stopped too abruptly. For if it cannot get out, it runs back inside and burns and gums up the limbs and putrifies the blood vessels. It also runs back and forth in the body and causes the sick a good deal of pain. Therefore, if it bursts out vigorously, do not stop it suddenly, but at first apply only a thin plaster, so that it can leak through the plaster." Oswald Gabelkover, *Artzney-Buch, Darinnen fast für alle des Menschlichen Leibes Anliegen und Gebrechen, außerlesene und bewehrte Artzneyen . . .* 5th ed. (Frankfurt am Main, 1680), p. 389.

41. Magnus Schmid, "Zum Phänomen der Leiblichkeit in der Antike: Dargestellt an der 'Facies Hippocratica.'" *Sudhoffs Archiv Beihefte* 7 (1966): 168–177. Karl Sudhoff, "Eine kleine deutsche Todesprognostik," *Archiv für Geschichte der Medizin* 5 (1911), and "Abermal eine deutsche Lebens- und Todesprognostik," ibid. 6 (1911), cites German material on the "facies." On the history of the word *Körper* (body) in German, which could describe both *lip* and *licham,* the living and the dead, see Helene Adolf's study, which is not limited to Middle High German: *Wortgeschichtliche Studien zum Leib/Seele-Problem* (Vienna, 1937).

42. To the Hippocratic signs Storch added some others derived from Halle or from the specific sense of modesty in the early eighteenth century: the fatal sign that women in childbed wanted to expose themselves: "they act very freely toward the *medicus* and set all modesty aside, they show the purpura without being asked to . . . and do not care whether they have soiled sheets under them . . . They have more pleasure in being seen exposed . . . And one can surely take this as a sign of impending mortification" (6:50).

43. Storch took the adjectives for describing the bad blood from humoral

pathology, e.g. "black" blood (= melancholic, thick blood), or yellowish-white, phlegmatic blood; on this, see Höfler, *Krankheitsnamen,* p. 60 (Blut). But Storch never explicitly referred to the doctrine of the four humors. It did not systematically determine his choice of terms; he merely dragged it along as an outmoded tradition.

44. Höfler, *Krankheitsnamen,* p. 61. Storch frequently used the word "Reliquien" [remains, relics] for clotted blood, the blood remaining behind, inside. See Zedler, *Universallexicon,* vol. 31, col. 526: "Reliquien . . . among physicians . . . [are] the crudities, phlegm, and bad moistures that collect in a person's stomach." With Storch the "Reliquien" remained in the womb.

45. In a contemporary work on self-treatment, anger was described as a feeling in which the soul felt "hatred and dislike" toward something it tried to drive out with all its might, something it "strove to get rid of." Anger therefore drove the blood *a centro ad peripheriam;* see Nicolai Börner, *Medicus sui ipsius oder Sein Selbst Arzt . . .* 2 parts (Frankfurt, 1747), pp. 552 ff.

46. An examination of the remedies suggested to combat anger and fright can give us some information about the bodily meaning of these "feelings." Here is one of the powders against anger from the widely known, popular pharmacopoeia of a Württemberg doctor: "An excellent powder for sudden fits of anger, fright and other bad cases," "administer it to someone who gets frightened, angered, or vehemently terrified"; Gabelkover, *Artzney-Buch,* p. 471. The remedy contained many parts of a stag caught while in rut; Storch believed rather more in purgatives and calming remedies.

47. Lelland Rather, *Mind and Body in Eighteenth Century Medicine: A Study Based on Jerome Gaub's "De Regimine Mentis"* (Berkeley, 1965), translates and discusses two texts from the eighteenth century, in which anger, fright, and distress were considered the prime causes of illness, and a person's mood was the decisive factor in preserving good health. Footnote 74, p. 224, reports on a case of repressed anger examined by Harvey. A man had swallowed his feeling of hatred. The hatred rose within, toward the heart, causing pains and illness there. During the autopsy Harvey found the heart to be enlarged: "so great is the power of confined or enclosed blood, so dynamic is it" (quoted by Rather, who sees this as evidence for the persistent survival of older notions even with the "inventor" of blood circulation).

48. A classic description of anger with all the signs of a frenzied person—rolling eyes, a hot head, swollen veins—can be found in Storch, *Weiberkrankheiten,* 4/2, p. 70.

49. I deliberately avoid addressing the historical forms of "hysteria." The "convulsions" of the Eisenach women do not interest me as a type of disease but as a common form of reaction within a continuum of reactions. Before medicine in the nineteenth century singled out "hysteria" as a psychiatric problem, the understanding of convulsions, epileptic fits, was tied into the entire imagined world of the inner body. An introduction to epilepsy can be found in Owsei Temkin, *The Falling*

Sickness: A History of Epilepsy from the Greeks to the Beginnings of Modern Neurology (Baltimore, 1971), chap. 7 on the eighteenth century, and in the classic book of Ilza Veith, *Hysteria: The History of a Disease* (Chicago: 1965).

50. Very useful and interesting observations on the external, concrete depiction of internal images conceived as real, and on the mutual exchange of the two (though relating to the fifteenth century), can be found in Michael Baxandall, *Painting and Experience in Fifteenth Century Italy* (Oxford, 1972), pp. 45 ff. Baxandall addresses two aspects (esp. pp. 60 ff.): the pictorial depiction in religious painting as a mirror of internal conceptions, and the gestures and facial expression (of the preacher and the orator, for example) as a depiction of internal states. It is hard today for us to imagine how the language of the body was ritualized in commonly known gestures and how these gestures mirrored the inner condition directly for everyone to see.

51. Börner, *Medicus,* writes about "fright" that it "presses the blood . . . back to the heart and lungs, and . . . there causes sudden coagulation." Anger throws "the humors that are ordered inside us for steady circulation into the greatest confusion by arousing them, or by producing a cramp in the outermost parts, that is, the vessels arranged for the circulation of said humors, thus driving the humors from the periphery to the center, that is, toward the heart and lung" (p. 551). See also Zedler, *Universallexicon,* article "Schrecken," with a precise description of the external signs of fright, since fright affected the body directly, without being mediated through the thoughts.

52. What the women named a "fright" must not be seen simply as the flinching we mean today when we say someone was frightened or startled. As my source shows, horror, nightmares, goosebumps, a surprise that struck a person dumb, and even the shivering caused by a chilly breeze were perceived as "fright." In Mexico today a quarter to a third of the mothers give "susto" as the cause for a child's death. On the bibliography, see Italo Signorini, "Patterns of Fright: Multiple Concepts of Susto in a Nahua-Ladino Community of the Sierra de Puebla," *Ethnology* 21, 4 (1982): 313–323. Libbet Crandon, "Why Susto?," *Ethnology* 22, 2 (1983): 153–167, addresses the question of whether it is possible not only to describe the ideas about "susto" and to explain socially the attribution of "susto" but also to say what "susto" *is.*

53. On the chlorosis of the nineteenth century as the clinical picture of "anemic" young girls of the middle class, see Karl Figlio, "Chlorosis and Chronic Disease in Nineteenth-Century Britain: The Social Constitution of Somatic Illness in a Capitalist Society," *Social History* 3, 2 (1978): 167–197. According to him, the medical concept of bloodlessness and anemia represented the desire for the social demarcation of the English bourgeoisie, who made their daughters "naturalized" symbols of their socioeconomic position.

54. MacDonald, *Mystical Bedlam,* describes "patient stories" from mid-seventeenth-century England that sound very similar to the Eisenach cases: excessive

sadness, great fear, and anxiety in widespread forms of visible somatic reactions and as expressions of conflicts and imagined misfortunes; see pp. 148 ff., "Disorders of Mood and Perception," and 112 ff., "Popular Stereotypes of Insanity."

55. Contemporary medical literature discussed "timor" and "terror," fear and fright, as causes for very diverse illnesses, from smallpox to measles. Terror also paralyzed resistance to the plague. H. Kölbing, U. Birchler, and P. Arnold, "Die Auswirkungen von Angst und Schreck auf Pest und Pestbekämpfung nach zwei Pestschriften des 18. Jahrhunderts," *Gesnerus* 36 (1979): 116–126, examine two tracts from 1722 and 1735 in which the physiological effects were precisely deduced.

56. The remedies for both cases often belonged together. See, for example, what the Prussian midwife Siegemundin recommended in her list of home remedies for midwives and mothers: "A powder against fright or anger: take crab's eyes, prepared mother-of-pearl, prepared red corals . . . sudorific antimony . . . a pinch taken with a cold drink after the fright or anger." The remedy mixed calming-sustaining and expulsive ingredients. Justine Siegemundin, *Die chur-Brandenburgische Hoff-Wehe-Mutter,* 2nd ed. (1756), p. 237.

57. Ivan Illich, *Medical Nemesis: The Expropriation of Health* (New York, 1976), p. 139.

58. It seems so self-evident to us that a woman is pregnant when, according to the science of embryology, an embryo has nested in the uterus. The medically ascribed biological condition today is regarded as a demand on the woman to know that she is pregnant or even to feel it. This identification of ascribed condition and experience makes it difficult for us to understand Dr. Storch and to grasp the fact that he treated as pregnant only those women who felt themselves to be pregnant. The uncertainty of the experience of being with child on the part of women has been discussed by P. Crawford, "Attitudes to Pregnancy from a Woman's Spiritual Diary, 1687–8," *Local Population Studies* 21 (1978): 43–45, and Sir John Dewhurst, "The Alleged Miscarriages of Catherine of Aragon and Anne Boleyn," *Medical History* 28 (1984): 49–56, who reports a case which today would be described as a phantom pregnancy. The many different signs of pregnancy in medico-legal literature are discussed by E. Fischer-Homberger, *Medizin vor Gericht: Gerichtsmedizin von der Renaissance bis zur Aufklärung* (Bern, 1983), pp. 222–228.

59. The concept and notion of abortion is determined largely by the historically conditioned nature of fertility, the interruption of which could begin even when the semen was spilled on the ground. On this, see John T. Noonan, Jr., *Contraception: A History of Its Treatment by the Catholic Theologians and Canonists* (Cambridge, Mass., 1966), chaps. 1–3. On the other hand, until the nineteenth century, procedures which by modern understanding are abortifacients could still be seen as "womb-cleansing," "promotion of the courses," relief of congestion. On this, see

Angus McLaren, *Reproductive Rituals: The Perception of Fertility in England from the Sixteenth Century to the Nineteenth Century* (London, New York, 1984). On the pharmaceutical remedies, see Edward Shorter, "Has the Desire to Limit Fertility Always Existed? The Question of Drug-Abortion in Traditional Europe" (unpublished manuscript) and Shorter, *Women's Bodies,* chap. 5. Basic reflections on the classification of remedies that "expel' or "retain" are found in C. H. Browner, "Criteria for Selecting Herbal Remedies," *Ethnology* 24, 1 (1984): 13–33. She illustrates her methodological reflections with observations from Mexico.

60. On the frequency of abortion in a practice around 1770, see Gélis, "La pratique," p. 195: in Reims in 1781, one of eleven interventions by the surgeon and obstetrician Robin concerned a mola or a "miscarriage."

61. Terms taken from Storch, *Weiberkrankheiten,* vols. 4/1 and 2. See also Zedler, *Universallexicon,* articles "Mutter-Kalb," "Mond-Kind," and others. Johannes Juncker discussed the expulsion of various foreign substances from the body in *Conspectus Therapiae* (1725), pp. 322 ff.: "De Expulsione Rerum Toto Genere Praeternaturalium." He gave the following gender-specific definition: "This is the specific form of evacuation, by which nature labors to expel clearly useless, harmful, even noxious humors from certain parts of the body. They are in particular wind, worms, stones, dead or alive fetuses, lumps of blood, wrong growths, after births, and so on (p. 322).

62. Berg, *Der Krankheitskomplex,* pp. 138–181, summarizes the ideas that lead to an analogy between womb and stomach in popular belief.

63. On the resemblance between womb and stomach, see Pouchelle, *Corps,* pp. 309 ff.

64. The sociogenesis of the fetus, which I could also call the history of the discovery of the true nature of the fetus, has been treated in some larger handbooks on the history of embryology. The book of Joseph Needham, *A History of Embryology,* 2nd ed. (Cambridge, 1959), allowed me to insert Storch as a scholar into the framework of the discussion between animalculists and ovulists, and to become aware that he did not let these new, and to him important, concepts keep him from seeing the fruit in the wombs of Eisenach's women as the product of coagulation and stagnation. Although in Storch's eyes the women of Eisenach were already equipped with ovaries (and not merely "womb-trumpets"), they clotted in the Aristotelian manner. Interviews have shown that even today women in Michigan (Wisconsin) believe that conception is the curdling of two fluids inside their bodies. See C. P. MacCormack, "Biological, Cultural and Social Adaptation in Human Fertility and Birth," in *Ethnography of Fertility and Birth,* ed. C. P. MacCormack (New York, 1982), p. 2.

65. Mireille Laget, *Naissances,* gives a detailed and impressive description of the images in which women's expectations and ideas about the fertility in their body are expressed. On the ambivalent perception of birth as either a woman's accouchement

or the birth of a child, see also Arlette Farge, "Accouchement et naissance au XVIIIe siècle," *Revue de médecine psychosomatique et psychologie médicale* 18, 1 (1976): 19–28. Judith Lewish Schneid, *Manners and Medicine: Childbearing in the English Aristocracy, 1790–1840* (Baltimore, 1978), allows access to this experience through her study of letters of the English upper class. See also Audrey Eccles, *Obstetrics and Gynecology in Tudor and Stuart England* (Kent, 1982).

66. Max Neuburger, quoted here from *The Doctrine of the Healing Power of Nature throughout the Course of Time* (New York, 1943), pp. 25 ff.

67. Quoted in ibid., p. 41.

68. Quoted in ibid., p. 37.

69. Boyle, quoted in ibid., p. 48.

70. Neuburger, in ibid., p. 55.

71. In his language Storch follows Stahl when he speaks of "nature." Yet Storch's "nature" is not the Stahlian *agens* that I find in medical history. Medical historians readily claim Stahl as a doctor, and as a doctor he did, in his immediate circle and in his generation, influence medical theory and practice. Medical history easily forgets that Stahl's phlogiston theory in chemistry remained an almost undisputed doctrine for more than eighty years. As a doctor he often used "nature," where as a chemical philosopher he would have said "phlogiston." Mikulás Teich, "Circulation, Transformation, Conservation of Matter and the Balancing of the Biological World in the Eighteenth Century," *Ambix* 29, 1 (1982): 17–28, believes he can prove that Stahl, beyond his influence on chemistry and medicine, influenced modern thinking even more fundamentally. Teich argues that Stahl added to the great themes in modern thought—gravitation, preservation of energy, evolution and descent—a fourth basic theme: the circulation of matter. According to Teich, this basic theme has been hardly studied. As I have mentioned, Storch translated some of Stahl's tracts, but they were lecture notes, third-hand records of Stahl's lectures. Despite the documented fact that Storch was a follower of Stahl, I had to beware of classifying him as a "Stahlian." Given the great complexity of the issue, any attempt to interpret Storch on the assumption that he adopted Stahl's concept of nature is impossible.

72. The best introduction to the change of remedies in the tug-of-war between the Galenic and the chemical apothecary of the seventeenth century is the work of A. Benedicenti, *Malati, Medici e Farmicisti*, 2 vols. (Milan, 1924), chap. 12, pp. 748 ff., on the development of the chemical pharmacy in the seventeenth century. Johann Christoph Sommerhoff, *Lexicon Pharmaceutico Chymicum Latino-Germanicum et Germanico-Latinum* (Nürnberg, 1713; repr. Hildesheim, 1977), allows the translation of Latin and German vernacular terms.

73. H. M. Nobis, "Die Umwandlung der mittelalterlichen Naturvorstellung: Ihre Ursachen und ihre wissenschaftsgeschichtlichen Folgen," *Archiv für Begriffsgeschichte* 13 (1969): 34–57, has traced this transformation, especially in the

example of the book metaphor: the Middle Ages wanted to read and decipher creation, the book of God, while, according to Bacon, nature was to be described and enciphered by the scientist.

74. Quoted by Neuburger, *Healing,* p. 24.

75. Georg Ernst Stahl, *Collegium Casuale Magnum oder sechs und siebentzig Practische Casus . . . ins Deutsche übersetzt von D. Johann Storchen, alias Hulderico Pelargo* (Leipzig, 1733), p. 20. (This is Storch's translation and commentary on the notes he was given to a series of lectures Stahl had delivered in 1705–1707).

Index